D1234595

Mediterranean Naval Battles that Changed the World

Mediterranean Naval Battles that Changed the World

Quentin Russell

Pen & Sword
MARITIME

First published in Great Britain in 2021 by
PEN & SWORD MARITIME
An imprint of
Pen & Sword Books Ltd
47 Church Street
Barnsley
South Yorkshire
S70 2AS

ISBN 978-1-52671-599-9

Typeset by Concept, Huddersfield HD4 5JL.
Printed and bound in England by TJ Books Ltd, Padstow, Cornwall.

Pen & Sword Books Limited incorporates the imprints of Atlas, Archaeology, Aviation, Discovery, Family History, Fiction, History, Maritime, Military, Military Classics, Politics, Select, Transport, True Crime, Air World, Frontline Publishing, Leo Cooper, Remember When, Seaforth Publishing, The Praetorian Press, Wharncliffe Local History, Wharncliffe Transport, Wharncliffe True Crime and White Owl.

For a complete list of Pen & Sword titles please contact
PEN & SWORD BOOKS LIMITED
47 Church Street, Barnsley, South Yorkshire, S70 2AS, England
E-mail: enquiries@pen-and-sword.co.uk
Website: www.pen-and-sword.co.uk

For James Russell MC and
Efthalia Russell MBE

Contents

Maps

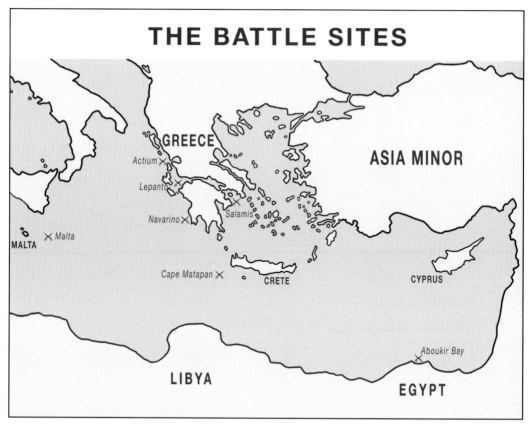

THE BATTLE SITES

GREECE

ASIA MINOR

Actium ✕

Lepanto ✕

Navarino ✕

Salamis

MALTA

✕ Malta

Cape Matapan ✕

CRETE

CYPRUS

LIBYA

✕ Aboukir Bay

EGYPT

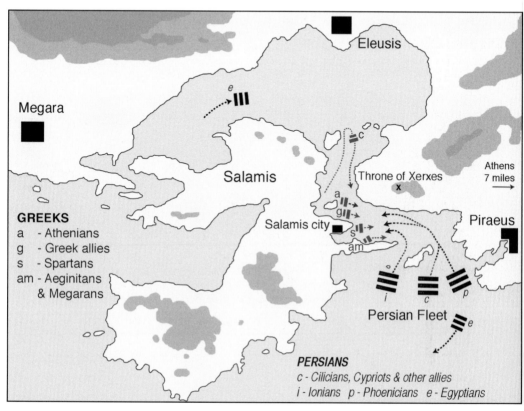

Eleusis

Megara

e III

Salamis

c

Throne of Xerxes
x

Athens
7 miles →

GREEKS
a - Athenians
g - Greek allies
s - Spartans
am - Aeginitans
     & Megarans

a
g

Salamis city

s
am

Piraeus

i   *c*   *p*

Persian Fleet

e

PERSIANS
c - Cilicians, Cypriots & other allies
i - Ionians p - Phoenicians e - Egyptians

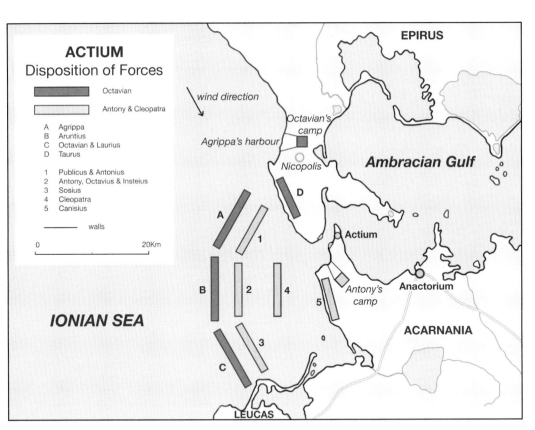

ACTIUM
Disposition of Forces

- ▬ Octavian
- ▭ Antony & Cleopatra

A Agrippa
B Aruntius
C Octavian & Laurius
D Taurus

1 Publicus & Antonius
2 Antony, Octavius & Insteius
3 Sosius
4 Cleopatra
5 Canisius

—— walls

0   20Km

EPIRUS

wind direction

Octavian's camp

Agrippa's harbour

Nicopolis

D

Ambracian Gulf

A

1

Actium

B

2

4

5

Antony's camp

Anactorium

3

ACARNANIA

C

IONIAN SEA

LEUCAS

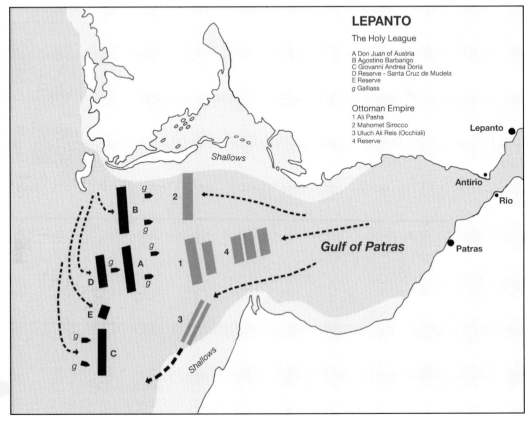

LEPANTO

The Holy League

A Don Juan of Austria
B Agostino Barbarigo
C Giovanni Andrea Doria
D Reserve - Santa Cruz de Mudela
E Reserve
g Galliass

Ottoman Empire
1 Ali Pasha
2 Mahomet Sirocco
3 Uluch Ali Reis (Occhiali)
4 Reserve

Lepanto

Shallows

Antirio

Rio

g
B
g

2

g
A
g

1

4

Gulf of Patras

Patras

D
g

E

3

g
C
g

Shallows

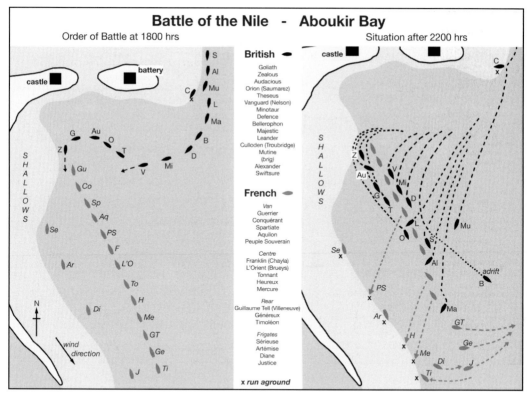

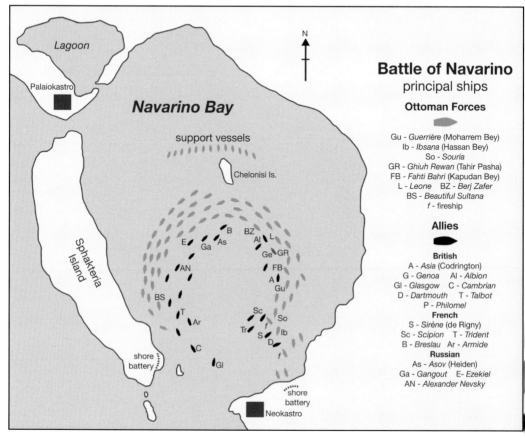

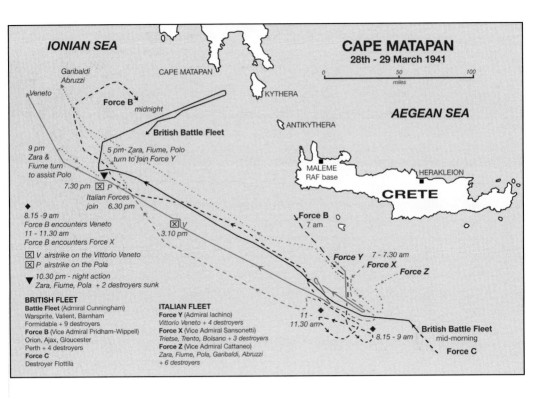

IONIAN SEA

CAPE MATAPAN

CAPE MATAPAN
28th - 29 March 1941

0   50   100
miles

AEGEAN SEA

KYTHERA

ANTIKYTHERA

Garibaldi
Abruzzi

Veneto

Force B
midnight

British Battle Fleet

9 pm
Zara &
Fiume turn
to assist Polo

5 pm - Zara, Fiume, Polo
turn to join Force Y

MALEME
RAF base

HERAKLEION

CRETE

7.30 pm ☒ P

Italian Forces
join   6.30 pm

◆ 8.15 -9 am
Force B encounters Veneto
11 - 11.30 am
Force B encounters Force X

☒ V
3.10 pm

Force B
7 am

Force Y 7 - 7.30 am
Force X
Force Z

☒ V airstrike on the Vittorio Veneto
☒ P airstrike on the Pola

▼ 10.30 pm - night action
Zara, Fiume, Pola + 2 destroyers sunk

11 -
11.30 am

◆

British Battle Fleet
mid-morning

8.15 - 9 am

Force C

BRITISH FLEET
Battle Fleet (Admiral Cunningham)
Warsprite, Valient, Barnham
Formidable + 9 destroyers
Force B (Vice Admiral Pridham-Wippell)
Orion, Ajax, Gloucester
Perth + 4 destroyers
Force C
Destroyer Flottila

ITALIAN FLEET
Force Y (Admiral Iachino)
Vittorio Veneto + 4 destroyers
Force X (Vice Admiral Sansonetti)
Trietse, Trento, Bolsano + 3 destroyers
Force Z (Vice Admiral Cattaneo)
Zara, Fiume, Pola, Garibaldi, Abruzzi
+ 6 destroyers

Introduction

The Contested Sea

During his long conflict with Britain, Napoleon Bonaparte often compared France to ancient Rome, and his enemy with Rome's obstinate adversary Carthage. This was not only because Rome managed to defeat Hannibal, his favourite general, but also to prove a point. Early in his military career when he was a precocious 19-year-old lieutenant on garrison duty in Auxonne, he reached the conclusion that a nation whose strength is reliant on its navy will always ultimately be defeated by one that is dominantly a military power. Carthage had achieved success through its shipping and commerce, whereas Rome was essentially an agricultural society. Napoleon argued that experience has nearly always shown that the maritime state was vulnerable because warfare destroys its commerce, leading to its exhaustion, whereas on the contrary 'its opponents are toughened and strengthened'.

When his theory was put to the test, despite his many victories it was Napoleon's land empire that was defeated. In the end France had proved unable to isolate and wear down Britain because it could not overcome the Royal Navy's mastery of the seas, leaving the Duke of Wellington to declare in 1814 that Britain's maritime supremacy had enabled him to maintain his army while strangling France. After his defeat and exile to St Helena, Napoleon was forced to concede that the inferiority of the French navy had cost him dearly, but he still maintained that the outcome was not inevitable. The great American naval historian, Alfred Thayer Mahan, writing in 1889, took the opposite lesson from history. Britain by this time was established as the premier naval power in the world and the possessor of a large empire, and it seemed to him that it followed that a naval power would always prevail.

In the West the beginnings of naval warfare start in the Mediterranean. The Mediterranean, being almost completely landlocked and thus the largest 'inland sea', offered a unique environment for the development of seafaring. At times a barrier and the boundary between continents and cultures, East and West, it was also a conduit for settlement and exchange, providing a highway for trade and ideas, and ultimately colonisers and invaders. The Mediterranean's numerous islands and limited expanses of open water were ideal for the development of the art of seafaring, allowing early mariners the luxury of never having to venture far from land. Once the sea was explored it nurtured communities that looked towards it for their livelihood rather than to the land. Plato noted (*Phaedo* 109) that the Greeks had settled around the Mediterranean 'like frogs around a pond'. Centuries later Cicero, in contradiction to Napoleon, put in the mouth of Cato (*De Res Publica* 2.10) the sentiment that Romulus had founded Rome on the banks of the Tiber because it gave the city access to the sea (around only 16 miles/26km away), and with the advantages of a coastal city he had the foresight that from this vantage it would 'become the centre of a world empire'.

By then skill at seafaring had become part of the common culture of the coastal civilisations that had grown up around the Mediterranean. Phoenicians and Greeks had left their homelands, searching for raw materials and then land to settle, and founded cities in suitable havens. The Greeks' most important colonies were along the coast of Anatolia, where their independent city-states, collectively known as Ionia, became torchbearers of Greek civilisation. There was a long history of conflict for control of the Ionian coast between the Greeks and the native Anatolians and an uneasy relationship of competition and respect grew up between the rival communities. In the 7th century BC, when Lydia became the dominant power in the region, it was the Ionian Greeks who were forced to submit. But Lydia's supremacy was short lived. A new and more formidable empire had emerged in the east. The early great empires of the Nile valley and the Fertile Crescent had been created by land armies, and they had been content to halt their expansion at the coast. The Egyptians, although knowledgeable sailors, built their whole society around the fluctuations of the Nile and were little interested in naval power except for defence, whereas this new power, successor to the Assyrians and Babylonians, would not be satisfied merely with taking the coastal cities. The armies of Cyrus the Great of Persia swept all before them, overrunning the Median, Babylonian and Lydian empires and bringing Mesopotamia, Anatolia and the Levant under their control. Egypt, that had been the most successful and dominant power in the eastern Mediterranean, fell to Cyrus' son, Cambyses II, in 525BC and by the reign of his grandson, Darius I (the Great, 550–486BC), Persia was the largest and best-organised empire in the world, stretching from the Indus valley to the shores of the Mediterranean. But Darius was not to be satisfied within the confines of his Asian empire. With his eyes on Europe, he pushed west across the Hellespont in 513BC and invaded Scythia.

With Phoenicia and Egypt already under its control, and the Ionian Greek cities of Anatolia subdued, the Persians were free to be masters of the eastern Mediterranean. Darius planned to control the whole Aegean by taking his armies into the Greek mainland, encircling it. Persia was a land power, and it depended on its subject peoples, Phoenicians, Egyptians and Ionian Greeks, to provide its naval strength. The Greek islands and small mainland city-states began to feel squeezed between the growing power of the Phoenician city of Carthage in the west and Persia in the east and as a result there were differences of policy between states, and differences of opinion as how to deal with the threat from the east, whether it was more expedient to confront or align with Persia. Many chose the latter course. The stage was now set for one of the great confrontations in history, a conflict as never before between a land-based power and a seafaring people, pitting East against West for the first time. This rivalry, initially between Greece and Persia, and then Rome and Persia, would last for as long as Persia had an empire – a thousand years. Against the odds, and in two rare moments of unity, the Greeks were able to inflict humiliating defeats on the mighty Persians as they attempted to invade the Greek mainland under Darius and then his successor Xerxes. Xerxes returned ten years after his father with an even bigger force bent not only on retribution, but on the invasion of the whole Greek peninsula. The defining moment of what the Greeks termed the Persian Wars was the victory of the allied Greek navy, under the leadership of Athens, over the Persian fleet at the Battle of Salamis (480BC). This was followed by defeat at the hands of a combined force under Sparta on land at Plataea, effectively ending any further attempts by Persia to expand into Europe.

The prestige of the leading Greek cities, Sparta and Athens, was greatly enhanced by victory over Persia. Sparta's professional hoplite army was recognised as supreme on land, and the Athenian navy ruled the Aegean, creating a maritime empire in all but name; a situation that before long meant the resumption of old rivalries and war between them. Although Sparta came out on top in the Peloponnesian War, no Greek city was powerful enough to maintain dominance, and further conflict between the city-states meant the Greeks were never again able to offer a combined front to future invaders. In 336BC the expansionist northern Greek kingdom of Macedonia was the first to take advantage of this disunity. With Greece under Macedonian control, their young commander and military genius, Alexander, presumptuously took the fight back to Persia, ostensibly to 'liberate' the Ionian Greek cities, but with conquest in mind. His liberation march did not end at the coastal regions; he went on to take over the whole Persian Empire, creating his own Hellenistic empire that stretched from Greece and Egypt to the edge of India and central Asia. The eastern Mediterranean was now briefly under one rule, but on Alexander the Great's death in 323 BC, his empire fractured into a number of competing Hellenistic states run by the descendants of his generals. These Hellenistic kingdoms proved as incapable as their Greek forebears of any semblance of unity. Under the descendants of Ptolemy, Alexandria, the city that Alexander had founded in Egypt, became the pre-eminent city-port in the eastern Mediterranean, but Egypt could not control the sea. The Hellenistic states surrounded the eastern Mediterranean keeping it within the Greek sphere of influence, but their rivalries kept it as a constant scene of war. In the west a new power was emerging that threatened Greek interests, and the Hellenistic kingdoms of Macedon and the Seleucids took it seriously enough to ally themselves with their Phoenician rivals at Carthage, while Pergamum decided to take the other side; the new emerging power was the city state of Rome.

A natural fault line had developed between the forces of East and West and it is no coincidence that decisive naval turning points took place in this region. The riches of Egypt and the lure of the East meant that Western armies would continue to be drawn to its coasts. For us on the western tip of Europe, our focus is on Rome's brutally efficient legions as they conquered Gaul and Britain and held the northern frontiers of the Rhine and Danube. But this loses sight that most of the richest provinces of its Empire were those of the coastal hinterland of the Mediterranean. In common with Napoleon's assessment, the Romans are often cast as land-lubbers, who, unlike the seafaring Phoenicians and Greeks, were not natural traders and owed their expansion to their armies; so it might come as some surprise that one of the most important battles in their history was fought at sea. In its early history Rome was heavily influenced by its Etruscan, Greek and Phoenician neighbours who were carrying out a three-cornered struggle for supremacy in the western Mediterranean. Despite Romulus's premonition, initially Rome had little access to the Tyrrhenian (Etruscan) Sea. The Etruscans, who dominated to the north, and the Greeks, to the south, held the ports. The Greek city-states had spread their influence from the 8th century onwards, colonising Corsica and Massilia (Marseilles) from where they could easily annexe the western coastal regions of southern Italy and Sicily. The Greeks became so dominant in the south that the region became known as Magna Graecia. For Rome to compete it had to match its rivals at sea. Archaeological remains suggest that Ostia, Rome's port at the mouth of the Tiber, was founded in the late-4th or early-3rd century BC, not earlier as tradition held, during the period of its landward territorial expansion. In Sicily, where the Corinthians had founded the important city of Syracuse, Greeks and Phoenicians had been in conflict for control of the island since the 7th century BC. Once the Roman Republic was able to overcome the Etruscans by land to the north and extend its influence into southern Italy, conflict with these powers came to a head in Sicily during the First Punic War (264–241BC). Carthage, founded in North Africa near modern Tunis by Phoenician colonists from Tyre, had become the centre of an extensive maritime commercial empire with its own colonies along the African coast, southern Iberia, Sardinia and Sicily. With the largest fleet at the time, the Carthaginians were loath to commit to land battles with what they thought to be the superior Roman legions. But they failed to make the most of their naval superiority, whereas the Romans responded by building a fleet to match the Carthaginians in a number of naval encounters.

Victory for the Romans gave them control of Sicily, Sardinia and Corsica, and they began to refer to the Tyrrhenian Sea as *Mare Nostrum*, 'Our Sea'. In the Second Punic War (218–201BC), Napoleon's hero, Hannibal, attempted to strike at the heart of Rome, but despite his tactical genius he was thwarted by Rome's delaying strategy that exploited his stretched resources, not allowing him to receive support by sea. In the end, a weakened Hannibal was at last finally defeated on land in defence of his home city. A humbled Carthage was left with only ten warships and would never be a major player again. Having inherited the old Carthaginian territories in Africa and Iberia, Rome now turned their attentions to the eastern Mediterranean, to conflicts in Greece and to the powerful Hellenistic kingdoms. The Romans adroitly played the divisions and conflicts in the region to their own advantage, until they were ultimately able to break Greek resistance in battle bringing Macedonian Greece (146BC) and Pergamum (133BC) under their nominal control. Such was their dominance they were finally able to end the endemic scourge of piracy in the region. In 67BC Pompey, in a concerted campaign lasting over three months, deploying 20 legions (approximately 120,000 men) and close to 500 ships, he simultaneously destroyed all the 400 major pirate strongholds, capturing over 1,000 pirate ships and imprisoning and enslaving tens of thousands of men. By 30BC, Rome had control of the whole Mediterranean, and the term *mare nostrum* was then used in this context.

Rome was an empire in all but name and control of the empire became the ambition of the generals that had built it. The struggle for power in the last years of the Republic came to a head when Mark Antony succumbed to the lure of the East. With his lover Cleopatra, the last Ptolemaic Pharaoh of Egypt, the greatest of the remaining Hellenistic states, he tried to revive the empire of Alexander in opposition to Rome. Together they took on a force under the young Octavian, grandnephew of Julius Caesar, sent by the Republic to thwart Antony's defiance. The decisive confrontation came at Actium (31BC) with the destruction of Antony's naval force. Victory secured Egypt for Rome and brought the nominally independent Hellenistic and Levantine states firmly under its rule. It also gave Octavian complete control. Under the pretence of safeguarding the Republic he effectively brought it to an end, installing himself as *Augustus* and *Princeps* and making Rome an empire in name as well as in reality.

For four hundred years the rule of Imperial Rome held sway and for at least two hundred years it could claim that it had introduced a period of rule known as the *Pax Romana*. It was the only power that was able to gain complete mastery of the inland sea and with the sea pacified for centuries, further internal and external wars were fought on land. In 410AD Rome was sacked by the Goths under Alaric and the empire in the west fatally wounded; a slow disintegration followed. In the east the empire continued from its power base in Constantinople from where a new Christian empire emerged under the name of Byzantium. Although their empire lasted 1,000 years, its glory days were short and it was soon beleaguered on all sides, staving off threats from the Arabs and then Turks in the east and opportunist Franks and Crusaders from the west. It was an empire in retreat and in the increasing power vacuum, piracy returned to the seas even worse than before.

Following their conversion to Islam in the 7th century, the Arabs surged out of their homeland in a dynamic period of conquest that gave them control of Byzantine Egypt and its lands in the Levant. They occupied many Mediterranean islands, including Sicily and Cyprus, and made incursions into mainland Europe through the Iberian peninsula that took them beyond the Pyrenees. The European response came in a series of crusades, beginning in 1096, while new vigour was given to the Muslim conquests by the arrival of the Seljuk Turks who took over Anatolia from the Byzantines (Battle of Manzikert, 1071) and the Arab Abbasid Caliphate centred on Baghdad. In Italy a new maritime power based on mercantilism was on the rise, the Republic of Venice. In order to secure her trade routes with the Levant the Doge Pietro Orseolo II cleared the Adriatic of the scourge of

Croatian pirates in 1000, ever since commemorated as a decisive moment in the city's history. At sea, the rival Crusaders and Muslims both resorted to piracy as the Crusaders endeavoured to retake the Holy Land. In the 14th century a new dynamic Turkic people arrived in Anatolia and within two hundred years the Ottomans had extended their domains into eastern Europe. The eventual fall of Constantinople came in 1453 and it made the Turks a European power and the dominant naval force in the eastern Mediterranean.

The naval historian Roger Anderson argued (*Naval War in the Levant,* 1952) that during the 15th and 16th century the Mediterranean could be regarded as two seas, an eastern and western. In the west the *reconquista* of the Iberian peninsula had created a strong monarchy in Spain and an expansive kingdom of Portugal, and the Christians still held or had re-taken the most important islands, such as Sicily and Malta. In Italy, the Byzantines' old maritime rivals, Venice and Genoa, precariously con-tinued to hold on to their commercial ventures and territories left over from the Crusades in the Adriatic and Aegean, including the important islands of Crete and Cyprus (Venice) and Chios and Samos (Genoa). But on the whole the other Western states hardly ventured east of Malta, or the Turks or Venetians to its west. What was common to both east and west was that conflict was typified by irregular warfare, particularly piracy. It was only when the western powers had grown enough in confidence to meet the Ottomans on more equal terms that they were drawn back to the eastern Mediterranean as both traders and belligerents. By then, on land Suleiman the Magnificent had taken his hitherto invincible Turkish armies as far as the gates of Vienna, and his naval power extended along the north African littoral to Algeria, which became an Ottoman vassal state in 1537. The Turks would never succeed in advancing beyond Vienna, despite a hundred years of trying, but at sea the situation was more volatile. No power could completely encircle the sea, and therefore control it. Venice remained a serious rival, and she had managed to create a maritime empire by the method of establishing a series of bases, particularly in the Adriatic and Aegean where they held some of the Greek islands and established ports on the mainland coast; and then there was the unfinished business of the old Crusader pirate bases held by the Order of St John, the Knights Hospitaller, on Rhodes and Malta.

In the West, Charles VIII of France was intent on making France the dominant power in the Mediterranean and to this purpose he established Toulon, east of Marseilles, as the base for his Mediterranean fleet. France's primary rivals were Genoa and Spain and Charles' immediate aim was to take the Spanish controlled southern Italian kingdoms of Naples and Sicily. When this failed, his successor, Francis I, was even prepared to make an alliance with the Ottomans in 1536 to thwart his Spanish rival, Charles V, the Holy Roman Emperor. Under Ottoman suzerainty the corsairs of the Barbary Coast continued to profit from their piracy and slaving with the Sultan's connivance, and the most famous amongst them, Hayreddin Barbarossa, was adopted into the Ottoman navy as their admiral. To harness the expertise of Barbarossa for himself, Francis went as far as permitting the Algerian fleet to winter in Toulon, where the Cathedral was temporally turned into a mosque. Barbarossa went on to make the Ottomans the dominant naval power in the Mediterranean, taking a number of Aegean islands from the Venetians and significantly defeating a far larger Christian fleet at the Battle of Preveza (1538), close to the site of the Battle of Actium. The Venetian and Spanish dominated fleet of the 'Holy League' had been formed by Pope Paul III as an act of holy war, but Francis was not interested in joining a Christian alliance; it was more useful to maintain his diplomatic relations with the Ottoman Empire. France would continue its alliance with the Turks for most of the next two hundred years until Napoleon invaded Egypt, and Toulon would remain the main port for its Mediterranean fleet.

As on land, the Ottomans had reached the limits of their power under Suleiman. Although they persisted in maintaining a large fleet, they were never again able to overcome their European enemies if their opponents could settle their differences and act in consort. Although the influence of Venice and Genoa was receding in the east, the power of Spain remained too great an obstacle, and though they forced the Knights of St John out of Rhodes (1522), they were unable to take Malta (1565). Without Malta no power in the Mediterranean could be secure. At the Battle of Lepanto in 1571 the forces of Christendom, at least some of those that were Catholic, briefly united in another Holy League to inflict a resounding defeat on the Sultan, Selim II, putting an end to any dream of the Mediterranean becoming an Ottoman lake. The victory of Lepanto and the defeat of the Ottomans at the Siege of Vienna in 1683 put an end to the aura of invincibility that surrounded the Turkish military. Unity after Lepanto was short lived however, and the last 'crusade' did nothing to free those Christians still under Ottoman rule.

While the peoples of the Mediterranean were squabbling for supremacy within their sea, those of the north Atlantic seaboard had embarked on an era of exploration and discovery that would take them round the Cape of Good Hope to the Far East, west to the Americas and eventually around

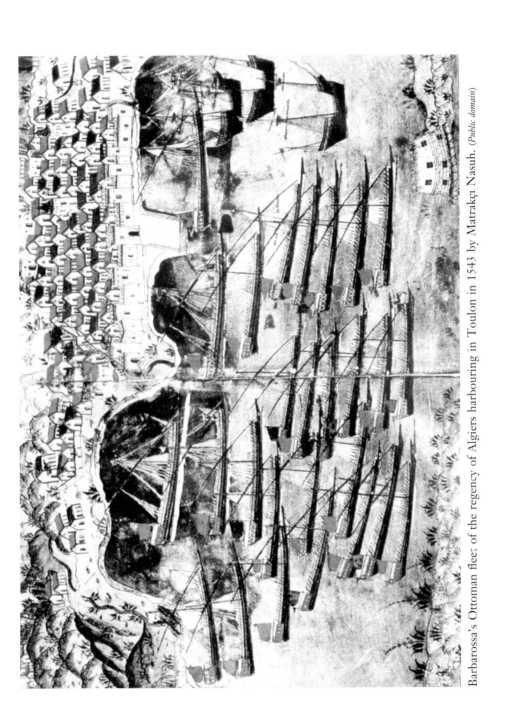

Barbarossa's Ottoman fleet of the regency of Algiers harbouring in Toulon in 1543 by Matrakçı Nasuh. *(Public domain)*

the world. Columbus' discovery of the Americas in 1492 brought prospects of new riches and territories, and the bypassing of the Ottoman controlled routes to the Orient opened up lucrative markets in silks and spices for western traders; increasingly the Mediterranean resembled what it nearly was, an inland sea or lake. Previously insignificant countries found themselves at the centre of the action while the importance of Venice and Genoa waned, and although the 16th century witnessed the arrival of English and Dutch sailing ships on the back of their maritime successes, trade in the Mediterranean became a trickle compared to that of the Atlantic. The English founded the Levant Company during the reign of Elizabeth I to facilitate trade with the Ottoman Empire and the company set up trading bases or 'factories' in the most important ports. The necessity of running the gauntlet between Barbary pirates and Spanish galleys meant that the English, who were not above a bit of privateering themselves, increasingly had to take protective measures and arm their ships.

The difficulties of dodging the pirates at one end of the sea and the growing inertia of the Ottoman Empire at the other meant the Mediterranean had begun to become a footnote in world events. Selim II had proposed a canal through Suez to give Ottoman ships from the Levant direct access to the Indian Ocean, but the idea was not taken up until Napoleon invaded Egypt in 1798, only to be postponed again due to his defeat by Nelson. The rise too of European nations with interests around the globe brought about a bitter rivalry for dominance of world trade and territorial gain. During the 17th century the English continued to harass Spanish ships wherever they could, including in the Mediterranean, and war with the Dutch and France meant that all three contested control of Tangier at the western end of the Straits of Gibraltar.

Britain (now England and Scotland), scored a particular coup when Spain was required to cede Gibraltar in perpetuity (Treaty of Utrecht, 1713) after the War of the Spanish Succession, giving the Royal Navy an important base at the entrance to the Mediterranean. This opened up the possibility once again of a shorter route to the Orient. The occupation of a number of strategic Mediterranean islands would become of central importance to Britain as its attention became increasingly drawn to maintaining its links with its expanding empire in the East, particularly India. At the same time the waning military prestige of the Ottomans was matched by increasing unrest within its Empire, particularly in its European possessions, leaving a power vacuum waiting to be filled. Though the Mediterranean was no longer the hub of activity it once had been, it was regaining its importance as a link between three continents.

During the protracted wars following the French Revolution, the one constant enemy for the Republic and then the Empire under Napoleon, was Britain. Napoleon's conquering army had taken him well beyond the 'natural' borders of France, but any attempt to negotiate a peace was thwarted by Britain's insistence on retaining the balance of power in Europe, which required him to retreat to the frontiers of 1792. This he would not do. The French navy could not match Napoleon's victories on land, leaving him unable to deliver the *coup de grace* on his foe, as he had done so effectively to his other European adversaries. France was an Atlantic and a Mediterranean maritime power, enhanced by its control over Spain and parts of Italy, but there remained no dominant navy in the inland sea.

The conflict between Imperial Russia and the Ottoman Empire around the Black Sea and in Central Asia convinced Peter the Great of the need to develop a navy and with a navy the Russians began to turn their attention to the Mediterranean. In 1770 its Baltic fleet defeated the Ottomans at the Battle of Chesme off the island of Chios, and after their annexation of the Crimea (1783) they saw an opportunity to enter the Mediterranean from the Black Sea. The Russian Tsars, as heirs to Greek Orthodoxy, saw the lands of their co-religionists in the Balkans and Levant as part of their sphere of interest and they had dreams of restoring the Ottoman capital of Constantinople, which guarded access through the Bosphorus, to its position as the seat of the Orthodox Church.

Napoleon had his eyes on the eastern Mediterranean too. Following his belief that the only way to humble Britain was by disrupting its trade, particularly with India and the Far East, he would have to invade Ottoman Egypt. Although Britain held Gibraltar, up until then she had not maintained a Mediterranean Fleet, but Napoleon's strategy finally brought the Royal Navy decisively into the Mediterranean. Nelson's victory at the Battle of the Nile (1798) effectively ended Napoleon's ambitions in Egypt and the taking of Malta (1800, formally ceded in 1814) and Corfu (1815) from the French gave the British secure stopping-off places on the way to the Levant. Nelson considered Malta as 'a most important outwork to India, that it will give us great influence in the Levant and indeed all the southern parts of Italy. In this view I hope we shall never give it up'. For the next hundred and fifty years Britain would be a Mediterranean power.

If Napoleon had turned revolution into empire, the French Revolution itself gave voice to Enlightenment ideals of liberty and brotherhood, and these found fertile ground in the oppressed Balkan communities of the Ottoman Empire. This new mood of national self-determination brought the navies of Britain, France and Russia together to fight the last decisive naval battle of the 19th century, one that determined the outcome of a war and the fate of a nation. The slow decline of the Ottoman Empire was becoming acute and its hold on the Balkans was fracturing. When Greece made a bid for independence, its unique status as the birthplace of European civilisation brought about a rare moment of cooperation among the 'powers'. Romantics might have cried out for Greek freedom, but the politicians were reluctant to get involved. In the end neutrality proved too difficult for Admiral Codrington to maintain and when their fleets were drawn into action the Ottoman navy was destroyed at the Battle of Navarino in 1827, leaving the Turkish land army high dry. Although the total realisation of a Greek state within its present borders would take a hundred years, from then on the Ottomans were in retreat. The Greek State was formally recognised in 1832 and other Balkan countries would follow.

The British navy may now be in its ascendency but there was a new presence in the Mediterranean, the navy of the liberated American states, and the US navy was prepared to express its growing confidence. The long history of piracy had had a devastating effect on coastal communities and trade, leaving many islands and coasts desolate after the inhabitants had fled or moved inland. The main culprits, the Barbary corsairs, continued to operate out of Algiers, and to deal with them the Americans established a naval base at La Spezia in northern Italy. La Spezia would later become the main harbour and arsenal for the Italian navy. After a combined naval bombardment of Algiers by the British and Dutch (1816) in an attempt to end slavery, it was the French who dealt the deathblow to the pirates and their activities when they occupied Algeria in 1830. Piracy was finally outlawed when all European countries signed a declaration in Paris in 1856 formally banning it in all its forms. The newly developed armed steamship appeared just at the right time to enforce the ban.

Ottoman decline allowed the British the opportunity to establish themselves in Egypt, first economically, prompted by the shortage of cotton due to The American Civil War, and then formally, after the Anglo-Egyptian War, as a protectorate in 1882. In 1869 British interests were increased with the opening of the Anglo-French Suez Canal, dramatically cutting the time of the voyage to India by reducing the distance from London to the Arabian Sea by approximately 5,500 miles. Britain's presence in the eastern Mediterranean was further cemented when Ottoman Cyprus was placed under its protection in 1878 following the Treaty of Berlin; it was formally annexed in 1914. The treaty marked the conclusion of the Russo-Turkish War of 1877–8 and France was another beneficiary, taking control of Tunisia as a protectorate. Despite these ructions, by mid-century an era of relative calm had descended on the Mediterranean and European tourists began to make their first appearance in the Levant, and from the 1880s they felt safe enough to embark on Thomas Cook & Sons' excursions up the Nile. The entente between Britain and France and their support of Turkey against Russia, manifested in their jointly taking on the Russians in the Crimea, allowed Westerners the security that they were under the protection of their navies. Malta's harbours were enlarged to accommodate the whole of Britain's Mediterranean Fleet, its largest single squadron with ten first-class battleships, double the number of the Channel Fleet. The 'powers' felt that peace could only be maintained through the display of military potential.

At the beginning of the 20th century, Britain's reputation as a naval power was well established, but there were others who vied for control of the inland sea, and they began to flex their muscles. Italy seized Libya from the Ottomans in 1911 and occupied the Dodecanese islands, including Rhodes, in 1912. They were supposed to hand the islands back to the Ottomans but due to the vagueness of the peace agreement they continued to administer the islands until Turkey formally handed them to Fascist Italy in 1923. The Italians held on to the islands until 1947 when they ceded them to Greece. France and Spain had been extending their influence in Morocco over a long period. In 1912 they formally divided the country into two protectorates, Spanish and French Morocco, giving France virtual control of the north African coast west of Libya.

But in 1914 the long European peace came to an abrupt end. Although the First World War is characterised in the popular imagination by the horror of trench warfare on the Western Front, the British believed there was an opportunity to hurt the Central Powers, Germany and Austro-Hungary, by attacking them through the eastern Mediterranean and the Balkans and Winston Churchill, as First Lord of the Admiralty, was a keen proponent of inflicting defeat on Germany's ally, Turkey. A daring amphibious landing by Australian and New Zealand troops assisted by the Royal Navy was attempted at Gallipoli and although the ensuing Dardanelles campaign (1915–16) failed, Allied successes on the Macedonian front proved to be crucial in defeating the Central Powers and finally bringing the Ottoman Empire to an end. The Empire's collapse enabled Britain and France to extend their power in the Middle East and in 1923 they formally became protecting powers; Britain in Palestine and France in Syria and Lebanon. Britain's rule of Egypt under various pretexts lasted formally until 1922 when the country became independent, but British forces were allowed to remain to protect the Suez Canal and for Egypt's external security; as a result, Britain retained its dominance over Egypt's political life. After centuries of conflict between East and West, the European powers had gained almost complete control of the Mediterranean coast with the exception of Turkish Thrace and Asia Minor; the greatest extent since the Roman Empire.

The peace would not last long. In Italy, the dictator Benito Mussolini's Fascists came to power on the back of a wave of expansive nationalism and he wasted little time in putting into effect his dream to create a New Roman Empire. This meant Italy regaining control of *Mare Nostrum*, repossessing areas he considered Italian (Nice, Corsica, the Dalmatian coast and Corfu), taking the British base of Malta and extending Italian rule throughout North Africa. The Second World War brought Fascist Italy and Britain directly into conflict in the Mediterranean, and in 1941 at the Battle of Cape Matapan the British fleet came out victorious against a powerful Italian fleet. It would be the last time a British fleet would engage with an enemy fleet.

Spain and Spanish Morocco were under Franco's Fascist dictatorship, and as the war progressed France and its possessions in the Middle East and north Africa came under the puppet Vichy government, Albania was invaded by Italy in 1939 and Greece and Yugoslavia fell to Axis forces in 1941, leaving Britain in danger of being completely squeezed out of the Mediterranean.

For Britain, and then Germany, the Mediterranean became a key element in defeating the enemy. Hitler believed, like Napoleon, he could attack Britain's empire through the Mediterranean, and Churchill still held the view that Germany's vulnerability was an attack from the south. In 1938 nearly 29 million tons of shipping passed through Suez and on any given day 185 British merchant ships were in transit through the Mediterranean or unloading at a port. As Grand Admiral Erich Raeder, C-in-C of the German Navy told Hitler in September 1940, 'The British have always considered the Mediterranean the pivot of their world empire ...' and he urged the Führer to order an advance southward to break British resistance in north Africa, take Suez and threaten Turkey, which if accomplished would render an invasion of Russia unnecessary.

Maintaining supply routes was vital to both sides and Malta was crucial for the British in keeping contact between Gibraltar and Egypt and in disrupting Axis naval activity. As Churchill put it in his history of the war, 'Since the days of Nelson Malta has stood a faithful British sentinel guarding the narrow and vital sea corridor through the Central Mediter-ranean. Its strategic importance was never higher than in this latest war.' The Mediterranean became the scene of the largest conventional naval warfare actions of the war outside of the Pacific theatre and despite the importance of the Battle of the Atlantic more warships of minesweeper size and above were deployed in surface engagements than elsewhere. At different times five navies were involved; the French, Italian, German, British and American. By the end of the war it was the American navy that was left as the dominant force, and the lesson learnt was that mastery of the seas would no longer rest on conventional naval power but on air supremacy.

Chapter One

Development of Naval Warfare in the Mediterranean

A striking feature of the history of naval warfare is that most battles were fought close to land, often near a harbour or place of shelter. In ancient times sailors preferred to sail near to the coast, where protection could be sought in bad weather and supplies of food and water taken on board. This was particularly true of warships, where there was little storage space or room for the crew to rest. It is no surprise then that naval strategy was determined by proximity to land. It was not until the age of steam and advances in communications that navies could pursue one another across the expanse of ocean. Previously the best way to gain the upper hand was by bottling up opposing forces, giving them little room to manoeuvre or escape. The enclosed nature of the eastern Mediterranean, with its numerous islands and welcoming coves, offered an ideal environment to develop seamanship, and it was here that the first navies in the West developed. The sea was an ideal medium for exploration and trade in an age when crossing difficult terrain was slow and arduous. But slow trading vessels were easy prey to pirates and it appears that the first developments of naval power were a response to this threat. The legendary King Minos of Crete was credited with creating a navy for this purpose. The Cretans used their navy to take their civilisation throughout the Aegean creating a *thalassocracy*, or maritime empire.

The Mycenaean Greeks learned from their Cretan neighbours and when it came their turn to seize control they used their ships to raid and colonise Asia Minor and beyond. Memories of Mycenaean exploration and raiding became immortalised in legend: Jason who ventured into the Black Sea with his Argonauts to steal the Golden Fleece from Colchis, and the exploits of the kings and heroes who sacked Troy. When the civilisation of the Aegean waned at the end of the first millennium, a confederacy of displaced Aegean sailors, known as the 'Sea Peoples', terrorised the eastern Mediterranean. The difference between piracy and organised warfare was never clear and piracy was endemic from the earliest times whenever there was a lull in trade or the lack of a strong power to exercise control. In later ages the pirates would be termed privateers or corsairs, but their purpose was the same. Throughout the Sea's history certain locations proved to be consistent havens for piracy; Rhodes, Crete, Cilicia and the Dalmatian coast in the east, Malta, Algiers, Corsica and the Balearics in the west.

Naval technology advanced slowly and most ships were transports and cargo vessels, and not designed exclusively for warfare, and the first response to piracy was merely to arm the ships. It was when ships began to be designed purely for military purposes that ambitious rulers and aggressive states began to build navies for offensive purposes. Often the early navies were used just as transports for armies, as in the fabled sacking of Troy by the Achaean Greeks sometime around 1100BC. When Darius of Persia invaded Greece over 500 years later he did not exploit the vast naval superiority at his disposal. The ships of his allies were used soley to perform the first recorded amphibious landing of an army in the build up to the Battle of Marathon.

The object of naval warfare was to disable or sink the enemy ships, but this was not easily accomplished, and usually the best ploy was to board the enemy vessel. This tactic was abandoned with the development of the ram on the ship's prow, turning the ship itself into a weapon. Ramming required a high level of skill. The earliest surviving image of a Greek galley, depicted on a 16th century BC sherd from Volos, already shows what would be recognisable later characteristics; the side-steering oar at the curved upward stern and the pointed ram at the prow. In Homer's (c.750–650BC) accounts of the Trojan War in the *Iliad* and *Odyssey*, composed well after the event, the Greek ships came in three sizes, twenty, thirty or fifty-oared galleys, with the rowers all on one level. The rowers would be aided in their efforts by a square-rigged sail.

The Greeks' rivals, the Phoenicians, had commercial ships with one and two banks of oars, the larger protected by soldiers. For warfare they had a masted ship with a bowed stern and ramming prow and two banks of rowers beneath the shields of the defending soldiers, and by the 8th century BC, their navy was already in possession of war galleys with three banks of oars. Thucydides tells us that around the same time the Corinthians were the first Greeks to introduce the *triērēs*, the three-banked warship known to us as the trireme (from the Latin *trirēmis*), and to build a navy. It is a matter of contention who built the first triremes but Herodotus implies the Egyptians soon followed suit.

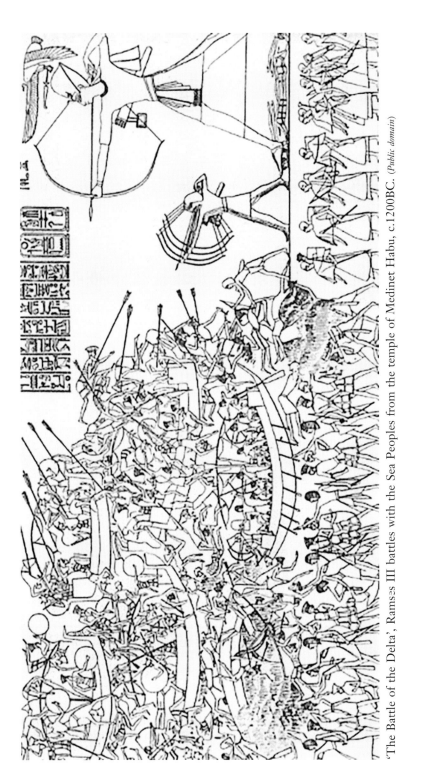

'The Battle of the Delta', Ramses III battles with the Sea Peoples from the temple of Medinet Habu, c.1200BC. *(Public domain)*

When the Persians took control of the coastal cities of Anatolia and the Levant they utilised the expertise of the conquered peoples to establish a navy, and the first recorded use of the trireme in battle was when Polycrates, the tyrant of Samos, contributed forty triremes to the Persian invasion of Egypt (c.525BC). The trireme would remain a mainstay of ancient navies until the first century BC.

Greek interest in the coast of Anatolia persisted after the Trojan War and their period of early exploration, and they began to colonise its coast around 800BC. At the same time their commercial rivals, the Phoenicians from the Lebanon, were exploring westwards. Acknowledged as the pioneers of navigation, they set up trading networks that stretched as far as the Pillars of Hercules (Straits of Gibraltar). Before the compass, navigation was performed using the constellation Ursa Minor, which the Greeks called 'Phoenician'. When exactly the Phoenicians settled in Spain is disputed, but they are believed to have founded Carthage (near modern Tunis) in the 9th century BC. It went on to become the most important trading centre in the Mediterranean.

In the east the Greek challenge to Phoenician control of the trade routes may have encouraged them to go further afield, and where they went the Greeks followed. In Sicily, Greeks and Phoenicians arrived more or less together to contest the island (c.800BC), and the Greeks established significant colonies in southern Italy and the south of France, including that of Massilia (Marseilles, c.600BC). Emboldened by their growing seamanship, Phoenicians and Greeks ventured beyond the Mediterranean into the Indian Ocean and the Atlantic. The Phoenicians were the first to explore the seas beyond the Straits, and the Egyptian Pharaoh, Necho II, whose native craft were only suitable for the calmer waters of the Nile and Red Sea, used Phoenician sailors to circumnavigate Africa around 600BC. They sailed from the Red Sea back to the Nile, entering the Mediterranean from the west. They were followed by two early Greek explorers from Massilia who ventured into the Atlantic; Euthymenes, who in the early 6th century BC sailed south along the coast of Africa, perhaps as far as Ghana, and around 325BC, Pythias, who was apparently motivated to acquire tin from Cornwall, but his voyages reputedly took him as far as circumnavigating Britain, venturing into the Baltic and even reaching what was thought to be the most northerly island, Ultima Thule, possibly Iceland.

The Phoenicians may well have been primarily traders, but they were not above a bit of occasional piracy, particularly the kidnapping of young boys and girls to be sold on as slaves in other countries. Slavery was seen as

Assyrian bireme from the palace of Nineveh 700–692BC manned by Phoenician sailors for Sennacherib rowing with their backs to the pointed prow for ramming, shields hang from the protective 'walls'. (*British Museum, CC BY-SA 3.0*)

a legitimate business in antiquity (as it would be off and on for over 2,000 years), and it was often slaves who manned the oars of the warships. It was of course the fabled kidnapping of the willing Helen by Paris that brought about the Trojan War.

In reality it was the need for resources (mainly metals), trade and land for settlement that was behind Greek incursions into Anatolia and their exploration and then colonisation of the wider Mediterranean and Black Sea littoral. Their success in this and the creation of a maritime network was largely created without direct resort to naval power, with the result that up until the 5th century Greek warships, despite the claims of the Corinthians, were still mainly *pentekonteroi*, fifty-oared vessels with the rowers seated on one long bench that went side to side, one man to an oar.

The Battle of Lade (494BC) was the first large-scale battle in which triremes were deployed. Fought off the small island of Lade, which protected the approach to the Greek city of Miletus in Anatolia, it was an opening encounter in the wars between the Greeks and Persia in which the Persians under Darius the Great were victorious. The coalition of Greek Ionian city-states in revolt against the Persian empire were defeated

The Siren Vase, Odysseus and the sirens 480–470BC, made in Attica and found in Lazio, Italy (*British Museum, CC BY-NC-SA 4.0, public domain*)

by a combined fleet of around 600 ships (according to Herodotus), out-numbering the Greeks by almost two to one, drawn from its subject peoples: Phoenicians, Egyptians, Cilicians and Cypriots.

At Salamis, sixteen years later, outnumbered Greeks turned the tables. Under the firmer leadership of the Athenians' commander, Themistocles, the mistakes of the previous encounter, where they had rowed out to meet their enemies in a chaotic engagement in which some contingents, notably the Samians, faltered, were not repeated.

Despite their proximity to the sea, Athenian recognition of the potential of sea power had been slow. During the 6th century BC they struggled to match the formidable mercantile supremacy of the island of Aegina, and their fierce economic rivalry eventually degenerated into open warfare. The dates of the encounters are disputed as our main source of informa-tion, Herodotus, appears to have conflated the timeline, but without a fleet Athens remained powerless to compete with its neighbour. When in 506BC the Athenians took the city of Chalcis and captured twenty ships, they burned them, not knowing what to do with them. It was not until Themistocles imposed his vision that the lessons were learnt. He realised that for Athens to be secure and successful it would have to develop a modern navy.

By the time of Salamis the trireme was a streamlined state-of-the-art warship built for speed, a 'bronze-rammed floating chariot' in the words of the poet Aeschylus, and it would reign supreme for another 200 years. The ships were up to 130 feet long and about 20 feet wide. Because the ship was long and narrow it was fragile and not suited to open water, and as a result trireme fleets hugged the coast. The rowers were arranged in three banks, the oars of the lower two protruded through the hull, while the oars of the upper deck were supported by an outrigger. The ram, made of wood and encased in bronze with three cutting blades at the front, was rather snub-nosed and protruded about seven feet from the prow at the waterline. The use of the ram reached its pinnacle under the Greeks. Until the development of a stronger bow, the tactic was to ram the enemy vessel from behind, which involved delicate manoeuvring. The attacker made for the stern section of the ship making sure not to get entangled with their oars so as to be able to back away easily. With their improved bows, the Corinthians introduced the practice of ramming head-on in 413BC. The Phoenician triremes carried a longer tapered ram, were broader and perhaps higher out of the water, and possessed no outrigger. Their wider decks made it possible to carry more marines, protected by a defensive bulwark lined with shields.

At her peak, Athens had a fleet of 400 ships, a force requiring close to 80,000 men. It is generally accepted that the Athenian triremes carried 170 rowers, though this figure has been disputed. A more likely number is estimated at 160 leaving room for officers, deckhands and marines to bring the number of crew up to 200. Triremes could either operate under sail or by rowing, but in battle the use of oars was preferable as it allowed greater manoeuvrability. These rowers, mainly drawn from Athens' poorer citizens, were paid and were seldom slaves. A short treatise on the relationship between its naval supremacy and democracy, the *Constitution of the Athenians* (c.440–410BC), purported to be by Xenophon, argued that by employing citizen oarsmen the State gave them a vested interest in the maintenance of Athenian democracy, giving 'poor' and 'ordinary people':

> more power than the noble and the rich, because it is the ordinary people who man the fleet and bring the city her power; they provide the helmsmen, the boatswains, the junior officers, the look-outs and the shipwrights; it is these people who make the city powerful much more than the hoplites and the noble and respectable citizens. This

being so, it seems just that all should share in public office by lot and by election, and that any citizen who wishes should be able to speak in the Assembly. [Pseudo-Xenophon, 1.1–2]

The writer goes on to say that Athens' influence amongst her maritime possessions and allies enabled these ordinary people involved in official capacities the opportunity to become adept sailors, learning to row and steer with great skill.

Having realised that they had to have a navy to take on the might of Carthage, the Romans were still slow to embrace the tactics of naval warfare. Initially during the First Punic War (264–241BC), more confident as successful soldiers, they tried to fight a naval engagement as if it were a land battle. To maximise the superiority of their army, they turned to the idea of boarding the enemy ships rather than sinking them. To do this they employed the *corvus*, or drawbridge, mounted on the prow, which

The Lenomant Relief (c.410BC) discovered in 1852 near the Erechtheum on the Athenian acropolis showing the centre part of a trireme. This with some other fragments showing twenty-five oarsmen, a helmsman, lookout and armed soldiers has enabled scholars to reconstruct a fifty-oared vessel. (*Photo: Marsyas 2006, Acropolis Museum, CC2.5 generic*)

when dropped allowed the legionary marines to storm the opposing vessel. Although this proved successful in defeating the Carthaginians, it was cumbersome and they soon resorted to taking on the Carthaginians in the ramming battle.

By now the trireme was being dwarfed by larger warships. The quinquereme (*penteres* in Greek), or 'five', was invented by Dionysius I of Syracuse and used against the Carthaginians sometime around 398BC. Modern scholarship has come to interpret the name as not referring to five banks of oars, but to the number of rowers per tier, usually taken as being in three banks, two to an oar on the upper levels and one man to an oar near the waterline. This arrangement is uncertain and there have been other suggested permutations of the number of banks and rowers per oar.

With a crew of 300 oarsmen allocated to 90 oars per side, the ample deck space of the quinquereme also allowed for a large fighting contingent aboard of between 70 and 100 marines and the deployment of such artillery as the one-armed catapult. Some 200 years later amongst the hundreds of warships at the battle of Actium, the deployment of huge quadriremes and quinqueremes reached its peak. The principle of doubling up could be extended to having three, four or more rowers per oar hence the terminology of hexareme, 'sixes', or even 'sevens', 'eights' and more, but by the 1st century AD these larger ships were mainly used only as flagships, having being supplanted by the lighter and faster libernian.

Following the collapse of the Roman Empire in the west during the 5th century, the eastern part continued on from its capital at Constantinople, the former Greek city of Byzantium. The Byzantines adapted the Roman version of the *liburna*, a small, fast and agile bireme initially used by pirates from Dalmatia. This development, the *dromon*, a galley with a full deck, a raised spur instead of a ram and later with a triangular lateen sail, became the mainstay of the Byzantine navy. In the 7th century the power of Byzantium was challenged in the east by Arab armies surging through the Middle East and into north Africa. Not content with their success on land, the Arabs took to the seas. Essentially a land people, like the Romans before them, they were happier with the tactic of boarding rather than ramming. By chaining their boats together they could create a fighting platform from which they could use grapnels and hooks to get at close quarters with the enemy. Using this method they achieved a victory over the Byzantine navy at the Battle of the Masts off Cilicia in Anatolia in 655AD.

But the Byzantines had a secret weapon, 'Greek fire'. Although incendiary weapons had been in use for some time, this was a new development

Roman bireme from the Temple of Fortuna Primigenia, Palistrina c.120BC, Pius-Clementine Museum, Vatican Museum. (*Photo: Jaques Élisée Reclus, 1830–1905, public domain*)

and it was used to great effect to repulse the Arab navy in their attempts to take Constantinople. The secrecy surrounding Greek fire has meant that its exact nature is open to conjecture, but it involved a number of moving parts, a siphon and oil or naphtha. The siphon would spurt the inflammable material, possibly onto the enemy ships, but more likely onto the surrounding water. Clay containers were also used as a form of hand grenade. The unpredictability of the oil or naphtha meant that Greek fire only saw limited use in the repulsion of naval sieges. To counter the incursions of the Arabs, the Byzantines had formed their first permanent navy and as their land possessions dwindled they became increasingly reliant on it for survival, continuing as a formidable naval power.

The difficulty of naval sieges meant that many defended coastal towns were safe from attack from the sea, but this did not mean that coastal communities could not be harassed by pirates and their people carried off into slavery; and the increasing instability of the medieval period gave rise to an increase in piracy. The incursions of Vikings into the Mediterranean saw the arrival of longships and in the 9th century the medieval galley appeared, with the capability of carrying the ever more reliable projectile

Βyzantines using Greek fire against a ship of the rebel Thomas the Slav in 821, from the c.12th Codex Skylitzes Matritensis, Bibliteca Nacional de Madrid. (*Public domain*)

weapons that were being developed; the crossbow or arbalest, and eventually guns and cannon.

In the Atlantic, the maritime nations relied more on sail, but the tideless nature of the Mediterranean and the long periods of relatively calm weather had suited the development of the oar-powered galley. Bulky sailing ships had been used to carry cargo and as military supply vessels, but the speed and manoeuvrability of galley fleets were perfect for warfare. When necessary a lateen sail, up to three on the larger great galleys, could be employed. This version of the lateen sail, which had been copied from the Arabs who had developed it in the Indian Ocean, proved more versatile than the traditional square rig. The ships of the Atlantic, built for rough seas, were less sleekly constructed and for defensive purposes they had 'castles' at fore and aft. These northern ships came into the Mediterranean in the wake of the Crusaders, and the rising naval powers of Venice and Genoa developed a number of types of galley, some of these with 'castles' for use in maritime sieges.

The northern Crusaders, often as much adventurers as holy warriors, utilised Venetian ships to take them on their excursions eastwards toward the Holy Land. These excursions brought them into conflict with the beleaguered Byzantine Empire, and in 1204 they took, and briefly held, Constantinople. By now the Venetian and Genoese navies had become a match for Byzantium, and as Byzantine power faded they were able to take over islands and coastal territories and establish 'Frankish' enclaves. But it would not be the Franks who inherited the last vestiges of the Roman Empire in Greece and the Aegean but the Turks. Constantinople fell to the Ottoman Sultan Mehmed II, the 'Conqueror', in 1453, giving the

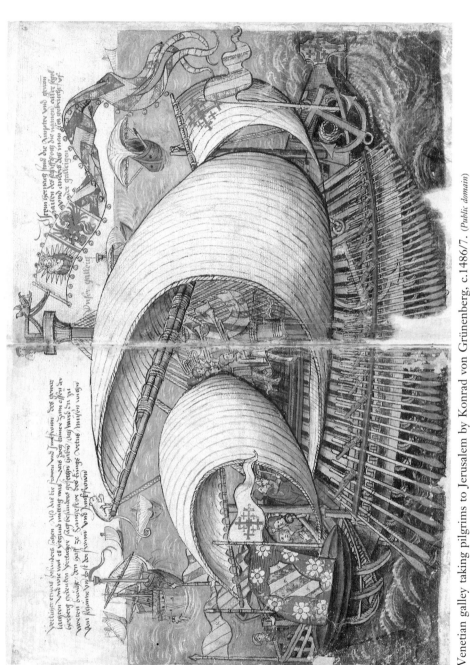

Venetian galley taking pilgrims to Jerusalem by Konrad von Grünenberg, c.1486/7. *(Public domain)*

Turks the prize of the most important city in the Mediterranean, linking the trade routes of East and West and controlling access to the Black Sea. From henceforth the capital would be known within the Ottoman Empire as Istanbul.

The Turks had already begun developing a navy and by 1402 their largest naval dockyard at Gallipoli had the capacity to take forty galleys. Like the Persians before them the Turks were not a maritime people, so they used workers and sailors from their conquered territories. As heirs to the Byzantine Empire it is little surprise that, as the Venetians record, most of their shipwrights were Greeks from Constantinople, Galata and the Greek islands and by mid-century they were even employing skilled Venetians in the capital's naval Arsenal with a resulting improvement in standards. An advantage of the galley was that to build the hull did not require a specialist dockyard, so in times of need the ships could be built at any suitable location. Furthermore, as they could be beached, they could be carried over land. But they had the disadvantage that they were unfit to carry large numbers of guns and when military sailing ships began to appear, their pre-eminence in the Mediterranean would be challenged.

The first recorded use of naval artillery during battle, three cannon and one hand gun, was by the English ship *Christopher* against the French at Arnemuiden in 1338 during the Hundred Years War. Around the same time in the Mediterranean Venetian galleys began deploying guns against their Genoese rivals. The guns were carried at the prow to fire on the enemy in the approach prior to the use of grappling hooks for boarding. Early in the 15th century, the French came up with the idea of cutting holes in the sides of a sailing ship so that guns could be placed below decks, which would lead to the tactic of the broadside. Sailing ships could now be turned into fully commissioned warships, solely designed to carry as many guns as possible with as many as three gun-decks, the heaviest guns at the lowest level. Cannon were developed to fire a variety of shot, stone or iron balls or exploding devices. By the end of the century artillery was in general use, leading to ships being categorized by the number of guns, perhaps up to a hundred, rather than the number of oars.

In the end, sailing ships would prove better adapted for the new technology, able to take the extra weight and with the space required by artillery, but in the early days it was in the balance as to which was the more effective, the galley or the sailing ship. The galley's vulnerability was less important in the Mediterranean where its manoeuvrability was superior to that of a sailing ship, dependent as it was on the wind and more ponderous under the heavy weight of its guns. The decline of the Mediterranean galley was slow and it would maintain its position in the fleet until 18th century gun technology was sufficiently improved to make artillery fire faster and more accurate.

Unlike their Mediterranean competitors the Turks had no established maritime culture. To become an Admiral in the Turkish fleet required no prior naval experience and the post would often be given to a governor of a coastal province. Similarly, captains and crew were not trained sailors. The captains typically rose through the ranks, from a crew that would also have had little previous nautical knowledge having been recruited through the levy of young men from the regions in the same way as the army. The only requirements to man the oars were regarded to be strength and health. On the other hand, tending the rigging and sails was a skilled job, so the riggers were usually levied from coastal areas where they might be assumed to have some knowledge of ships. Europeans regarded the Ottoman navy as inefficient, but when in 1539 the Turks had to recruit 23,538 oarsmen for a fleet of 150 ships it would be impractical for all of these to be experienced sailors. Criminals and prisoners-of-war were also used to make up the numbers. The Imperial galleys would also carry a complement of around sixty troops.

Typically, Italian galleys had around twenty-five pairs of oars, one oar per man, supported by an outrigger, with two to three rowers sharing the

Model of Barbarossa's galley c.1543 in Istanbul Navy Museum. (*Photo: Uploadalt, CC BY-SA 3.0*)

same bench. This method, *alla sensile*, favoured by the Venetian Republic, required skill, and the oarsmen were often professional free men. Other less democratic regimes preferred the use of slaves, convicts or prisoners of war and a simpler method was developed known as *al scaloccio*, where all the rowers on the bench pulled the same oar. The skill of the oarsmen was matched by their shipwrights, who were so skilled that using a forerunner of modern assembly-line techniques they could assemble a galley in a day. The final development of this type of vessel was the galleass, a low vessel of over 200 tons, rowed by more than 200 *galiotes* and carrying as many armoured soldiers. The merchant Richard Chiswell (1696) described seeing a galleass under construction in the Venice arsenal; 'they are very great and unwieldy Vessels, carrying 700 Soldiers and Seamen, beside 300 rowers, and are mounted with 32 brass demi canon.' An even larger ship, as the name implies, was the gallygrosse. As the oars grew larger they required more men to manipulate them, rising to as many as seven, and they were grouped together in threes. By the 16th century the increased numbers required meant that even the Venetians had to resort to the use of slaves.

The advances in naval technology and warfare were spurred on by the great age of global maritime exploration and discovery during the 15th and 17th centuries. By the end of the 16th century, the requirements of protecting their colonial interests in the Americas and fighting off English buccaneers meant the Spanish had to maintain two largely separate fleets, one in the Atlantic mainly of large ocean going and heavily gunned sailing ships, and one in the Mediterranean, where naval warfare had hardly advanced, still reliant on the fighting galley.

A portent of things to come, which went largely unheeded at the time, came during the Holy League's defeat by the Ottomans at the Battle of Preveza (1538) when the cannon of a great Venetian galleon soundly repulsed the enemy's galleys. The two great naval encounters of the century epitomised the difference between the Mediterranean and Atlantic methods of warfare. At the Battle of Lepanto (1571) the Spanish and their allies of another Holy League took on the Ottoman navy in the last great battle using oared galleys, and won; in 1588 the galleons of the Spanish Armada took on the English sailing ships in the Channel, and lost. The lesson was that, by maintaining two distinct types of fleet in each theatre meant that they had fallen behind the technical advances of the English who had developed faster, more manoeuvrable ships capable of carrying heavier guns. The English seamanship and gunnery was also superior, and utilising the latest tactics that took advantage of the wind and deploying the ships in a line (hence 'ships of the line') they could fire devastating broadsides from distance, negating the need to board the enemy ship. This success of a smaller organised navy over larger opponents finally swayed the balance towards sail. Although Lepanto did not end Ottoman dominance in the eastern Mediterranean, their continued reliance on galleys meant they fell behind western advances. The new English and Dutch warships that began to penetrate the Mediterranean were far superior, so much so that in 1607 the privateer Sir Thomas Sherley boasted that one English warship could defeat ten Turkish galleys. To face the increased western threat, the Turks had to modernise, but to make such large-scale changes meant levying an extraordinary tax burden on its population fostering discontent and unrest. The easier course of action was to avoid naval confrontations.

Before the arrival of the English and Dutch, an important tactic of galley warfare was to attempt to separate the quicker galley from its slower moving escort under sail. To counter this, hybrid vessels were developed that combined sail and oars. These hybrids found particular favour among the pirates who continued to plague the Mediterranean, and the Barbary pirates of the north African coast developed their own version of a galliot or half-galley known as the *fusta*. Light, narrow, and nimble it was typically powered by up to thirty-six rowers per side, two to a bench, and one or two lateen sails. Like a traditional galley, it was the oarsmen's job to bring the ship in and out of harbour and to engage with the enemy in battle when manoeuvrability was needed, while the sails could be used to save the rowers' energy. With its shallow draft it was perfect for coastal waters, where it could hide ready to pounce on any passing ship, and combined with its speed and mobility, and its up to ten small calibre cannon, it was ideal for both war and piracy. The fusta was used by Barbarossa and his brothers in their conquest of Algiers, which they eventually handed over to the Turks, and it continued to be used by other north African corsairs to terrorise Christian shipping and the islands and coastal areas during the 16th and 17th centuries. The Ottomans found it useful, particularly in the west, to augment their navy by co-opting the Barbary pirates into their ranks.

Whereas the Atlantic navies had developed tactics designed for naval warfare, the opposing commanders at Lepanto, who were better versed in land warfare, had treated their fleets like armies. They required their oarsmen to manoeuvre their ships into position facing one another and then proceeded to slug it out. The only sophistication was to attempt to out-flank the enemy or to make a breakthrough, which was achieved by having

Model of a 16th century Maltese galley built for the Knights of St John, in the Museo Storico Navale di Venezia. (*Photo: Myriam Thyes, CCASA 3.0*)

the fleets line up abreast or in a crescent formation. A hundred years on, the innovations of the 16th century had changed the nature of naval warfare considerably. Now that the gun batteries were universally deployed on the sailing ships' sides, the 'line ahead' formation, all the ships in a line, had become the default. The line of attack was now sideways for maximum deployment of the guns rather than prow ahead for ramming or for a boarding bridge. The continued use of galleys by the Venetians and Turks meant they presided over an ever-diminishing sphere of influence, while the Atlantic powers were becoming global operators.

This did not mean the Mediterranean was entirely forgotten, the Spanish and the French had seaboards in both seas and by the mid-17th century their rivals, the British, confirmed their desire to be a permanent presence there by establishing a Mediterranean Station or Fleet. This became firmly established by the capture of Gibraltar, which became its base, in 1704, formalised by the Treaty of Utrecht in 1713. Such successes during the War of the Spanish Succession (1701–14) left Britain as the strongest European naval power. It may not have had a standing army; but, as other nations invested their money elsewhere, it maintained a permanent professional fleet, with a bureaucracy housed in the Admiralty, in the belief that it would guarantee its future liberty and its greatness. Britain enjoyed its role of pre-eminence in the Mediterranean until mid-century when it was challenged by a resurgent France.

The British may have had more ships, manned by first class crews, but complacency had let them be overtaken by the French in warship design. The French began building larger two-decked ships capable of delivering a heavier broadside than its equivalent 74-gun British third-rate ship (ship of the line). With a state of the art hull, it was faster and more seaworthy, but it had disadvantages. Its rigging was inferior and it could not withstand an enemy barrage as effectively. The race was on to develop a hybrid ship that combined speed, manoeuvrability and firepower with the durability and internal strength, and the cheapness, of the British ship. The result was the new 74-gun ship introduced in 1755 that combined the speed and power of the French ship with the robustness of the British model. At the Battle of the Nile, thirteen out of Nelson's fourteen ships would be these 74s. The personnel were modernised too, introducing more formalised ranks, and conditions for the men, particularly provisions, improved. This did not mean men were no longer press-ganged (forced compulsory service) in times of war; the practice continued until 1815.

A favoured policy of the British during the wars with France that followed the French Revolution was the use of the 'open blockade' to confine the enemy fleet in harbour. This required the crews to spend many days of inactivity afloat. Despite the improvements, conditions for the ordinary sailor were often harsh, and the strains imposed on them during the long years of the French wars came to a head in a series of mutinies, the most famous of which was at Spithead in 1797. After a number of demands were met by the Admiralty most of the sailors returned to their duties, but it did not quell all the discontent. The most effective officers decided that the best remedy was to keep the men active at all times. Nelson, an admirer of the ordinary seaman, was able to maintain discipline where crueller and weaker captains were not.

The British warship was a strangely egalitarian institution. Many of the officer class were of aristocratic birth, promoted through their family connections, but there was opportunity for a man of humble origins to rise up on merit. The lower deck was a community of all nations. On board the 120-gun first-rate frigate, HMS *Caledonia*, which took part in the blockade of Toulon in 1814, there were Swedes, Frenchmen, Portuguese, North Americans, Brazilians, Germans, Italians, Russians and Africans. In the novel *Mr Midshipman Easy* (1836), Captain Marryat describes his fictionalised experiences aboard the frigate HMS *Imperieuse*, commanded in

A French ship under attack by Barbary Pirates c.1615 by Aert Anthoniszoon (1579–1620), National Maritime Museum, Greenwich.
(Public domain)

HMS *Victory*, the most famous British ship-of the line and Admiral Nelson's flag ship from 'The Fleet Offshore', 1780–90, anonymous folk art. (*Compton Verney Art Gallery, CC BY-SA 4.0*)

the Mediterranean by the colourful Thomas Cochrane between 1806–8. The young 17-year old midshipman is taken under the experienced protection of Mesty, 'a great man in his country', who after coming to Britain to escape slavery has enlisted in the Royal Navy. He may have found freedom, but despite his admirable qualities of bravery and leadership there is a limit to equality. Mesty is given limited responsibility, but it is Easy who will be promoted to captain.

Nelson was not only a great leader but also a tactical innovator. He believed that if his subordinates were well briefed he could rely on them using their own initiative to seize the moment, giving him greater flexibility while remaining in control. His favoured method was simple enough, to attack 'from to-windward', i.e. with the wind behind, and then to break through the enemy line. At the Battle of the Nile this meant that as the leading ships at the front of the French line were being attacked those at the back were unable to tack up-wind in time to help them. The victory re-established British supremacy in the Mediterranean and with the addition of Malta, which became the Royal Navy's principle base there, the British sphere of influence had moved further east.

By the early-19th century the Ottoman navy had begun to modernise. They were still using galleys when their fleet was crushed by the Russians at Chesme (1770), an encounter notable for the use of fireships. Fireships had a long history, they had been used to great effect by the English against the Spanish at the time of the Spanish Armada, but by the early 1800s their use had gone out of fashion in Western navies. When the Greeks rose up in revolt against their Ottoman masters in 1821, they pitted their meagre resources against the might of an Empire. Their small navy of mainly converted merchant ships were challenging a far larger and superior fleet for dominance in the Aegean. To help their land army they blockaded ports and one of the tactics they resorted to was the use of the fireship. The Western allies were then somewhat taken aback when the Ottomans deployed fire ships against them at the Battle of Navarino, no doubt prompted by their successful use by the Greek rebels. This time the tactic gained the Turks little. The allied victory was the last major battle fought completely between traditional wooden sailing ships; steam ships were used in addition to sailing ships by the Russians and Turks at the Battle of Sinop (1853) during the Crimean War.

The 'long peace' (a misnomer because there is always a war somewhere) between the Napoleonic and First World wars did not mean that the countries, particularly the great powers, neglected their armed forces. For the British this primarily meant the navy, but all the naval powers embarked on a fierce competition to out-do one another. The first steam-powered warship, the *Demologos*, was a floating battery used to protect New York harbour from the British during the Anglo-American war of 1812, and the Royal Navy began to experiment with a number of small steam warships from the 1820s. Ironically it was the Greek irregulars that deployed the first steamship in war. The *Perseverance*, built in Deptford in

1826 under the instruction of the English Philhellene Frank Abney Hastings, was renamed the *Karteria* and under his command it successfully took part in a number of engagements during the Greek War of Independence. Thomas Cochrane, who was now employed by the Greek navy, ordered five more steam-powered warships from London but due to delays two arrived too late to take part, while the other three never made it. The deployment of the *Karteria* was so effective that George Finlay wrote in his *History of the Greek Revolution* (1861):

> The battle of Salona afforded the most satisfactory proofs of the efficiency of armament of steam-boats, with heavy guns, which Captain Hastings had so long & warmly advocated. The terrific & rapid manner in which a force so greatly superior to his own was utterly annihilated by the hot shot & shells of the 'Karteria' silenced the opponents of Captain Hastings's plan throughout all Europe. From that day it became evident to all who studied the progress of naval warfare, that every nation in Europe must adopt his principles of marine artillery, & arm some vessels in their fleets on the model he had given them.

Steam was the future and with the introduction of the Paixhans naval gun by the French in 1824 the days of the wooden sailing ship were numbered. Explosive shells, fired at a high trajectory and low velocity from howitzers or mortars, had only been used in ground warfare until this point. Naval guns required a flat trajectory and for some time cannon balls had been augmented by canister shot, a container filled with small metal balls that burst open upon firing giving the effect of a shotgun. The Shrapnel shell invented in 1784 was a development of canister, using a time fuse to break it open over the target. The Paixhans gun's ability to fire explosive shells at a flat trajectory was used for the first time by the Russians to devastating effect on Turkish wooden ships at Sinop. The first steam ships used paddles for propulsion, but by mid-century the paddle had been superseded by the screw propeller, which gave more space amidships and better scope for the firing of broadsides.

The race was now on between Britain and France, each trying to outdo the other. The French took the lead when they launched the first 'ironclad', *Gloire*, in 1859, but it was soon followed by the improved British ship, *Warrior* (1860), larger and built of iron rather than ironclad. The ironclads were first tried out in battle off the Dalmatian island of Lissa in 1866 when the Austrians defeated a larger Italian force. With its occupation of the Dalmatian coast Austria, later Austro-Hungary, had become an increasingly important player in the Mediterranean since the end of the 18th century, and the *Regia Marina*, had been formed in 1861 on the unification of Italy. The Battle of Lissa was the united Kingdom of Italy's naval baptism of fire. The ironclads still had some features of the old galleys; they carried sails in case of need and they had a ram shaped bow. Lissa was the last naval battle to feature ramming as a tactic; while the mast was phased out, its success meant the ram shaped bow remained a feature for the next fifty years of warship design.

As Alfred Thayer Mahon pointed out, there were similarities between steam power and the galley as opposed to sail; both can move in any direction independent of the wind. The wind could also cause high waves, rendering the lowest gun deck out of action. During the American Civil War warships were deployed with guns in armoured turrets to considerable advantage, but this development was impractical for sailing ships and by 1870 sails were being abandoned altogether. Manoeuvrable turrets also meant the abandonment of guns along the ships' sides on a number of decks. This gave the steamship the ability to both attack head-on and to deliver a broadside as a ship of the line.

To protect its interests overseas Britain was prepared to back up its concerns with a show of naval force. The term 'gunboat diplomacy' became common usage for interference by the imperial powers in lesser nation's affairs after Lord Palmerston despatched a naval squadron in 1850 to protect a Gibraltarian British citizen from rioting in Athens. During the controversial action known as the 'Don Pacifico Affair' the gunboats blockaded Piraeus and bombarded Athens. Britain's confidence in its navy meant it was not only able to protect its citizens wherever and whoever they were but also able to impose its will. In the Mediterranean it protected the Italian leader Giuseppe Garibaldi during his revolt that would lead to Italian independence; it maintained the balance of power between Russia and Turkey; and it assisted in the annexing of Egypt to 'protect' the Christian population and look after European interests.

By the turn of the century the arms race, which had led to the development of ever more powerful guns, better armament and bigger ships, culminated in the launching of the *Dreadnought* in 1906, the fastest and best armed ship afloat. From now on every other navy would be measured by how many dreadnoughts they could build. The dreadnoughts were followed by 'super-dreadnoughts', and so on, and by 1914 the Royal Navy had forty dreadnoughts and battlecruisers carrying more accurate 15-inch guns. Meanwhile a new force was rising in the East and the Japanese had

HMS *Dreadnought*'s 12-inch guns with anti-torpedo boat guns on the turret roof, 1907–22. (*Library of Congress Bain collection, public domain*)

shown the accuracy of their guns utilising their own new director system in their victory over the Russians at Tsushima in 1905.

Torpedo boats and submarines had been in development since the early 19th century. In the War of 1812 the Americans used torpedoes, i.e. a bomb on the end of a pole, to ram the British ships, but the modern self-propelled torpedo was perfected by the English engineer Robert White-head in 1866 from an Austro-Hungarian design. It was first used in the Russo-Turkish War of 1878, the fallout from which procured independence from the Ottoman Empire for the Balkan states of Romania, Serbia and Montenegro, autonomy for Bulgaria and handed Cyprus over to the British. Initially the use of torpedo boats against battleships was slow to find favour, but they would come into their own during the Second World War.

The first successful use of a submarine to sink an enemy ship was during the American Civil War. The French were the first to substitute mechanized power for human propulsion in 1863 and the installation of the Whitehead torpedo turned the submarine into a viable weapon (the last Whitehead torpedo was used operationally in Norway in 1940) but it would take almost fifty years of development before the submarine came into widespread naval use. By 1914 the German navy was leading in submarine technology and the *U-boat* was ready to emerge into the mythology of the two World Wars.

The British battle fleet formation of 1914, favoured by Admiral Sir John Jellicoe, was based around the dreadnoughts at the centre proceeded by a mobile squadron of cruisers for scouting, with further forward the light cruisers to make contact with the enemy, all protected by flotillas of destroyers to ward off *U-boat* torpedo attacks. It was highly organised and rigidly planned, the antithesis of Nelson's system. After the great fleets of Germany and Britain had barely came into contact in the Atlantic, it was decided to send a large fleet to the Dardanelles. The battleships proved ineffective against Turkish mines and heavily defended shore batteries in their attempt to gain access to the Black Sea. Back in the Atlantic, the battle fleets finally engaged at the Battle of Jutland in 1916. Although it left the British Grand Fleet heavily bruised with the loss of three battlecruisers and eleven other ships, the German ships were so badly damaged that they had to remain in harbour for weeks. As a result, the Germans decided to rely on their submarines and it became the Royal Navy's turn to enforce a blockade on Germany.

The First World War saw the introduction of many of the elements that would play a more significant role when war resumed in 1939: convoys of merchant ships with naval escort, the depth charge, asdic for the detection of submarines, naval aircraft. Flying boats or aircraft launched from cruisers were used for bombing and reconnaissance, or in the Mediterranean with limited success to make torpedo attacks. In 1918, HMS *Argus* became the first carrier able to launch and retrieve aircraft, and in 1924, the year of the formation of the Fleet Air Arm, it was followed by the *Hermes*, the first purpose-built full-length aircraft carrier. But in the inter-war period it was the USA and the Japanese who were the front-runners in the development of aircraft carriers.

In 1922, the naval powers, Britain, France, Italy, Japan and the USA, signed the Washington Treaty, an agreement limiting the construction and number of warships of each nation. This effectively ended Britain's supremacy as a naval power. Matters reached a low ebb for the Royal Navy when, during the austerity of the 1930s, wages and conditions had deteriorated so much that the ratings mutinied. Despite the Washington Treaty other navies, particularly Japan and Germany were modernising and expanding and the Royal Navy was no longer able to intervene as before in world affairs, standing by as Mussolini used the Suez Canal to transport his troops for the invasion of Abyssinia. By the end of the 1930s Britain had reversed its policy and began to reinvest in the navy, making it still the largest in the world, with more battleships and aircraft carriers than any other, but outnumbered in each ocean and sea.

The British went into World War II trusting that the concept of the battle fleet still held good. Germany's attempt to starve out Britain by submarine attack on the convoys had failed, and, it was believed, would do so again. The greater threat was thought to be the German 'pocket battleships', heavily armed but theoretically lightly built to be in accordance with the restrictions of the Treaty of Versailles (1919). Britain also relied on its soft power, the bases and financial links around world and its control of fuelling stations and sea-lanes for merchant shipping. In the Mediterranean this meant Gibraltar, Malta and Suez, which enabled it to put pressure on neutral trading nations and to starve out belligerent ones. But the nature of warfare was about to change significantly; it would be mass bombing and the importance of air cover that would dictate the course of events and without aerial support both armies and navies would struggle. Although submarines (and frogmen with mini-submarines favoured by the Italians) would play their part, air supremacy would prove more decisive. Germany relied heavily on its *U-boats* in both wars, but lost even though their submarines were undefeated. It was the failure of the Luftwaffe that was the real blow.

James Sommerville, commander of Force H in Gibraltar and a veteran of the First World War, was initially sceptical as to the use of naval aircraft and the deployment of aircraft carriers, but after the success of the air attack from the carrier HMS *Illustrious* on the Italian fleet at harbour in Taranto, the first of its kind, he changed his mind. As Admiral Andrew Cunningham, commander of the Mediterranean Fleet, was to put it: 'Taranto, and the night of 11–12 November 1940, should be remembered for ever as having shown once and for all that in the Fleet Air Arm the Navy has its most devastating weapon'.

Communications had improved considerably since 1918, allowing aerial reconnaissance and bombardment to become more effective. As the Italian and German airbases were within range of Malta they were able to bomb the island and to harry the Mediterranean convoys, making it necessary for the RAF and Fleet Air Arm to give both protection and to support offensive actions. The combination of the possibility of attack by submarines and aircraft forced a change in naval tactics. The line-ahead and 'ship of the line' was abandoned in favour of close defensive formations, with aircraft carriers and other essential ships protected by a ring of gunships and torpedo boats reminiscent of the ancient Greek tactic of the *kiklos*, a circular formation with all the warships with their prows turned outward employed 2,500 years earlier.

Chapter Two

Salamis, 480BC

Defeat of the Persians heralds in the Golden Age of Athens

> Messenger:
>   Persians, the whole barbaric host is fall'n …
>   In heaps the unhappy dead lie on the strand
>   Of Salamis, and all the neighbouring shores …
>   O Salamis, how hateful is thy name!
>   And groans burst from me when I think of Athens.
>   [Aeschylus, *Persians*]

Classical Greece is so rightly admired for the beauty of its art and architecture and the insights of its poets and thinkers that it is easy to overlook that the same society that produced such wonders was also locked in almost constant and extremely bloody warfare. The historian Xenophon described the blood-stained battlefield after Coroneia (394BC), possibly from first-hand knowledge, as having 'the dead bodies of friends and enemies lying close to one another, shields broken to pieces, spears snapped asunder, daggers without their sheaths, some on the ground, others sticking in bodies, and others still in the hands of the dead'. Herodotus, our main source for the period of the Greeks' conflict with Persia, gives the Persian commander Mardonius the following lines concerning Greek warfare in his *Histories*: 'When they declare war with each other, they go off together to the smoothest and levellest bit of ground they can find, and have their battle on it – with the result that even the victors never get off without heavy losses, and as for the losers – well, they're wiped out.' The slaughter was such that identifying bodies in the aftermath was only made easier for the Spartans when they employed the method of attaching nametags to their wrists.

Every summer was the marching season, and there was a ready supply of enemies, whether fellow Greeks from competing city-states or from barbarian nations. Athens, the city that came to be seen as the pinnacle of Greek civilisation, was no exception, and at the end of each combat-season they set up memorials listing all the city's dead, whether citizens, allies, slaves or foreign mercenaries.

For one brief moment in their history, though, the Greeks were able to put aside their constant internecine warfare and come together against a common enemy; the time known as the Persian Wars. And it was this moment that forever sealed Athens' reputation as the foremost Greek city.

The geography of the Greek peninsula, with its mountain-encircled plains and the sea never far away, was well suited to the growth of the city-state. The relative isolation of these communities made them intensely competitive, even if they shared an underlying sense of common identity and uniqueness, which they collectively saw as setting them apart from the

A kylix from around the 5th-century BC showing a Greek hoplite and Persian warrior fighting. (*Archaeological Museum of Athens, public domain*)

'foreigners' or barbarians, those who did not share their language, culture and religion. By the early 5th century the Greek city-states and their colonies in southern Italy and Asia Minor had grown in self-confidence and prestige. This inevitably brought them into conflict with the interests of other colonisers and empire builders, the most powerful of which was the expansionist Persian Empire to their east. Persian military might had carved out an empire stretching from the Indus to Asia Minor, the Levant and Egypt. With the Eastern Mediterranean under his dominion, the Persian King of Kings, Darius I, set his sights on Europe. He invaded Thrace in 512BC, threatening to encircle the Aegean so that it would no longer be a Greek lake.

Darius was not only interested in military conquest; if he could get what he wanted by other means he did so. He realised that the endemic rivalries and faction fighting of the Greeks could be exploited and that he could win over leading members of the political class with bribes and promises of friendship. His offers of great rewards to those who would become servants of the Empire worked on some, but when the Ionian Greek cities of Anatolia rose up in revolt against their Persian masters, the Athenians and Eretrians (from the island of Euboea) were bold enough to send twenty-five triremes in support of their fellow Greeks (499BC). The venture failed, and having crushed the revolt Darius felt he now had a pretext to invade the Greek mainland to teach the upstart cities a lesson.

Despite being able to call on a vast combined navy drawn from those of his subjects with maritime expertise, he put his main effort into subduing the Greeks by land. Thrace was re-invaded and the already pliant kingdom of Macedonia became a client state. Most of the other Greek cities then submitted or were paid off, and once Eretria had been quickly annihilated and its citizens enslaved, Athens was left isolated. The threat to Greek liberty was now so great that when Athens asked the Spartans for their help, they put aside their differences and made ready to march. Spartan intervention proved unnecessary when the Athenian citizen infantry, aided by a small contingent from neighbouring Plataea, inflicted a shock defeat on the far larger Persian army at the Battle of Marathon (490BC). The Persian force, variously estimated at between 25,000 and 100,000, had made the first recorded amphibious landing in the bay and in the ensuing battle 6,400 of them died at the hands of the Greek hoplites, or foot soldiers. The mere 192 Greek dead were given the heroic honour of being buried where they fell in the two mounds that remain as their memorials today and, to mark the victory, work began on the Athenian Acropolis on a temple that has become known as the 'Old' Parthenon (as opposed to the temple visible today begun in 447BC). Marathon, famed as one of the great turning points in history, may have saved Greece from Persian sub-jugation for the time being and enhanced the reputation of Athens, but, like a horror movie trope, the Athenians had not killed the beast, only wounded it; Persia would be back with a vengeance. The defeat of its military might by an army outnumbered by between three-to-one and ten-to-one was a humiliation for Darius. This was something he and the Persians could not forget, so by 480BC a huge Persian combined land and sea expedition, drawn from warriors from across the empire, was again advancing on Greece under Darius' son Xerxes.

Xerxes' decision to invade Greece was not taken lightly. After first having to be persuaded by Mardonius, Darius' principal commander, to embark on an endeavour of such magnitude, for the Persians did nothing by half, he had to set in motion preparations that would take several years. Meticulous forward planning would be needed for the logistically complex endeavour of transporting his immense army through Thrace and into Greece in coordination with naval support. Once the invasion began, the Hellespont had to be bridged by a pontoon capable of taking the vast army, a canal wide enough for two ships abreast carved through the Chalkidiki peninsula at the narrow point before Mt Athos, and roads built. The size of the invading force can only be estimated. The ancient sources put the figure in the millions; according to Herodotus, perhaps 2.5 million troops, with the same number in support. He also says the Greek spies reported counting 1,207 triremes. Modern historians prefer more cautious estimates of between 120,000 and 300,000 men. Either way it is no surprise it took three months for the army to travel 360 miles (600km) through Thrace to Therme (modern Thessalonika) collecting their Balkan allies along the way. There was no doubt that the Great King meant to send a message to the small and irritating Greek states. With Macedonia and Thrace and many of the islands under Persian control, the door was open for the invasion of the southern heartlands by land and sea. The only problem it would seem was keeping the army fed.

The problem for the leaders of Sparta and Athens, was not having too many mouths to feed but having too few allies to resist such a force, and then where to make a stand against the enemy. It was uncertain how many other of the cities would resist the Persian's coercive diplomatic advances and pledge their allegiance to free Greece. Thessaly, to the south of Macedonia, could not be relied on, overrun as it was with spies and col-laborators. As the threat of the Persian advance drew closer, the Athenians turned to the oracle at Delphi for advice.

From her vapour-induced trance the Pythia, the mouthpiece of the god Apollo, uttered her prophecy to the Athenian envoys. Herodotus (7.141) informs us she was as enigmatic as usual, but her doom-laden words contained a telling glimmer of hope. The enemy might cross into Attica and take it, but 'the wooden wall only shall not fall'. Furthermore, the Athenians were not just to sit and wait for the approaching army, they should:

... turn your back and withdraw from the foe.
Truly a day will come when you will meet him face to face.
Divine Salamis, you will bring death to women's sons
When the corn is scattered, or the harvest gathered in ...

The Spartans too had hoped for consolation from the Pythia, but left with the message that even the strength of lions or bulls could not withstand the enemy. Either their city was to fall and their country made a wasteland, or they would 'mourn the death of a king of the house of Heracles'. Xerxes would not be stopped until one of these came to pass. When the Delphians themselves asked if anything could stop the Persians, they were told to 'pray to the winds'.

The Greeks were well aware of the Persians' intentions. Among the first to realise that the Persian menace was not over was Themistocles of Athens, an astute politician with populist appeal amongst the lower classes who had fought with honour at Marathon. Recognised as being clever, his weakness was that he was perhaps too clever for his own good. As early as 493BC, when he was elected as the Archon Eponymous, the supreme magistrate, his response to the continuing threat from Persia was to order work to begin on a new harbour and fortifications at Piraeus using money from the treasury earmarked for the construction of the Old Parthenon. Any problems with this strategy were forestalled by a stroke of good fortune. A new rich vein of silver was discovered at the nearby Laurion mines (c.483) and Themistocles persuaded the populace that, instead of each citizen receiving a dividend from their windfall, they should use the funds for the more urgent need to build a navy. He argued cleverly that this was necessary to protect Athens from its rival, the nearby island of Aegina. Athens at this stage was not the most powerful of the Greek city states, lagging behind maritime Corinth and Aegina. The chance to outstrip Aegina's formidable fleet was a message that went down well with his audience.

What set Attica, with Athens its capital, apart from the other Greek states was its experiment in democratic rule. Introduced into Athens by

Cleisthenes in 508–507BC, democracy as a form of government was still in its infancy. The Persian threat would be a test as to how the citizens of Athens, that is those allowed to vote, would react in a crisis. Themistocles the wily politician had quickly learned how to sway the assembly and he achieved his real aim of preparing against the future threat of the Persians by focusing on the here and now. Of course he was happy to receive the credit for his foresight when the Persians made their move into Europe. As Thucydides cynically viewed it in his history of the Peloponnesian War, written in the latter years of the 5th century, the famed Athenian collective spirit was merely a reaction to danger. Describing their reaction to the destruction of their army and navy in the calamitous expedition to Sicily (413BC), he tells us that the distressed citizens decided to 'procure money and timber by whatever means they might, and build a navy. As befits a democracy, they were very amenable to discipline while their fright lasted'. When the Persians appeared on their doorstep, the political wrangling stopped and the city united. Marathon had been a triumph for the citizen army, in which every male from eighteen to sixty served, but this time around the onus would be on the navy. Aeschylus, a native of Salamis who would achieve fame later as the first tragic dramatist, served as a young man at Marathon with his brother (who died there) and ten years later at sea at Salamis with his younger brother.

Flush with Laurion silver, the Athenian dockyards were swiftly put to building a fleet of triremes. The riches from the mines were loaned to wealthy citizens who were then responsible for fitting out the ships, and as a reward they were given titular command. By 480, Athens possessed at least 147 triremes on active service, with around 53 in reserve, a fleet of 200 ships; ships that would require 40,000 men to crew them. Themistocles drafted in men from the heavy infantry as oarsmen and marines, earning the criticism, according to Plutarch, that he was turning noble warriors into 'vile-galley slaves'.

Slaves they were not: it is thought slaves in Athens were used only for the most menial tasks aboard ship. The oarsmen were brought together on an equal footing, a crew of citizens, though to what extent has been debated. In a few months these landlubbers had to be turned into highly trained oarsmen who, for their pains were financially rewarded. In contrast the army's hoplites had to provide their own armour and the cavalry to keep their own horses. The prospect of payment meant that the rowers were drawn in the main from the *thetes*, the poorest citizen class. Free men they may have been, but with no land or particular skills they would have had little to lose compared to their wealthier Athenian brothers. Crewing a trireme, particularly for the oarsmen, was an uncomfortable experience. The ships were cramped and there were long periods of inactivity and boredom before any action took place; and when it did it was swift, terrifying and gory. It is no surprise then that the security and intense way of life aboard ship created a new subclass with its own solidarity.

With the north of Greece pretty much in their pocket, the Persians were aware they were likely only to encounter resistance from the other Greeks once they had passed through Thessaly. In 481, when the danger of invasion became real, those Greeks who, according to Herodotus were 'loyal to the common cause', met in Sparta and, as the Persians were crossing the Hellespont, again in Corinth the following year. The Cities formed a Hellenic League or Alliance led by Athens and Sparta, but it was a show of Greek unity in name only. The Persians could call on their Greek vassal states, including the chastened one-time rebels from Ionia, while even the Spartans' fellow Peloponnesians from Argos were moved to stay out of it. Many cities remained neutral, waiting to see what happened, and the Thebans were split. Meanwhile the Persians had managed to persuade their Phoenician ally Carthage to act as the other half of a pincer movement from the west by threatening the Greek cities in Sicily. As a result, Gelon, the Tyrant of Syracuse, the leading city on Sicily, could not be persuaded to assist the Greek Alliance with his 200 triremes. Those left to defend Greece resolved to bury their differences, even Athens and Aegina.

Sparta assumed the natural role of leader of the land armies, but when it came to the navies, it was a more delicate decision. Although it might have appeared obvious for the Athenians, who were now in a position to provide most of the ships, to take command, this could have provoked unease amongst the captains from Corinth or Euboea with their long maritime traditions. So in order to maintain the necessary unity, Themistocles swallowed his pride and diplomatically handed the command of the sea to land-locked Sparta as well.

Themistocles had to use his diplomatic skills at home too, where those of the hoplite class preferred to relive the glories of Marathon rather than commit their fate to the uncertainties of the waves. This problem was taken off his hands when it was decided to send a combined force of 10,000 men led by the Spartan Euainetus to hold the northern border of Thessaly at the Vale of Tempi, a narrow defile between the mountains of Olympus and Ossa. The plan backfired when they were informed by king Alexander I of Macedon that the gorge was easily by-passed, and they discovered they could also be undermined from the rear by the possibility of civil war in

Bust of Themistocles. *(Photo J.P.A Antonietti, 1926, CC BY-SA 4.0)*

Thessaly, which was riven by rival pro-Greek and pro-Persian factions. The army was forced to make a humiliating withdrawal and the commanders to have a rethink. It is uncertain when the oracle at Delphi was consulted, and it has been argued that it was probably more than once, with this the most likely defining moment.

On the return journey Themistocles noted the strategic significance of the fortified coastal pass at Thermopylae at Thessaly's southern border, just across the narrows from the island of Euboea. Using his assessment of the terrain, the League decided it was the place to make a stand and a combined force of 4,000 Peloponnesians was despatched under the Spartan king Leonidas. The Theban loyalists and contingents from the other small states south of the pass joined the defenders bringing the total up to around 7,000. In an illuminating aside, Herodotus says that the Phocians only showed such great loyalty to the cause because of their hatred of their northern Thessalian neighbours and it was they who had built the wall across the pass seen by Themistocles. To coordinate with the army's advance, the supporting Greek navy was sent to the north coast of Euboea, where the new Athenian ships were drawn up on the beaches at Artemisium at the ready to be launched. Artemisium held the approaches to Thermopylae, the straits between Euboea and the mainland and the seaward route south around the island.

The approaching Persian navy was so large that the Greeks had little hope of halting its approach in a set battle, and the first skirmishes with the triremes of the Sidonian advance party were ominous as the Greek patrols were easily beaten back. With the Athenians dominating the fleet, it was now that Themistocles began to show his potential skill as a naval commander. He slipped the fleet back to Chalcis, in the hope of tempting the Persians into the narrows between Euboea and the mainland, but the Persians failed to take up the challenge and when the Greek ships returned to guard the straits, the expected enemy fleet were still nowhere to be seen. It was August, a time notorious for unpredictable weather, and the Greeks prayed for winds.

Meanwhile, as the odds against them began to sink in, the Greek defenders at Thermopylae understandably began to feel uneasy. The slow and dreadful approach of the Great King could easily be tracked from the cloud of summer dust kicked up by his colossal army as it crossed the Thessalian plain; but Leonidas and his elite contingent of 300 Spartans remained calm. When a Persian scout reported back to Xerxes, the king was bemused to learn that the Spartans were preparing for battle by under-taking light exercise and combing their long hair. Xerxes, who did not want the bother of an annoying delay, was prepared to be magnanimous on his own terms, and he offered the Greeks various bribes to encourage them to quit their position. The Spartan resolve swayed the others, and when the Persians then demanded the Greeks hand over their arms, Leonidas replied, 'Come and take them' (Plutarch: *Spartan Sayings*).

Eventually the prayed-for break in the weather arrived and the storms came. During the first Persian invasion under Darius, his commander

Mardonius had suffered heavy losses in a storm rounding the tip of the Mount Athos peninsula. To avoid a repeat Xerxes had built the canal across the peninsula, but unfortunately for the Persians the weather played its part again, only this time the fleet was caught by the gales out in the open sea. The severe losses meant a change of plan and any hope of out-flanking the Greeks at Thermopylae or supplying the ground army was put on hold. For four days there was a standoff between the two armies, during which Leonidas bided his time waiting for the expected Persian onslaught. When finally Xerxes unleashed his forces, in the narrow confines of the pass wave after wave of Persian troops were shattered against the spears and shields of the Greek phalanx. While the Spartans were holding firm, the danger at sea was not over. The Persian fleet had been battered, perhaps losing 20 per cent of its number, but it was by no means destroyed and the Greeks at Artemisium found themselves confronted by a similar hostile horde, an approaching fleet of around 800 triremes. Against such odds, Themistocles had to use all his skills to persuade his fellow commanders to hold the line, even if it meant a little bribery.

With intelligence that the Persians were planning to send a detachment around the seaward coast of Euboea to cut off the Greeks' escape route through the channel between the island and the mainland, Themistocles had to come up with a plan to avoid being bottled up in the straits. It was agreed that part of the Greek fleet would sail south by night through the straits to confront the Persians by surprise and trap them between the Greek ships patrolling the coast further south. To do this without giving the game away the remainder of the fleet would make a diversionary attack on the main body of the Persian fleet in the open sea. Initially the skilled Persian crews from Phoenicia in their lighter and faster triremes seemed to have the upper hand, but the Greeks had come prepared. They had developed a tactic, the *kiklos*, whereby the ships formed a circle with their rams facing outward like the spines of a hedgehog, thereby nullifying the superiority of the enemy ships, and then at the right moment they would attack. The tactic was so successful they captured thirty triremes, and took the honours at the end of the day. This was an important morale booster for the Greeks who now knew they could take on the best of the Persian navy. However, the next part of the plan, the night-time dash down the channel, had to be abandoned because of more bad weather. Unfortunately for the Persians, as they made their way around the island they were again caught out by a north-easterly gale that lasted three days and caused the loss of many ships, 400 according to Herodotus, dashed to pieces on the rocks. In relief the Athenians gave thanks to Boreas, the north wind, who in myth was married to an Athenian girl.

For a moment it seemed as though the Greeks might halt the Persian advance then and there in central Greece. Reinforcements were on the way, fifty-three fresh ships from Athens, and a hit and run raid on a squadron of Cilicians had proved successful. Meanwhile Leonidas was holding out for another day. The Greeks had enjoyed the luck so far, but the full frontal assault was yet to come. This time the massed ranks of Phoenician, Egyptian and Ionian ships bore down on the Greek line, which although it suffered severe losses held firm. It was obvious though that with their smaller numbers taking a heavy battering they would not survive a war of attrition. Then the news from Thermopylae made up their minds. The Greeks had been betrayed. A local had led a contingent of 10,000 elite Persian troops, the Immortals, by way of one of the little known mountain paths to outflank the defenders. Once he heard of their approach, Leonidas realised the game was up and he decided the priority was to save as many of his troops as he could. He ordered the majority to retreat, while he and his Spartans, aided by the Thespians and Thebans were to hold the Persian army at bay for as long as possible. As was their tradition

Persian king killing a Greek hoplite, possibly Leonidas, cylinder seal, c.500BC–475BC.
(Photo: Marco Pins, Metropolitan Museum of Art, New York, Livius.org, CC0 1.0, public domain)

the Spartans and Thespians fought to the death, the remaining Thebans surrendered and as prisoners were branded with the royal mark. With the pass taken, the route to Athens was open, but the valiant rear-guard action had cost the Persians dear, perhaps 20,000 men to the Greek losses of around 2,000. Now was the time for the Greek fleet to slip away by night. Once again the fate of Greece would be settled in Attica.

In Athenian myth, during the war between gods and giants the goddess Athena had tossed Draco, a huge serpent, into the sky, turning it into a constellation and thereafter the snake was associated with the goddess. So when the priestess who tended the sacred snake kept in her honour on the Acropolis as a guardian of Athens said it had disappeared, in effect abandoning the city, it was taken as a particularly bad omen. Plutarch took it to mean the goddess herself had abandoned the city; either way, for the populace it was taken as a sign to do the same. As the prophecies of the Pythia seemed to be playing out one by one – the death of a king of the house of Heracles, Leonidas, and the intervention of the winds at Artemisium – it would now appear provident to trust to the 'wooden wall', which some took to be the walls of the Acropolis. Themistocles had argued that the 'wooden wall' referred to the fleet and his advice to the people was to retreat to 'Divine Salamis'. This may have appeared fanciful at first, and on his return to the city he was disappointed that few had listened, so it was fortunate that the priestess made a timely intervention and he won the debate. This and the impending arrival of the Persians focused the mind enough to persuade the Athenians to decamp to the island, joined by refugees fleeing from across Attica.

Salamis, only one nautical mile (2km) from Piraeus, virtually blocks off the Bay of Eleusis, leaving two narrow straits at either end. Here the Athenians established what amounted to a city in exile, from where they could clearly see the rock of the Acropolis above their city. It was a near total evacuation, taking about a week to complete. As much of the finances and city's treasures that could be moved, the grain supply and of course the ships were transferred to the island. To leave Athens and the Sacred Rock of the Acropolis to the mercy of the Persians was a heart-wrenching and difficult decision, and a bold show of unity for the fledgling democracy. Nevertheless, the Assembly voted that the Acropolis should not be left totally empty, the treasures of the gods were to remain under the protection of the stewards and priestesses. These guardians were joined by a few stubborn defenders, unable or unwilling to leave and they put their faith in their own 'wooden wall', hastily thrown up across the entrance to the citadel in preparation for a siege.

The Athenians still had the support of the allied ships loyally keeping a watchful eye in the straits, but the inclination of their captains was to retreat to the Isthmus. For the Peloponnesians the logical step was to return to this narrow strip of land near Corinth that joined the peninsula to the mainland, and make preparations for its defence. The land forces, under Leonidas' brother Cleombrotus, were there already, digging in. Themistocles saw this division of the Greek forces as a potential disaster. However brave the Spartans and however vigorously the Corinthians might defend their homes, he thought they would eventually succumb to the might of the Persian army. For his strategy to work, he had to persuade the Spartan Eurybiades, the overall commander of the fleet, and the other Peloponnesians to put aside their natural desire to safeguard their homelands by taking the fight to Attica.

At the first war council of the returned fleet, Adeimantus, a Corinthian, urged that the allied navy combine forces with the army at the Isthmus, from where they could strike in concert. The captains from Aegina and Megara, north of the Isthmus, were none too enthusiastic with this prospect. Along with Athens they contributed three-quarters of the fleet and their view was important, but Themistocles knew the Greeks could not afford a split. The Athenians could not take on the Persian fleet alone. A united front was imperative if there was to be any chance of victory, and victory was what he had in mind.

Once again Themistocles would have to draw on his political skills honed in the Athenian council and assembly meetings to persuade his allies of the wisdom of his plan. With so many commanders of the contributing ships in the allied fleet there were many conflicts of interest to address. He argued that to make a stand in open water, as they would have to if they retreated to the Isthmus, would suit the enemy. And he had learned the lesson of Artemisium; in confined waters their heavier ships had the advantage. During a vital meeting, news arrived that the Persians had entered Attica and were devastating and burning their way across the country. It was to be assumed then that the Persian navy must surely be close at hand, but for the time being, Themistocles' arguments were enough to persuade the allied commanders to remain united at Salamis. The defenders on the Acropolis were well aware of the location of the Persian army as they had a fine view of the fires burning across the plain that signalled the Persians' approach and before long the streets of the city were aswarm with the enemy and the Sacred Rock surrounded.

Xerxes took up a viewing position on the Areopagus, a hill opposite the citadel's main entrance where the Athenians held their court, and ordered his archers to shoot flaming arrows at the wooden ramparts. The rock was also defended by huge bronze-age walls, but when Xerxes tired of this tactic they proved to be an insufficient defence when some of his elite mountain troops managed to scale the sheer eastern cliff of the citadel which had been left unguarded. Once inside, they succeeded in opening the western gate and their comrades flooded in; a bloody massacre of the defenders and priestesses followed. Some of the guardians preferred to throw themselves from the eastern walls rather than trust to the mercy of the Persians. The temples, including the Old Temple of Athena and the unfinished Old Parthenon, its columns only two or three drums high, were then destroyed and the whole citadel set on fire with the help of the wooden scaffolding from the building work.

Miraculously, it was said the next day the olive tree planted by Athena herself by the north porch of the Erechtheion grew a new branch signifying that the city would rise again. The legend persists; succeeding armies may have tried to cut the tree down but it can still be seen, or a version of it, today. The Athenians had been prepared for a violent reaction from the Persians, but the total devastation of their city and the desecration of their holy sites took them by surprise. For the Greeks on Salamis or at sea it was a signal that could not be missed, as the flames and smoke were clearly visible in the night sky. This was an atrocity beyond the Greeks' comprehension, as it ignored their long held convention that the sacred sites of their enemies should be respected and spared during war. It was an act that in their view tempted divine retribution. For the Persians it was a risk worth taking, for they followed the teachings of Zoroaster and worshipped another god, Lord Mazda. Seizing the Acropolis may have been a strategic move but its destruction was an attack on the soul of the city, aimed at wiping out the collective memory represented by the storehouse of treasures accumulated by the Athenians over centuries.

The captains of the repaired Persian fleet too would have seen the flames of the burning city. For them it was a sign of success and a message that it was safe to approach the Athenian harbours. On their arrival at Phaleron, Xerxes called a conference of his admirals. He did not heed the advice of Artemisia, the Queen of Halicarnassus, renowned for her bravery and highly respected by the king, to starve the Athenians out, or that of Demaratus, the exiled ex-king of Sparta who had thrown in his lot with the Persians, to launch an amphibious attack on the Spartan homeland, forcing them to save their homes and split the alliance. The Great King was impatient to get the job done here and now and he was not prepared to sit out a long winter in a devastated Athens or weaken his navy on an expedition to the Peloponnese. He wanted to deliver the fatal blow at Salamis. Had not the Persian navy routed 350 Greek triremes in a similar situation at the Battle of Lade (494BC) off Miletus during the Ionian revolt? His view that this was the best course of action was bolstered by reports from his spies of dissention in the Greek camp.

The sight of Athens in ruins had affected the morale and unity of the Greeks. The Peloponnesian commanders were again on the verge of splitting the alliance and making for home and Themistocles had to persuade Eurybiades to call one more council, appealing to his honour as a Spartan and not to accept defeat. Once again the argument for making a stand at the Isthmus was raised, and once again Themistocles had to bring all his skill to bear to defend his position. The debate became heated. The Peloponnesians were not keen to fight for an abandoned country. The Corinthian commander, Adeimantus, belittled Themistocles as 'a man without a country', a mere refugee, and when in his enthusiasm Themistocles out of turn embarked on an impassioned speech, he was interrupted by Adeimantus who said: 'in the races, the man who starts before the signal is whipped', to which Themistocles replied, 'but those who start too late win no prizes'. Although Themistocles knew that if the fleet left Salamis it would mean the dissolution of the Greek forces, the Greeks no longer fighting for 'one country' but for their own interests, this time he made his plea directly to Eurybiades saying, 'It is now in your power to save Greece'. He then outlined his plan for defeating the Persians at Salamis by stating the advantage of fighting a larger enemy in narrow waters, and by doing so, not only saving Athens but Sparta as well. The Peloponnesian commanders had to weigh up the prospect of Themistocles' threat to withdraw the Athenian fleet and sail off into exile in Italy against the prospect of being bottled up in the straits by the Persians and stranded on an overcrowded island. For the time being Themistocles had again won the day.

The Persians were experienced at exploiting Greek division, and Xerxes' advisors came up with a ploy to test their resolve. Approximately 30,000 troops were ordered to march towards the Isthmus with as much pomp and display as possible in the knowledge that they could easily be seen from Salamis, while squadrons of the fleet took up threatening positions at the entrance to the straits. The results were as the Persians had predicted. The Peloponnesian sailors became restless, fearing they would be stranded in Salamis and forced to defend Athens while their homes burned. With the

Greeks once more at each other's throats, arguing over the same old ground, in the late afternoon the Persians withdrew in full view leaving the straits temptingly unguarded.

As the Persians would have backed up their attempts at sowing disunity with bribes through their agents in the Greek camp, it came as no surprise to them when Sicinnus, a loyal (and wealthy) slave in the household of Themistocles and tutor to his son, appeared with a message. Sicinnus had secret information to pass on from his master who, tired of his comrades' lack of unity and fighting spirit, was now hoping for a Persian victory. The Greek admirals were planning to save themselves and abandon Salamis overnight, all the Persians had to do was block the escape routes and the Greek fleet was there for the taking. Tom Holland argues that in order for Sicinnus to be able to return to the Greek camp he must have been carrying terms of amnesty for Themistocles and the Athenians. Herodotus makes no mention of this, only the bravery of Sicinnus in risking capture and his life. The Persians were delighted with the news and immediately ordered the fleet to put their plans into action, but of course they were naïve to take the words of the wily Themistocles at face value.

It was a busy night for the Athenian leader, who had absented himself from the bitter arguments still going on between the Greek commanders. Waiting outside the meeting he was taken aside by Aristides, nicknamed 'the Just', a one-time rival who had been ostracised from Athens by popular vote. Following an amnesty for exiles Aristides had been reinstated as a *strategos* (general) and had just returned from a mission to Aegina. Aristides put aside their old animosity, for he was eager to tell Themistocles that he had seen the Persian fleet silently taking up position to block the straits. Aristides wanted him to inform the Peloponnesians they were trapped, but Themistocles replied that he had anticipated this would happen, because it was he who was responsible, saying 'for as our men would not fight here of their own free will, it was necessary to make them, whether they wanted to or not'. He then asked Aristides to go into the council and to report the news, for they would be more likely to believe him. And even if they did not, the die was cast.

According to Herodotus, the admirals remained unconvinced of the news until it was corroborated by sailors on a ship from the island of Tenos that defected that night from the Persian fleet. This was the second Greek defection; a ship from Lemnos had previously changed sides at Artemisium. That the Greek admirals reacted to the news with surprising equanimity and no show of panic casts doubt on them being mere pawns

in Themistocles' game all along. It may be that the whole episode of dissention within the Greek camp was exaggerated to create one enormous
bluff, for the Greeks had already shown at Artemisium that they had
learned their strategy. The Persians obviously had not learned theirs, and
fell for it. As dawn approached the Greek ships were ready and primed for
action, whereas the Persians had spent all night taking up their positions.
Xerxes ordered 400 troops to be put ashore on the small island of
Psyttaleia that guarded the eastern strait, with the majority of the fleet
strung out behind from the coast of Salamis to Piraeus. In the meantime,
an Egyptian squadron was sent to guard the western escape.

It was now late September, and at around 7am as dawn broke the Great
King had already taken up position on Mount Algaleus, which overlooks
Piraeus, from where he had a clear view of the straits and the disposition of
his forces. Seated in splendour on a gilt throne and surrounded by his
retainers, he had his scribes at the ready to record the forthcoming victory.
The Greeks too had prepared for what the day would bring and, as was
their custom before battle, made animal sacrifices to the gods. Plutarch
tells us Themistocles' sacrifices were said to also include three captured
Persian princes, nephews of Xerxes. As human sacrifice was not common
practice among the Greeks, it is thought that if the act took place it would
more likely have been the killing of captives taken in time of war. The
uncompromising nature of ancient warfare is reinforced in Aeschylus'
account of the battle when he has Xerxes warn his captains that they would
lose their heads if any of the Greeks escaped.

As always with accounts of battles, especially the further back one goes,
precision of detail is difficult. In ancient warfare no individual would have
had an overview of the action, with the result there are differences in the
reports that were then handed on to succeeding generations. The first
casualty of detail is the number of participants. Herodotus gives the
number of Greek triremes as 380, Aeschylus, who was there and could be
assumed perhaps to be a more reliable source, put the fleet at around 310,
but he was writing poetry. He also tells us the Persian fleet was around
1,200 strong, a figure generally agreed in the sources, plus an even larger
number of support vessels. Of these Aeschylus says 207 were 'ships of
exceptional speed', presumably a lighter and faster form of trireme. The
Athenians provided the bulk of the Greek ships with 180 triremes, far out-
numbering the other major contributors. Corinth and Megara mustered
the same as at Artemisium, forty and twenty, and a further thirty came
from Aegina. The island of Euboea contributed twenty from Chalcis,

The *Olympias*, a reconstruction of a Greek trireme belonging to the Hellenic Navy showing the ram. *(Photo: George Alaniaris, CC-BY-SA 3.0)*

seven from Eretria and two from Styra. Aside from Corinth, the other Peloponnesians contributed forty-nine (Sparta sixteen, Sycion fifteen, Epidaurus ten, Troezen five and Hermione three). The Corinthians' allies along the Ionian coast, the island of Leukas and its mainland neighbour, Ambracia, provided three and seven respectively. A few of the small Aegean islands had managed to remain free of Persian control, so Naxos provided four triremes, Keos (Kea) two and Kythnos one trireme and one fifty-oared pentaconter. Some of their fellow Cycladic islanders contributed a few pentaconters, two from Melos and one each from Serifos and Siphnos. One pentaconter from Magna Graecia came from Croton (in what is now Calabria), the city famous for the school founded by Pythagoras. The ship was paid for and captained by the wealthy Phayllos, a fifty-year-old famous former athlete. The number, not including the pentaconters, was brought up to 380 with the ships from Tenos and Lemnos. As those who are good at maths will note, Herodotus' numbers do not add up, so he was either not including all the contributing ships in his breakdown or he made a mistake. Even so it was a larger fleet than at Artemisium, which finally totalled 333 ships, but it would be assumed no match for Xerxes' fleet when facing odds of more than six to one. Herodotus breaks down the contributors to the Persian fleet of 1,207 ships as follows:

Phoenicia	300
Egypt	200
Cyprus (Greek)	150
Cilicia	100
Ionia (Greek)	100
Caria	70
Aeolia (Greek)	60
Lycia	50
Pamphylia	30
Doria (Greek)	30
Cyclades (Greek)	17

Again this does not add up, and most estimates, taking into account losses at Artemisium and reinforcements, put the figure at between 600 and 800, reducing the odds to two or three to one. As can be seen there were probably more Greeks fighting on the Persian side, willingly or not, than on the side of the Hellenic League. The Ionian and Carian squadrons were under the overall command of Ariabignes, another son of Darius and the Great King's half-brother. Other contingents were commanded by their own kings: Sidon by Tetramnestus, Tyre by Matten and Aradus by Merbalus. Queen Artemisia of the Greek city-state of Halicarnassus led her own Carian squadron as she had done at Artemisium. Having so many leaders proved to be a disadvantage to acting quickly together when the forthcoming battle began not to go to plan.

The strategy for the Persians had always been to engage in the open sea. So when the Greeks appeared lined up in their battle formation in the narrows of the straits and not hurrying in disarray for the exits, the Persian command must have been somewhat nonplussed. It is therefore a mystery as to why they would so readily abandon their strategy and fall into Themistocles' trap. It may have been over-eagerness on the part of the admirals to impress the Great King, or Xerxes himself from his vantage point who impatiently gave the signal to engage, so sure of their superiority that it was worth the risk. He would have also seen the Corinthian triremes break from the Greek battle-line as if to make for the western exit, which was guarded by the Egyptians, and concluded that Themistocles was telling the truth.

For whatever reason, the Persians forgot their strategy and lurched into the attack. Rounding the islet of Psyttaleia the fleet passed into the strait, flanked by the Phoenicians on the right and the Ionians on the left. The Phoenicians were under the command of two Persian admirals, Megabazus and Prexaspes, a sign of a lack of faith on the part of Xerxes. To their surprise, the leading ships were confronted by the sound of singing coming from the opposition and then the sight of the ships drawn up in battle formation. The song was a paean, a mix of a hymn of triumph and a war cry sung by soldiers going into battle.

The Greeks had emerged from their narrow harbours in single file and then taken up position in two lines abreast. Due to a 5ft rise in sea level the straits were even narrower than today and the Greeks had more than enough ships to block the way, and the second line would guard against the *diekplous* manoeuvre, which the Persians had successfully used at Lade, whereby their ships would sail line abreast between the gaps in the opposing line and then turn on them from behind. There seems little doubt that the Athenians were drawn up on the left flank against the Phoenicians. In the centre was a mix of the smaller contingents, while it is suggested that the Aeginetans were either next in line to the Athenians or they opposed the Ionians on the right, or they may even have been lurking further east down the strait were they could pick off stragglers. It is also argued that the Spartans held the right flank. It is probable that in the haste and heat of the moment such details became confused.

If it now dawned on the Persian captains that they were being propelled headlong by their swift oarsmen into an ambush, it was too late to turn back, sandwiched as they were between the Greeks in front and the mass of the rest of the fleet speeding up from behind. Their alarm may have been allayed for a moment when it looked as though the Greeks were not fully prepared. For a moment it seemed as if they were backing off and reluctant to engage, but in reality this would have been wishful thinking; it is more likely they were either manoeuvring to close ranks or it was a ploy, for all the while the Persians' ships were being drawn deeper into the confines of the straits and within range of Greek onshore archers.

When the Greeks were on the verge of running aground, an Athenian trireme broke ranks and headed straight at the enemy, ramming one of its opposite number, at which point it became entangled in the enemy's oars. Whether this was a signal or not, it had the effect of spurring the others to join the action, rushing to its assistance and saving the captain Ameinias and his crew. The Athenians' old rivals, the Aeginetans, of course laid claim to their being the first to engage the enemy when a phantom woman appeared to one of their number, a late arrival carrying statues of the patron heroes of Aegina, the sons of Aeacus, and loudly asked for all to hear if they intended to go backwards all day. She then urged them on to attack the enemy.

An epigram by the contemporary poet Simonides of Keos, quoted by Plutarch in his *Moralia*, states that Democritus of Naxos was the third to join the fray, taking and destroying five ships and recapturing a sixth that had been taken from the Greeks. In Aeschylus' play *The Persians*, however, it is the Spartan right wing under Eurybiades that attacked first in an orderly fashion, urging each other on with the shout 'Charge! … set your country free! Save your children, your wives …' and then, 'Ship crashed her bronze beak upon a ship, the first being a Greek one that sheared off the figurehead of a Phoenician ship'. With the two fleets approaching one another head on, it was not necessary for the heavier Greek ships to build up speed in order to do great damage. This is when the discipline of the rowers, working blind in cramped conditions, came to the fore. There was no time for split-second decisions, and any sign of panic would make any manoeuvre impossible. The rowers, concentrating all their effort like athletes, could only trust to fate that they would come out alive.

Just before impact the pilot would order the rowers to back water in order for the ram not to penetrate too far. Ramming was not enough to sink the opponent, only cause it to take on water. The next stage was a volley of arrows and javelins from the marines, followed by hand-to-hand combat. The soldiers on the great Persian flagships, in Plutarch's phrase, shot their 'arrows and javelins as though from a city wall', emphasising the greater height of their vessels out of the water. The Greeks had an advantage over most of their Persian and Mede opponents; they knew how to swim. If they survived the mêlée, they could escape the foundering ship. In the ensuing confusion of battle, they held their discipline, acting as one and coming to each other's assistance, against a force that engaged at random, if bravely, whilst under the cruel eye of Xerxes. Plutarch credited Themistocles with not only picking the battleground but the time of day to best advantage. It being autumn, a knowledge of the local wind conditions was useful, so he took 'care not to send his triremes bow on against the Barbarian vessels until the hour of day had come which always brought the breeze fresh from the sea and a swell rolling through the strait'. The local breeze was known as *aura*, the name of a minor deity, so once again the gods or fate would play a part.

As the Persian fleet pushed further into the strait, the restricted space forced the ships to jockey for space so that they lost their positions. With the danger of fouling one another's oars, the ensuing disorder gave the attacking Greeks, who were holding their own line, the advantage. The swifter enemy ships could no longer twist and turn, or build up speed to bear down on a chosen target. As predicted, between 8.00 and 10.00am the breeze began to pick up and the heavier Greek triremes, lower in the water, were able to hold their line while the Phoenician ships with their high decks and sterns were skewed round to present an easy target for the Greek rams. The increased swell also created havoc for the famed Scythian archers who were unable to take steady aim. Eventually the Phoenician line cracked before the Athenian onslaught. Those ships that could, turned tail for safety, leaving crewmen in the water hoping to be picked up by a friendly ship or, if they could, to swim for shore.

On the left flank, Herodotus claimed the Ionians and Carians fared better than the Phoenicians against weaker Greek opposition. It was only when the Phoenicians had been dealt with that the left flank could be defeated with the aid of the Athenians and the smaller contingents from the centre. Most of the Ionians had committed themselves wholeheartedly to the fight, more so than they had done at Artemisium, perhaps in the knowledge that they were in full view of the ever-watchful Xerxes. They captured a number of Greek ships, and the Samians took the honours amongst the Persian ranks. Some captains though remembered Themistocles' plea not to aid the Persians, and held back from the action. There was no love lost between the Phoenicians and the Ionian Greeks, so it was understandable for those Phoenician captains that had escaped the carnage to claim to Xerxes that the Ionians were not pulling their weight, or that they had deliberately turned on Phoenician triremes. Unfortunately for them, their pleas fell on deaf ears, as Xerxes had made careful note of any outstanding actions and to whom to attribute them. As a result, it was the Phoenicians that lost their heads.

The Corinthian ships that Xerxes had seen making a feint as if to escape by the western strait returned to add their weight to the Greek cause, in the knowledge that the Egyptians guarding the exit were too far off to be a threat. Herodotus records that some of the Athenians accused them of turning up late on purpose, thereby missing the action; but this was not believed by the rest of the Greeks. As the battle turned into a general mêlée in favour of the Greeks, the retreating Persian ships created chaos as they mingled with those coming up behind. More destruction was caused during this confusion than at any other moment of the battle. The retreating vessels became easy targets for the Aeginetan contingent lurking in the narrows as they made their way out from the strait. The Aeginetans distinguished themselves to such an extent that the rest of the

Greeks recognized their bravery and awarded them a prize for valour. In order for the Aeginetans to successfully ambush the fleeing Persians, Aristides landed with a contingent of heavy infantry on Psyttaleia, where they set about slaughtering the Persian soldiers who had been stationed on the island that morning. Those Persians that did not flee were cut to pieces by the Athenians.

The strict hierarchical nature of Persian command meant that once a commander was incapacitated or killed, there was a tendency for discipline to collapse. In contrast the individuality of the Greeks allowed them to improvise and take the initiative when called upon. The Spartans at Thermopylae had fought on even after Leonidas had fallen. The Greeks would have known the Persians' dependency on the chain of command, and the enemy flagships were singled out as desirable targets. Artemisia was picked on for special treatment, in part because they resented a woman taking arms against them but mainly because there was a reward of 10,000 drachmae on her head. She managed to escape due to a bit of good fortune and a mix-up in identification. Xerxes' half-brother, Ariabignes, was not so lucky. He was the most notable Persian fatality, and his loss would have further undermined the morale of the fleet. Herodotus does not record how he died, but it is possible that Plutarch in his *Parallel Lives* misnamed him as Ariamenes, the 'strongest and most just of the King's brothers'. In his colourful account Ameinias and Socles, who were together on one ship, bore down on him:

> … and as the two ships struck each other bow on, crashed together, and hung fast by their bronze beaks, he tried to board their trireme; but they faced him, smote him with their spears, and hurled him into the sea. His body, as it drifted about with the other wreckage, was recognised by Artemisia, who had it carried to Xerxes.

Having survived the initial onslaught, Ameinias and his crew had gone on a successful rampage through the Persian ranks, epitomising the individual endeavour and duelling nature of what in essence became single-combat between ships. Spurred on by the need to impress their king, the Persian captains competed with one another to make a kill, whereas the Greeks managed to put their rivalries to side and work for the common good. Despite taking the distinction of being the outstanding Athenian captain on the day along with Eumenes, Polycritus of Aegina taking the overall honour, it was Ameinias who let Artemisia off the hook. Artemisia, when she saw Ameinias' trireme bearing down on her, took evasive action in the crowded waters, crashing her vessel into a fellow Carian trireme.

Ameinias, not realising who he had had in his sights, assumed the manoeuvre was an attack on purpose made perhaps by one of their own ships or a Carian ship that had changed sides. Artemisia's motives were open to question; was it merely evasive action, did she in fact take the opportunity to ram a rival, King Damasithymus, with whom she carried a grudge, or was she playing a duplicitous game. The lucky part of her escape was that she also avoided Xerxes' wrath because he was informed by his watchers, who had in their turn misidentified Damasithymus' ship, that Artemisia had rammed one of the enemy. The unhappy king replied, 'My men have become women and my women have become men.'

The battle lasted all day and during the lulls the weary oarsmen could stretch and take a rest, oars could be replaced with spares carried on board, and quick repairs could be made by the ship's carpenter. With the shore close at hand, the Greeks were able to replace their wounded with fresh men and take on supplies. Confined in a small space the progress of the battle could easily be followed from the shore and those of Xerxes' sailors lucky enough to make land, if they reached the wrong shore, were easy prey to the Greek soldiers. The retreating Persian fleet made for Phaleron, leaving the straits filled with floating corpses and the wreckage and debris of battle. The numbers of ships and lives lost can only be estimated. Herodotus says that the following year the Persian fleet only numbered 300, and the losses may have been somewhere in the region of around 300, depending on the starting figure. A disaster when compared to the Greek losses of around forty ships. Salamis, like Thermopylae, proved the wisdom of choosing your battleground on your own terms, both exploiting the constricted arena to advantage to even up the odds between a smaller and a larger force, and the effectiveness of maintaining a disciplined and unified force.

In a council of war Mardonius comforted Xerxes by absolving the Persians and laying the blame on the cowardly Phoenicians, Cypriots, Cilicians and Egyptians. He put forward the option of carrying the fight to the Isthmus, or, in his view the better plan, for the main army to march home and leave him with a select force to finish off the Greeks. The next day, Xerxes toyed with the idea of building a pontoon bridge to Salamis, but in the end resolved to heed Mardonius' advice. Xerxes' despondency was only increased with the news that Gelon of Syracuse had inflicted a heavy defeat on the Carthaginians at the Battle of Himera on the same day, putting an end to his ambition to conquer the west and making his priority maintaining control over his Greek possessions in the Aegean and Ionia. He left Mardonius in Greece, who was hoping the opportunity would restore his reputation. Mardonius retreated to Thessaly for the winter and returned to sack Athens again the following year. He then fell back to Boeotia in the hope of luring the Greeks into battle. He got his wish, and victory over the Persians was completed when his land army, now deprived of its naval support, was defeated at the Battle of Plataea by troops from Sparta, Athens (under Aristides), Corinth and Megara. This time the victory was credited to the steadfastness of the Spartan foot soldiers, and the Thebans also distinguished themselves, but in fighting on the wrong side. As for the Persian navy that had been ordered back to guard the Hellespont for the retreating army, the surviving ships made it to Samos only to be defeated, supposedly on the same day, at Mycale on the Ionian mainland after beaching their ships.

*   *   *

Salamis was a defining moment for the Greeks. As with the cenotaphs and war memorials of the First World War, the Greeks of the Alliance commemorated their heroes in stone and verse. For Phayllos, far from his native home of Croton in Magna Graecia, he advertised his achievement of capturing a number of enemy triremes during the battle on a statue he had erected on the Acropolis at Athens. For the Athenians, once Attica was cleared of barbarians, the first task was to rebuild their city. A programme was initiated by Themistocles to quickly construct new defensive walls for the city, using blocks that had survived the Persian destruction, including those from the Acropolis. The regeneration was also an act of commemoration and masonry still standing was incorporated into the rebuilding programme out of respect. Statues from the temples were collected and buried within the sanctuary and war trophies and booty stored and displayed on the Acropolis, including a stretch of the enemy's ship's cables. The sword of Mardonius who died at Plataea was displayed in the new Parthenon.

The rebuilding programme would take years and the new Parthenon was not begun until 447BC under Pericles, when he diverted Athens' increasing wealth to beautifying the city. The spoils of Salamis though did finance the huge bronze statue of Athena that faced the scene of the battle. Built in the 470s by the sculptor Pheidias it was 130ft (40m) tall, and visible from Sounion 43 miles away. The memory of Salamis was kept alive in other ways. During the Great Panathenaia, a summer festival held every four years that continued into the 3rd century AD, a huge *peplos*, or body-length woman's dress from one piece of cloth, was embroidered with figurative scenes and transported to the Acropolis in the form of a sail

Column drums from the Old Parthenon used as a memorial in the rebuilding of the Acropolis wall under Themistocles. (*Photo: Seligmanwaite, CC BY 2.0*)

hung from what was believed to be one of the Persian triremes mounted on a cart. The naval tradition was remembered in a regatta held in the Munychia harbour at Piraeus during which a mock sea battle was performed. Eventually the tomb of Themistocles was positioned overlooking the rowing races and the collective spirit of the oarsmen recognised by the prizes being awarded not to individuals but the winning team.

The memory of Salamis hung heavily over the next generation. Those who were youths or born at the time of Salamis or just after were destined to mould the golden age of Athens and of what we associate with Greece. In the following years Athens became the intellectual and artistic hub of Greece, even continuing its influence into the years of the Roman Empire. Sophocles was 16 years old when he led the male chorus in the *paean*, a victory poem or chant. He would go on to be one of the three major classical tragedians and do his bit fighting for Athens when it went to war with the island of Samos. Of the other two great tragic dramatists who reflected on morality and the human condition, Euripides, born like Aeschylus on Salamis, would have been about ten at the time of the battle. Aeschylus of course fought in the battle and imaginatively reflected on his experience through the reactions of the enemy to their defeat in his play *The Persians*. Pericles, the son of the politician and general Xanthippus, who led the Athenian navy at the Battle of Mycale, was a teenager at the time of Salamis. His first public act was to finance a production of Aeschylus' play in 472BC to celebrate the battle. He went on to become such an influential figure in Athenian and Greek history that the period of his dominance is referred to as the 'Age of Pericles'. Herodotus, for whom we are indebted for most of what we know about Salamis through his *Histories*, came from Halicarnassus and was aged 4 at the time. Before going on his travels and being drawn to Athens, his youth spent in Ionia gave him a Persian perspective on the events of the Persian Wars.

Defeat of the largest empire of the time confirmed to the Greeks their superiority over barbarian despotism. The Athenians in particular put their victory and strength down to their democratic system of government and the ethos behind it. After Thermopylae, when the Persian general Tritantechmes asked what the Greeks were up to, he was informed that they were celebrating the Olympic festival, during which the victors were awarded a laurel wreath as a prize. He then exclaimed 'Alas, Mardonius, what kind of men are these that you have brought me to fight against – men who compete with each other for no material reward, but only for honour.' The Athenians laid great store on honour but more importantly on the unity granted by citizenship. The ideal of self-sacrifice for the common good became so strong that it resonated down the ages. The words of St John the Evangelist, 'Greater love hath no man than this, that a man lay down his life for his friends', are an echo of the sentiments expressed by Euripides in his recently discovered play *Erecthius* (c.423BC) in which Queen Praxithea, whose daughter has sacrificed herself to save the city, articulates the idea that Athenian patriotism is not expressed through personal glory but by giving up one's life for the common good: 'At the cost of just one life I shall surely not fail to save our city ... I love my children but I love my fatherland more.' These lines so memorably captured the Athenian democratic spirit that Lykourgos quoted them a hundred years later during a lawsuit *Against Leokrates* (330BC), in which the defendant was accused of abandoning his comrades. The sentiment was taken up again by the Roman poet Horace in his *Odes* (23BC), from which the quotation *Dulce et decorum est pro patria mori*, 'It is sweet and proper to die for one's country', became a common expression of patriotism at the beginning of the First World War; it was used ironically by Wilfred Owen in his poem of the same name. The one defining thing the Greeks possessed which the Persians lacked was a unified purpose and love of country. As Aristotle said in his discussion on the nature of courage (*Nichomachean Ethics*, VIII, 3.2):

> But professional soldiers prove cowards when the danger imposes too great a strain, and when they are at a disadvantage in numbers and equipment; for they are the first to run away, while citizen troops stand their ground and die fighting ... This is because citizens think it disgraceful to run away, and prefer death to safety so procured; whereas professional soldiers were relying from the outset on superior strength, and when they discover they are outnumbered they take to flight, fearing death more than disgrace. But this is not true courage.

War with Persia did not end with Salamis and Plataea. The Greeks were now on the front foot, and Xerxes' Ionian possessions were under threat. Themistocles had laid the foundations of Athenian naval dominance, making them strong enough to take the war to the enemy. For mutual protection, and then to break Persian naval power and push them out of the Aegean altogether, they formed a confederation of allies, the Delian League (478BC), in which they were the dominant player. This was followed by an Athenian League to raise funds from its allies to build a more formidable navy that over time transformed it into a mini-empire. Athens' increased wealth under Pericles that funded the rebuilding of the Acropolis temples was also used to create a city that would be both beautiful and awe-inspiring. Although Themistocles was the Athenian hero of the hour at Salamis, his reputation meant he never rid himself of his enemies and after being accused by jealous opponents of being too clever and taking bribes, he was eventually exiled in c.472BC and, ironically, eventually found refuge in the Persian empire where he was given a governorship by king

Artaxerxes I and died at Magnesia in 459BC. Such was the nature of Greek politics.

Once the dust settled the old rivalries opened up again, and by 431BC Athens was at war with Sparta. Humbled by Sparta during the Peloponnesian wars, the power of Athens faded, and a hundred years after Salamis, Artaxerxes II was able to exploit Greek divisions to such an extent that he took back control of the Greek cities of Anatolia without a fight. It was left to Alexander the Great to take up the challenge to finally humble the Persians in retaliation for their invasions of Greece. His campaigns into Anatolia began as an expedition to liberate the Ionian Greek cities and his victory at Granikos (334BC) was payback for the destruction of the Acropolis. Some 300 Persian shields from the battlefield were sent to be displayed in Athens along with the booty from the dead soldiers for the Parthenon. And after the decisive battle at Gaugamela (331BC) in northern Iraq that brought down the Achaemenid Empire, he even had time to remember Phayllos, sending a portion of the booty to his home city of Croton.

Chapter Three

Actium, 31BC

Victory for the future Augustus Caesar over his former ally Mark Antony marks the end of the Republic and the beginnings of Imperial Rome

Then came the day of the great conflict, on which Caesar and Antony led out their fleets and fought, the one for the safety, the other for the ruin, of the world.   [Velleius Paterculus (19BC–31AD)]

All Italy swore allegiance to me voluntarily, and demanded me as leader in the war in which I was victorious at Actium.
                                                                [Augustus (14AD)]

If later generations had only the autobiographical testament of Caesar Augustus, the *Res Gestae Divi Augusti* ('the achievements of the deified Augustus'), the battle of Actium, the stake to the heart of the Roman Republic, would hardly be remembered. The bare allusion to his victory by the subsequent emperor of the Roman world, quoted above, is a monument to understatement, giving no more away than the name. There is no indication if the encounter was on land or at sea, or of whom the antagonists were. Augustus makes an oblique reference to his opponent Mark Antony a few lines above: 'In the temples of all the cities of the province of Asia, as victor, I replaced the ornaments which my antagonist in the war had appropriated privately after he despoiled the temples.' The *Res Gestae* was written by Augustus to be published on his death as his memorial, and copies were inscribed on stone monuments and temples throughout the Roman Empire. As a piece of propaganda it was in his interests to play down the more controversial aspects of his career and his absolute hold on the reins of government, so the *Res Gestae* glosses over certain aspects of his rise to power as sole ruler, in particular the ruthless elimination of his enemies, while elsewhere, extolling his achievements at some length. Luckily, other writers were more forthcoming in filling in the blanks. It is

Roman trireme from a Tunisian mosaic. *(Photo: Mathiasrex, CC3.0)*

largely from their accounts, usually written to glorify the first emperor, that the events of the battle have been reconstructed and the doomed romance of Antony and Cleopatra turned into legend.

The poets contemporary with events were the first to eulogise the victor of Actium as a hero and paint his opponents as worthless foreign adversaries, disguising in the process that this was the last act in a protracted civil war. Virgil in his epic the *Aeneid*, begun two years after the battle, welcomes in the new regime and describes Augustus standing heroically on the prow of his ship as it heads towards the enemy. Propertius, whose elegies first put expression to the formula of Western romantic love, established the idea of Antony's total infatuation with the fickle Egyptian queen amidst verses that allude to Paris and his love for Helen of Troy. Horace's tributes to Augustus are more enigmatic, for in his youth he had had republican sympathies. In his first book of *Odes*, he pays tribute to Agrippa, Augustus' commander at Actium, comparing him to the god Mars, while denigrating Cleopatra as a mad queen who nevertheless dies bravely. Antony he never mentions by name but only alludes to in his *Epodes* as the defeated admiral 'enslaved to a woman'. The first historians to tackle the subject did so well after the event; Augustus' contemporary Livy (64 or 59BC–AD12 or 17) who's account only exists in a heavily abridged version, Velleius Paterculus (see above) followed by Plutarch (c.46–120AD) and Suetonius (c.69–after 122AD) in the mid-first century AD, and then Dio Cassius (c.155–235AD) around 100 years later. The further away from the events the fuller the accounts become.

Gaius Octavius Thurinus was the great-nephew of Gaius Julius Caesar, the most powerful man in Rome. From a modest branch of the family, few would have picked the rather sickly young man as a likely successor. What he did have in his early life was steely ambition and good fortune. When a group of conspirators assassinated Caesar in 44BC, there was no legitimate heir to take up his mantle, so when his will was read out it came as a surprise that he had named a precocious eighteen-year-old as his adopted son and therefore heir. Octavian (in the anglicised form) changed his name, as was Roman convention, to Gaius Julius Caesar Octavianus to maintain the noble and patrician elements of the Julii Caesares name. To differentiate himself from his adoptive father he continued to be generally referred to as Octavian. The executor of Caesar's will was the aristocratic Marcus Antonius, commonly known to us as Mark Antony. Twenty years Octavian's senior and a previous supporter of his adopted father, Antony was put out by the arrival on the political scene of a young upstart and scoffed that Octavian was 'a mere boy' who owed 'everything to a name'. But the name carried clout and access to the complex world of Roman political intrigue.

Fear of despotism was the conspirators' motivation behind their drastic step of committing murder on the notorious 'Ides of March'. The self-named 'liberators' were a collection of former rivals, 'Republicans' and supporters of Caesar's late rival Pompey, but in the ensuing power vacuum following Caesar's death it was not clear if they could command public support. A jostle for control followed between the Senate, led by the intellectual statesman Cicero, a supporter of maintaining the Republic, and Antony, who proclaimed himself leader of the Caesarean party. Unfortunately for the conspirators and their Senatorial backers, the populace showed a disappointing lack of support for their actions. Initially Antony was prepared to compromise, even making overtures of reconciliation to Brutus and Cassius, the leading assassins, but when at Caesar's funeral the angry mood of the Roman crowd became apparent he was quick to harness their passion for retribution for his own ends.

Now sole consul (Caesar had been the other one), Antony seized the state treasury and put through measures to ingratiate himself with the people. To gain access to more funds he alienated Octavian by getting his hands on most of the young man's financial inheritance and, eager to exploit Octavian's resulting hostility to Antony, Cicero launched into a series of diatribes against Antony (*Phillipics*). He fulminated, as was his style when attacking his political enemies, against Antony's loose living while making sure to court Octavian's favour by comparing him to a god-sent boyish saviour. But Octavian was not to be so naive as to be easily taken in. He was more interested in cultivating military support from the veterans of Caesar's armies.

When Antony's term as consul came to an end, he was given command of the province of Macedonia. This was not to Antony's liking because the post came without an army. His preference was for the military assignment of Cisalpine Gaul in northern Italy which had been given to Decimus, Brutus' cousin and one of the assassins. He persuaded the Senate to order Decimus to give it up. Decimus refused, and so Antony set off to seize the province and its legions. In the volatile situation, under Cicero's influence the Senate changed its mind and declared Antony an outlaw. Octavian, who had no legitimacy to command an army, along with the two new consuls, Hirtius and Pansa, was sent off in pursuit to deal with the situation. Octavian came out on the victorious side against Antony at the Battle of Mutina (43 BC), and as fate would have it with the death in action of Hirtius and Pansa, was left in sole charge of the army. Events were moving in Octavian's favour, and, with the approval of the populace beginning to shift from Antony towards Octavian, the Senate fretted that it was Octavian who was becoming too powerful.

In the end power would rest with whoever could command the respect of the army. Brutus and Cassius emerged from their temporary hiatus to illegally take control of Macedonia and Syria respectively, where they still had some support. Sextus Pompey, the son of Pompey the Great, who largely operated as a free agent in Sicily, was off and on the legitimate commander of the navy. Amongst the legions in the west there was a strong affiliation to the memory of Caesar and a desire to revenge his death. As for the ordinary people, no one cared as they had no appetite for a return to civil war.

Octavian, realizing that Cicero and the Senate were intent on merely using him for their own ends, demanded to be made consul and began marching his veterans towards Rome. Meanwhile, in the north Antony had recovered his position and together with Marcus Aemilius Lepidus, a close ally of Caesar, had managed to gather a large army. Any hope that Caesar's death would herald a return to a Republican normality was severely dented when Octavian switched to join forces with Antony and Lepidus. Octavian was not prepared to ally himself to the Senate for the sake of Cicero. Throughout his career Octavian made a pretence of returning Rome to a Republic, but he found that the time was never quite right to give up the reins of power. On the pretext of maintaining order Antony, Lepidus and Octavian formed a Triumvirate, a five-year rule of three, later endorsed in Rome, that gave them the dictatorial powers 'to restore the state'. Their first priority was a purge of their political enemies and the ringleaders behind Caesar's murder. The unfortunate Cicero found his name added to the list of enemies of the state. He was hunted down and murdered, along with up to 300 other senators and 2,000 equestrians (knights).

On the Ides of March, Cleopatra VII Philopater, Queen of Egypt in the ninth generation of Ptolemaic rulers descended from Ptolemy Soter, a general in Alexander the Great's all-conquering Macedonian army, was staying in Rome in Julius Caesar's villa. The epitome of Oriental decadence in Roman eyes, she was the mother of Caesar's illegitimate son Caesarion. Moreover, she owed her position as queen to Caesar. Egypt was one of Rome's client-kingdoms, and, even if the richest and most populous, subject to Roman meddling in its affairs. A Roman army had put Cleopatra's father, Ptolemy XII, back on the throne after he had been deposed by his daughter, Berenice IV. There was little sentiment amongst the Ptolemies when it came to politics and Berenice was duly executed. In 48BC, Pompey sought refuge in Egypt after his defeat by Caesar at the Battle of Pharsalus in Thessaly. Hot on the heels of his rival Caesar arrived only to step into the midst of a civil war between Ptolemy's heirs, the twenty-one-year old Cleopatra and her younger brother and co-ruler Ptolemy XIII. Ptolemy, who had the upper hand, made a mistake when he ingratiatingly presented Caesar with Pompey's head. Caesar's reaction was one of disgust, and Ptolemy further alienated himself by refusing to stand his army down and make peace with Cleopatra. Cleopatra was not so gauche. She made good use of Caesar's time in Alexandria, working her youthful charms on the 52-year-old philanderer to such good effect that she succeeded in getting him to embark on a notorious affair with her, to the scandal of Roman society. Caesar settled the Ptolemaic familial conflict in her favour at the Battle of the Nile (47BC). Their combined Romano-Egyptian force defeated her siblings, Ptolemy, who drowned, and Arsinoe IV, who was exiled to the Temple of Artemis in Ephesus. Cleopatra was then installed as ruler of Egypt, but not alone. She was 'married' as was the Egyptian custom, to her other brother Ptolemy XIV, ten years her junior, for it was against tradition for a woman to rule alone.

In later years, the Romans liked to create an image of Cleopatra as a pleasure-seeking despot ruling an indolent nation in a manner that ran contrary to Roman virtues. This portrayal was seen as resonant of the clash of cultures between East and West that would inevitably lead to war. The reality was more nuanced. The Romans were generally great admirers of Greek culture, and Cleopatra was amongst the last in a line of sophisticated Hellenistic rulers installed when Alexander conquered Persia and Egypt. In the wake of his conquests came Greek culture and the East was 'Hellenised'. Although Cleopatra embraced Egyptian culture and religion in a conscious effort to be ruler of all her subjects, her capital, Alexandria, remained a Greek city. She was well educated, probably by scholars from the city's famous Museum and Library, and said by Plutarch to be conversant in the languages of Egypt's neighbours, the Persians, Medes, Parthians, Jews, Ethiopians, Troglodytae (to the south of Egypt), Arabs and Syrians. Her first language remained Greek, but significantly she was the first of her line to speak Egyptian. Latin was not included in her list of achievements, so it was lucky that Caesar spoke Greek too. By the time he was called away from Egypt to Asia Minor to deal with another troublesome Hellenistic monarch, Pharnaces II, King of Pontus, Cleopatra was pregnant. Their son, Ptolemy XIV Caesar, known as Caesarion, was born later that year.

With her sponsor Caesar murdered, Cleopatra was once again vulnerable; her position as queen dependent on the approval of the Senate. At this stage, even though Egypt was heavily in financial debt to Rome, there was no great desire to formally make the country a province. However, she had felt obliged to spend perhaps nearly two years on and off in the city to shore up her position while maintaining her liaison with her married lover. Caesar's three marriages had only produced one daughter, and his many other affairs had been childless, so if there was genuine feeling between them she would have hoped that Caesar might formally recognize their son as his heir. The contents of his will would have come as a bitter disappointment, as Caesar had no desire to break with tradition by recognizing the illegitimate child of a foreigner. During her sojourn in Rome, Cleopatra had found it harder to charm the Senate than she had Caesar; Cicero in particular hated her. The anxiety that Caesar was becoming seduced by the luxurious ways of the Hellenistic monarchs only fuelled their fear that he was preparing the ground to become king in the Eastern manner. As the leading Romans became increasingly preoccupied with avoiding civil war, Cleopatra decided it was time to return to Alexandria to ensure that there had been no undermining of her own position while she had been away. She was gone after Caesar's will was read and before the arrival of Octavian, who would have been glad to see the back of a potential rival to his claim. Soon after her return to Egypt, her young brother Ptolemy XIV conveniently died, according to the Jewish historian Josephus (37–c.100AD) from poison. Coincidence or not, her priority was that Caesarion should be recognized as her heir in Egypt rather than being acknowledged as Caesar's heir in Rome.

In Alexandria she still had to keep an eye on events in Rome. The powers of the Triumvirate had not been equally distributed. Lepidus, left in charge of Rome, had fewer legions, while Antony, the dominant partner, and Octavian were given the job of eliminating Brutus and Cassius and securing the eastern territories. Cleopatra knew that as Egypt was home to a large Roman army it would be difficult to keep out of the unfolding struggle. She was already well versed in diplomacy and astute enough to play a waiting game before committing to the winner. As a client state with a Roman army, Egypt could be called upon for aid in Rome's defence. A delicate balancing act was required when first she was asked to send legions in support of the consul Dolabella, on his way to Syria to protect its border with Parthia. After a plundering journey through Asia Minor that did little for his popularity, Dolabella came up against Cassius who had managed to raise an army. Dolabella was defeated. Now it was Cassius' turn to ask Cleopatra for ships and supplies. Cleopatra knew that neither Antony nor Cassius could be depended on for future support, both were already eying up the possibility of enlisting her sister Arsinoe to their cause if it suited them. To keep from getting embroiled in Rome's civil war, for the moment Cleopatra had to make a show at least of helping the murderer of her lover.

Cassius and Brutus were gathering their forces for what they realised would be the final confrontation. Stronger at sea with the help of Sextus Pompey and his renegade navy, they hoped to lure the triumvirs eastwards so that they could harass their supply lines. After stalling for as long as possible Cleopatra answered their call. She set off leading her squadron of ships in person, the first woman to do so since Queen Artemisia at Salamis, but the weather intervened and her fleet was forced back to Alexandria. Her actions were called into question, for, before being forced back, it had appeared she was about to change tack with the aim of aiding the triumvirs instead. The fortuitous intervention of the weather meant that before she could refit her navy, Sextus had been knocked out of the equation and Octavian and Antony had marched into Macedonia and defeated Brutus and Cassius at the Battle of Philippi (42BC). The battle, in which Octavian did not cover himself in glory, being either ill or absent, was a personal victory for Antony who greatly enhanced his reputation as a commander after his defeat at Mutina. His opponents rather than facing defeat both committed suicide. The triumvirs were left in control of the world, which they split between them. Octavian took Spain and Sardinia, Lepidus, north Africa, and Antony, Transalpine and Cisalpine Gaul and the East; Italy was to be held in common. The East was the richest and the most important region and the one that carried with it the fulfilment of Caesar's ambition to conquer Parthia.

Antony was made for the East. He had studied in Athens, where as a young man he had fled to escape his debts and happily adopted Greek ways. As a dashing young cavalry officer he had served in Syria, and been in Egypt during the Roman intervention in the civil war between Cleopatra's father and elder sister. In Alexandria he was said to have noted the fourteen-year old Cleopatra, and he would certainly have come across her during her time in Rome. His first task was to raise money. Protracted wars were expensive, and soldiers had to be resettled and paid off. There was also the campaign against Parthia to be financed. And it fell to the East, already stripped bare by Brutus and Cassius, to supply the funds. So in 41BC, during his progress through the provinces, Antony summoned Cleopatra to Tarsus in Cilicia. As Egypt was the major source of grain and money in the eastern Mediterranean this could be expected, but Antony also wanted to know if her intentions had really been to take her fleet to Cassius. With her sister Arsinoe in nearby Ephesus, Cleopatra had to reassure Antony that his best interests lay in friendship with her. She knew of his taste for hard drinking, luxury and excess, so she determined to put on a performance that would impress even the hardest of hard-boiled Romans. The Egyptians were masters of display and Cleopatra's spectacular arrival on a pleasure barge specifically designed to excite the senses has gone down as one of the iconic encounters in history. Antony tried to reciprocate in kind with a lavish dinner, but was forced to concede it was no match. Having succeeded in turning Antony's head, the diplomatic posturing soon moved on to a deeper personal relationship. Cleopatra was now in a position to persuade Antony to finally eliminate Arsinoe, who was taken from the sanctuary of Artemis and executed, and confirm her and her son Caesarion as joint rulers of Egypt. Cleopatra was 28 and at the height of her charismatic powers. She had made her play to commit herself to Antony, the man she believed most likely to be the most powerful in the world. Like Caesar before him, he offered her security combined with an undoubted attraction; that they had become lovers is in no doubt because she bore him twins, a boy and a girl, within a year.

Antony wintered in Alexandria, enjoying its delights, before external events dragged him away. The Parthians had invaded Syria, spurred on by Labienus, a surviving republican ally of Brutus and Cassius. In Rome, Octavian was struggling to contain the discontent created by trying to re-settle his veterans and to deal with Sextus Pompey, who remained a prob-lem, and Antony's wife Fulvia and brother Lucius who had openly turned against him. Fulvia's rebellion petered out when Antony, tied up with the Parthians, refused to give it his support. She fled to Athens only to receive a reprimand from her husband for her behaviour. For his part, Lucius received a pardon from Octavian, but neither lived long enough to enjoy their freedom; both became ill soon after and died.

Although Antony felt compelled to return to Italy with an army to secure his position he was more intent on patching things up with Octavian than starting an all-out war. The Triumvirate was renewed and another division of the world agreed, one that further side-lined Lepidus. To cement the bargain, Antony took Octavian's elder sister Octavia as his wife. Any immediate hopes that this marriage might usher in a new dynasty were thwarted by the arrival of two daughters. The triumvirs' priorities were for Antony to return to the East to continue his Parthian campaign and Octavian to finally end Sextus' piratical activities. It was at this time that Octavian dropped the names Gaius Julius and began styling himself *Divi filius*, 'son of the divinity', the divinity being *Divius Julius*, Julius Caesar himself, and as *Imperator Caesar* to promote himself as a victorious commander.

As yet he was not living up to his own hyperbole. After his navy was twice defeated, he was forced to ask Antony for ships. Despite Antony's compliance, Octavian decided to draw on the expertise of his close friend Marcus Vipsanius Agrippa, who first made improvements to the fleet, bringing in larger ships with turrets, artillery and grappling hooks, before victoriously taking on Sextus at the Battles of Mylae and Naulochus off the Sicilian coast (36BC). Sextus managed to escape as far as the island of Miletus before being captured and executed the following year on the orders of Antony. Agrippa was given the honour of a Triumph at Rome during which he was awarded a naval crown decorated with the beaks of ships. Lepidus, who had supported Octavian's campaign, felt he had not been treated as an equal. When the two quarrelled over the stationing of Lepidus' troops in Sicily, Octavian accused him of trying to usurp power and persuaded his legions to defect. Lepidus was forced to retire; now there were two.

During his absence, Antony's generals had led successful campaigns against the Parthians. Once back in Syria, Antony re-immersed himself in the dynastic complexities of Rome's fractious client-kingdoms and began preparations for his own war with Parthia, for which he needed supplies and legions. Octavian proved to be less than amenable in sending the troops he had promised in exchange for ships as agreed, so Antony turned to where he knew he could get help; Egypt. In the winter of 37 BC, with Octavia in Rome delivering their second child, Antony invited Cleopatra to Antioch. They had not seen each other for three years and he took the opportunity to recognize his paternity of their twins, Alexander Helios and Cleopatra Selene, named after the Sun and the Moon in the Parthian manner. Such symbolic acts and the names chosen pushed him further from Rome, and intentionally or not, on an inevitable collision course with Octavian. When Cleopatra returned to Egypt she was pregnant again with their third child. As for Octavia, Antony would never see her again. Henceforth he and Cleopatra would appear to the world as man and wife. She was given increased dominion over Cyprus and Crete and parts of the Cilician and Syrian coast, as well as Cyrenaica, to the west of Egypt. In name at least she had regained control of the lands ruled by her ancestors at the height of their power. These were not merely the gifts of a besotted lover, as some in Rome might have wanted to believe, but strategic. Cilicia was rich in timber and Nabataea in bitumen, useful for building ships and advantageous to have under the control of a trusted ally. Cleopatra did not always get her way. She had long had her eyes on Judea, in whose affairs she meddled, but was never able to persuade Antony to give it to her.

Cleopatra's ambition was to restore the glory of her Macedonian inheritance while maintaining a strong Egypt, Antony's was for foreign conquest in the manner of a latter-day Alexander, for true military glory could only be achieved against a foreign adversary. In 36 BC he led a large army against Armenia, which capitulated without a fight, and then into Media, in the depths of Parthian territory, but he failed to bring the Parthians to battle to gain the victory he wanted. With his supply lines stretched and winter approaching he was forced to make an ignominious retreat back to the Syrian coast. He immediately summoned Cleopatra, but this was not merely as an amorous imperative, for she came bringing with her much needed supplies for the troops. Octavia too had set out with supplies, reaching Athens before being ordered back to Rome by Antony. From her brother Octavian there was no help. As Antony was busying himself through most of 35 BC with Cleopatra, either in Antioch or Alexandria,

Bust of Cleopatra VII c.40–30BC. *(Photo: Louis le Grand, Altes Museum Berlin, public domain)*

Octavian made sure he was well occupied campaigning in the Balkans, close to Antony's territories. As was already apparent, he was not a born soldier. He had a propensity for becoming ill during campaigns, so it was important for him to create the impression of a strong and victorious military leader, and with the spoils of war he could begin an ambitious building programme to beautify Rome where his popularity was still low.

Cleopatra, whose political skills were well honed, saw the danger of Octavian and she was frustrated that Antony was concentrating on foreign ventures rather than his rival in Rome. He had already missed the chance to take on Octavian by supporting Fulvia, or to intervene with Lepidus in the war with Sextus. Even if Antony was loyal to the spirit of the division of powers, it was obvious to her that Octavian was not. He had returned only 70 of the 150 warships Antony had lent him, while Antony's pleas for legions fell on deaf ears. Antony was far from Italy and the source of recruits, so it was in Octavian's interests to starve him of manpower. To make up for his humiliation in Parthia, Antony turned again on Armenia, captured the king, Artavasdes, and returned to Alexandria to celebrate in triumph.

He most likely did not mean this to be a Triumph in the Roman sense, an official recognition that could be only held in Rome before the people and the gods, but his critics were soon to seize on this apparent disregard for sacred tradition. To add further insult, a few days later Antony and Cleopatra held a ceremony in the gymnasium of Alexandria in which they sat together on golden thrones, she dressed as the New Isis, with Caesarion, the twins and their two-year-old son, Ptolemy Philadelphus on smaller thrones beneath. Antony then formally proclaimed Cleopatra 'Queen of Kings, whose sons are kings'; Caesarion ruler of Egypt, Cyprus and part of Syria, and the twins Alexander king of Armenia, Media and Parthia and Cleopatra ruler of Cyrenaica and Libya. All this was good theatre in the Hellenistic tradition, but it did little for Antony or his reputation in Rome. It earned him a rebuke from Octavian, and it mattered little that in reply Antony claimed his rights to troops levied in Italy and allotments for his veterans, or that Octavian was standing in the way of the restoration of the Republic. Instead Antony's actions provided Octavian, ever eager to make the best of any propaganda opportunity, with ammunition to blacken his name. To the people of Rome Antony's motives were a puzzle. He seemed to be turning his back on Roman values, acting like a king and giving away hard won territories to a foreign monarch.

The stories of Antony's excesses at the Alexandrian court increased to circulate. Alexandrian court life was certainly luxurious, and Antony was not one to hold back. It was also artistic and learned, but his critics were not interested in that, only anything that could be linked to drunkenness and debauchery. In contrast Octavian was slowly getting a grip on the grievances of the malcontented farmers and veterans in Italy. Following the death of Sextus, the populace even dared to dream there might be the prospect of peace. Still only in his late twenties, Octavian had already accumulated his own chequered past of broken marriages and indiscretions, but after his marriage to Livia Drusila he began to put himself forward as the epitome of the solid Roman citizen and family man, whose upright sister was being publicly slighted by the open affair of Antony and his Oriental mistress. There was no longer any attempt to cover up the contempt felt between the two rivals. In the continuing propaganda war Octavian held the advantage of being based in Rome.

As the formalities of the Roman constitution were still being adhered to, if only in name, Octavian and Antony continued to hold the joint consulship. As consul in 33BC Antony was legitimately entitled to lead an army into Mesopotamia on the assumption he was about to resume his campaign against Parthia. Unpredictably, he suddenly turned about and began to march west as if making for Italy, his justification being that he needed land for his veterans. Octavian tartly countered that he should have plenty of land from his 'conquests'. When the official term of the Triumvirate lapsed, Antony continued to use the title; Octavian calculatedly 'retired'. Octavian's retirement did not prevent him from illegally entering into a war of words in the Senate with Antony's supporters, backed up by a not-so-subtle show of force. Antony's spokesmen, the consuls Lucius Domitius Ahenobarbus and Gaius Sosius, concentrated on Octavian's political abuses, to which Octavian responded with personal attacks on Antony, corrupted as he was by Cleopatra and her magic potions. Octavian's flaunting of convention and show of force was the signal for the consuls and those of Antony's supporters fearful for their lives, including about a third of the Senate (300–400 men), to flee from Italy.

Most damaging to Antony's reputation was the illegal leaking of his will, which Octavian had been informed was deposited at the Temple of Vesta. The contents were private, but Octavian managed to get hold of a copy by force, and had selections read out in public. This proved to be a pivotal moment in the lurch towards all-out war. As Suetonius' succinctly put in *The Twelve Caesars* (121AD):

> Eventually Augustus broke his friendship with Mark Antony, which had always been a tenuous one and in continuous need of patching; and proved that his rival had failed to conduct himself as befitted a Roman citizen, by ordering the will he had deposited at Rome to be opened and publicly read. It listed among Antony's heirs the illegitimate children fathered by him on Cleopatra.

Octavian had finally got what he wanted. There is no knowing if the contents were true, or why even Antony would have created such a document, one that served no purpose. He had already made no secret of his relationship with Cleopatra, his donations of territory, the declaration that Caesarion was the true son of Caesar. There was only the shocking revelation of an illegal attempt by a citizen to make a non-citizen his heir. Antony's wish to be buried with Cleopatra only added spice. Using these 'revelations' Octavian spread rumours that Antony and Cleopatra planned to rule the Republic as their personal empire, moving the capital from Rome to Alexandria. The strategy was to marginalise Antony by preying on the Romans' distrust of Easterners, Greeks and powerful women. His propaganda machine went into overdrive: Antony was weak and having 'surrendered to a woman' was in thrall to his scheming mistress, perpetually drunk or drugged and no longer in control of himself. In late 32BC what remained of the Senate duly outlawed Antony, revoking his powers. It was important for Octavian to create the illusion to a population tired of civil war that the state was under threat from a foreign power. He made it clear he was not at war with Antony, but with Egypt.

Octavian's unconstitutional heavy-handed use of force in the Senate may have given Antony the moral high ground to declare war on Octavian as a usurper and fraudster, but he was a long way away. After wintering in Alexandria, he returned to Anatolia to begin the transfer of his army to Greece. Contingents from client-kings, including Thrace and Syria, were gathered at Ephesus, plus nineteen Roman legions (around 70,000 men). Four legions were left in reserve in Cyrene and a further seven in Egypt and Syria. Although the political war was over, and lost, the war of words continued. The final outcome though would only be settled on the battlefield and preparations were set in motion for a final showdown between the two most powerful men in the Roman world.

Antony could no longer afford to be as generous to the local communities as in the past and once more the East was squeezed for revenue, the populace bearing the burden for another Roman civil war. In addition to money, he needed supplies, men for the army and timber and crew for the warships hastily being built. As Antony did not have the luxury of being able to raise an army in Italy, locals were conscripted or quickly given citizenship to encourage them to serve. Cleopatra emptied Egypt's coffers to finance the war and in addition contributed 200 vessels and crew, including both large warships and grain ships, to the fleet of 500 warships and 300 merchantmen. It was now that Octavian's accusation of Antony's despoliation of the temples for his own ends was said to have occurred as a form of reciprocation to Cleopatra for her assistance.

Bust of Mark Antony from the Flavian age (69–96AD). *(Vatican Museum, CC BY-SA 4.0)*

In the summer the pair were in Athens, where Cleopatra had a statue of herself as the goddess Isis erected. It was at this late stage that Antony decided to divorce Octavia, perhaps in the belated realisation that things had gone too far for reconciliation with her brother. Whether Antony and Cleopatra ever married is an open question. His Roman supporters found their relationship troublesome; they were happy to fight for Antony as long as they felt they were fighting for a common goal, but the more he became closely identified as a Hellenistic ruler it stirred up opposition. The Romans were used to dealing with kings as long as the kings were subordinate, as with the client-kings Antony left to look after the eastern frontier. Cleopatra's continuous presence in his company and active involvement in the war councils was unsettling. Ahenobarbus, Antony's major military supporter, would only address her by name, not as 'Queen', and tried in vain to get her removed from the army. As leader of a large naval contingent, to her own troops and the Hellenistic Greek world she was a figurehead. For the legions she was seen as undermining to morale and another gift for Octavian in the propaganda war. Antony's military reputation since his victory at Philippi had waned, so Cleopatra was useful to him both for support and to take his mind off matters by providing festivals and entertainments. For her part, she needed to keep close to the action to look after her own interests. If a truce was brokered or victory secured by whichever side, she did not want to be a pawn in the peace settlement. Whatever the reason, Antony's slow response allowed Octavian to solidify his authority in Italy, Africa and the western provinces with oaths of allegiance. By late summer Octavian was psychologically ready, if not militarily. Not averse to a bit theatre of his own he revived, or even invented, an ancient practice where, acting as a priest at a sacrifice to Bellona, the war god, he dipped a spear into the blood of the dead animal and hurled it at a patch of earth representing Egypt. War was thus declared, the Republic against Cleopatra, no mention of Antony.

In late 32BC, Antony had finally reached Patras on the Gulf of Corinth in western Greece. Here he struck coins announcing himself as triumvir and consul, despite Octavian having resumed the consulship with Valerius Corvinus as his partner. In Italy the prospect of Antony's forces gathered across the Ionian Sea was easily seen as a provocative move, and Octavian made the most of it. Neither side had really prepared for war. Octavian had an experienced navy of up to 400 ships at his disposal and a ready supply of troops, but he was busy having to raise taxes to fund his army. Even though Antony had nineteen legions, they were not at full strength. As winter approached Antony thought the better of making a pre-emptive strike on the uninviting Italian east coast with its few landing points. He did not want to provoke the situation further by 'invading' Italy with his 'Eastern' army, so he preferred to wait and let Octavian come to him in the belief that he could harry Octavian's convoys as they made the crossing to Greece. Handing the initiative to Octavian put him in the position of having to defend a long coastline full of natural harbours while protecting the sea-lanes to Egypt and the East vital for his supplies. Antony spread his forces from Methone in the southern Peloponnese to the island of Corcyra (Corfu) in the north, stationing his largest naval concentration at Actium in the Gulf of Ambracia. Leaving Rome in the hands of his trusted vice-regent Gaius Maecenas with strict instructions to allow no disturbances, Octavian made his move.

Early in 31BC, Agrippa attacked Methone. It was a particularly risky venture involving a long sea crossing, but it paid off. Antony had expected the attack to come in the north, near to where the Via Egnatia, the major route to the interior, Macedonia and the East, reached the sea. This was the route that Caesar had used to attack Pompey at Pharsalus and Octavian and Antony himself taken to take on Brutus and Cassius at Philippi. It is thought that Antony's strategy may have been to entice Octavian to do the same so that he could take him on in a land battle, something more to his liking than an engagement at sea.

With Methone in his hands and its ships destroyed or captured, Agrippa was free to launch a series of raids along the Greek coast as far as Corcyra, a diversionary tactic that allowed Octavian to land his army, including 80,000 infantry, unmolested somewhere to the north of Corcyra at Panormus, possibly modern Porto Palermo, in Albania. Across the strait, Corcyra was easily taken after being abandoned by its garrison. Antony's immediate reaction was one of positive indifference. Normally an impetuous commander he was suddenly lethargic, whether through overconfidence, indecision, or too many advisors in his camp, or a combination of all three. In an attempt to present an air of calm to his followers he preferred to belittle his enemy and boast of his superiority as a commander and the quality of his men. If his reaction was slow, he also needed time to gather his dispersed army. Octavian on the other hand was wasting none and making direct for Actium and Antony's fleet.

The expansive Ambracian Gulf is 25 miles (40km) long by 9 miles (15km) wide, but its entrance is barely a half-mile (700m) in width. The channel, which lies between two narrow promontories, widens out before slightly narrowing again to form a self-contained area flanked by two bays to north and south. Large areas of the interior of the Gulf are shallow and marshy, so the most suitable location for a harbour or anchorage is either within the entrance channel at either of the two bays, to the north near the modern town of Preveza or to the south by the ancient sanctuary and temple to Apollo at Actium, or just inside the Gulf proper on the southern shore at Anactorium, modern Vonitsa. The Gulf may have offered a safe haven in which to base his fleet, but it was not an ideal strategic location. In the confines of the bays lay most of Antony's eight fighting squadrons, some of his ships having been based elsewhere to guard the coast. A squadron consisted of sixty ships plus five scout ships, which meant over 500 ships in all, with between 125,000 and 150,000 crewmen. Amongst the ships' number were quinqueremes, or even larger vessels of Levantine design with high decks that allowed archers to shoot down on the enemy in close combat. The *octareme* war galleys, or 'eights', implying eight oarsmen per bank of three oars, would have space for around 200 heavy marines and archers plus at least six *ballistae* (large catapults). Some ships sported the addition of a 'castle' or tower on the prow to carry artillery in the form of heavy catapults. Antony's flagship was said to be a 'ten' or *dekareme*. Recent archaeological research by Dr Konstantinos Zachos has borne out that Antony favoured large ships, either in an attempt to intimidate or to out-muscle Octavian. Some are estimated to have been 131ft (40m) long, the largest carrying bronze rams 8ft long by 5ft tall (four times the size of any from antiquity found so far) in the shape of beaks and built with reinforced metal-sheathed timbers to counter the ramming of the enemy. Such powerful rams were strong enough to break down harbour defences, but for the present, holing an enemy below the water line would be good enough. To guard the fleet Antony fortified the entrance to the Gulf with towers and artillery.

The Gulf's northern promontory forms a long narrow peninsula and at its centre Octavian occupied a hill known today as Mikalitzi, overlooking both the entrance and the bays and close to a sea-facing bay that offered safe access to the open water. Agrippa's navy co-ordinated its arrival and they set about fortifying their positions. The vanguard of Antony's army began to arrive a short time later and set up camp near to Actium on the southern promontory. It took time for all of Antony's troops to muster, but when he had sufficient numbers he set up a second fortified position on the northern side, threatening Octavian. Octavian had strengthened his position with earthworks, creating a protective corridor to maintain contact with his ships. A standoff followed, neither side wishing to commit to battle before they were fully ready.

As spring turned to summer, Antony's army, cramped together in the lower marshy ground, began to succumb to the effects of malaria and dysentery, which often proved fatal. Apart from some raiding and a few skirmishes on both sides, Antony was unable to draw Octavian out, so he decided to cut off his access to fresh water. Earthworks were thrown up across the peninsula to Octavian's rear blocking the route to the river

The Ambracian Gulf from the air with modern Preveza at the north of the narrow channel. Actium was in the SE corner beyond the entrance. *(Photo: David Monniaux, CC BY-SA 1.0)*

Louros, but Antony's troops proved unable hold the positions effectively enough to maintain a blockade. In two cavalry encounters, the second led by Antony himself, he was beaten back. But still Octavian would not commit to battle. To make matters worse, Antony was beginning to lose men through desertion. Given his situation, with his army becoming slowly depleted and morale waning, a long waiting game was proving a hard ask for his men. All Octavian had to do was sit tight.

Agrippa, continuing his raids, took the island of Leukas just south of the entrance to the Gulf. Here he had access to a safer anchorage than the exposed bay close to Octavian's camp. To further turn the screw, he took Patrai (Patras), followed by Corinth, severing Antony from the Peloponnese and threatening the land routes through Greece. In virtual control of the western coast and the seas around the southern Peloponnese, Agrippa was free to harass Antony's supply ships bringing grain from Egypt. Rather than Antony blockading Octavian, it was Antony who was becoming hemmed in. If ill health was not enough, his troops were faced with malnourishment, forcing him to confiscate food from the Greek cities. The consequences fell heavily on the local population and no doubt coloured the account of Antony by Plutarch, who came from Chaeronea near Delphi. Plutarch's great-grandfather Nicarchos told him how:

> ... stripped of money, slaves, and beasts of burden ... his fellow-citizens were compelled to carry on their shoulders a stipulated measure of wheat down to the sea at Anticyra [a port on the Gulf of Corinth] and how their pace was quickened by the whip ...

In the worsening situation, Antony began to consider abandoning his position to take the fight inland where he would have the option of reinforcing his army from Macedonia and Thrace. To assess the prospects for a land war, Quintus Delius, who had served on many diplomatic missions for Antony, was despatched north to look for recruits. The move would mean abandoning the navy in the Gulf with Agrippa's fleet guarding the only way out. Antony received a brief moment of encouragement when Gaius Sosius, who was in command of a squadron of ships, managed to slip out and fight off an opposing squadron under Tarius Rufus, but the victory was short lived. With reinforcements from Agrippa, Rufus forced Sosius to flee back to safety. During the battle the client-king of Cilicia, Tarcondimotus I, one of Antony's important allies, was killed.

On land the continuing skirmishes were not going Antony's way either and he narrowly avoided being captured in an ambush. He was slowly losing control. The small northern camp was abandoned, forcing the entire army within the confines of the unhealthy southern encampment. There seeming no way out, the number of defections grew. When Ahenobarbus became ill, he too took a small boat and rowed over to Octavian, only to die a few days later. Antony, ever honourable to his one-time comrades, sent Ahenobarbus' friends, servants and baggage after him. More frivolously, Dellius, who had served Antony for ten years, defected to Octavian claiming that Cleopatra was plotting against him because she did not like his jokes. Other senators and client-kings, including the rulers of Paphlagonia and Galatia, began to drift away, the latter with 2,000 cavalry, and in retaliation Antony began to execute those he felt he could no longer trust.

Matters were now so bad that there were not enough crew to man the fleet. Again Antony considered his options; abandon the fleet and save the army for a campaign inland or break out with his ships to either fight a naval battle or, accepting the situation as lost, to head back to Egypt to fight another day. The calculation was made the more difficult because some of the ships were Cleopatra's and her bulky war chest could not be left behind. Compared to the navy the legions, under the command of Publius Canidius Crassus, were still in relatively good shape and a formid-able fighting force. Canidius, who had been consul in 40BC and served both Lepidus and Antony faithfully as a general, pushed for a land battle, advising Antony to send Cleopatra away. Unsurprisingly, Cleopatra was said to prefer the latter naval option. This was a narrative that would suit later writers who wanted to show Antony bowing to her wishes. Antony decided to stay with her and leave the army in sole command of his lieu-tenant with the intention of marching it to safety. It was a course of action that was perceived as flying in the face of all the accepted aristocratic virtues of a Roman general. To retreat was not to accept defeat but to regroup and continue the fight.

Bad weather delayed any attempt of a naval breakout for a few days, during which time surplus ships, those without enough men to form a crew, were burnt or destroyed so as to keep them out of enemy hands and the marines were brought up to complement; 20,000 plus 2,000 archers, with additions from the land army. On the morning of 2 September the weather calmed, and after being bottled up for months the fleet made for open water. The ships were formed into three squadrons, with Cleopatra's own squadron, carrying her treasury and courtly entourage, held in reserve at the rear. Sosius commanded the left wing, Antony the centre with the aid of Marcus Insteius and Marcus Octavius, a distant relative of Octavian who had fought with Pompey against Caesar, and Gellius Publicola the right.

Cleopatra's ships and some of the others carried sails on board. This was not usual practice; as the most effective way to manoeuvre galleys when going into battle was through the expertise of the oarsmen, masts were left on shore to lighten the load and create more space. The motives therefore behind the breakout remain uncertain. The crews may have known already whether they were going out to fight or were making a dash for safety, but the troops ashore were certainly kept in the dark. In effect they were being abandoned. In all likelihood, Antony had no intention of taking on Agrippa's ships in battle, outnumbered as he was against a fleet that had already proved itself. The suggestion that he had planned to take up a defensive position to lure Agrippa on to him, with the option that if he was being worsted he could always turn back, makes little sense of his preparations. Most likely was the attempt to make a break for it, taking down as many of the opposition as possible on the way if necessary.

As Antony's ships emerged from the narrows in close formation, Agrippa's fleet was waiting for him. It appears that he already knew of Antony's plan, having been informed in advance by a deserter, possibly Dellius, or merely forewarned by Antony's preparations. It would have taken most of the night to prepare and board the ships. Initially Agrippa had not attempted to match Antony in numbers or size of ship. The numbers employed in ancient warfare are always a matter of dispute, but it is acknowledged that Antony began the campaign with the larger fleet. After the ravages of the summer, this was no longer the case. It is estimated that Agrippa had around 400 ships at his disposal, carrying 16,000 marines and 3,000 archers, crewed by rowers with years of experience in comparison to Antony's recent conscripts, a serious advantage as the performance of the oarsmen would be crucial in the battle's outcome. In addition, Agrippa had proved himself a skilful naval commander. If Antony's fleet had been reduced to as few as 170 ships, as has been argued, Agrippa did not need his full force and he may have dispensed with his light squadrons, putting only around 200 ships into action.

Up against Antony's reliance on brute power, Agrippa had chosen to put his trust in the use of *liburnae*, the light and swift biremes that had originated in Illyria as pirate ships. He lined these up in a shallow arc to face Antony's oncoming ships, which had spread out in battle formation two rows deep across a broad, approximately three-mile (4.5km) front secured by the shoreline on either flank. Taking the left wing himself, he assigned the centre to Lucius Arruntius, one of his successful admirals in the war against Sextus Pompey, and the right to Marcus Lurius along with

Octavian, who was happy to leave command of the battle in the able hands of his general.

For four hours they faced one another in light on-shore winds, jostling for position and skirmishing, with neither side wanting to fight too close to shore. Octavian had argued that they should let Antony through and then attack from the rear, but Agrippa only wanted Antony to come out far enough into the open so that he could use his superior numbers to outflank him. If Antony was going to make a dash for it, he in turn was waiting for the wind to pick up, which it usually did in the afternoon, blowing north-northwest, to give him the impetus to outpace Agrippa and carry him past the island of Leukas. To do this he had to position himself far enough away from the coast to catch the wind. About noon, the wind veered in the right direction and Antony ordered the advance. To allow more space for his outflanking movement, Agrippa gave the order to back water, and then when he was satisfied he gave the order to attack. In response Antony had ordered his ships to create more space between them, spreading the line to counter being enveloped by Agrippa's longer line of ships. Having anticipated this move, Agrippa sent his swift biremes to pass by close to the heavier and slower quinqueremes in order to smash their oars and rudders. In a head on collision of two fleets it usually came down to a matter of one-on-one close combat and Agrippa's superior numbers meant he could deploy more than one of his biremes to attack an opposing quinquereme. Once the ship was successfully damaged it was out of action and the bireme could disengage and move on, leaving the drifting quinquereme as easy prey for the ships carrying *ballistae* to bombard them with flaming projectiles. Once softened up the boarding parties would follow to finish the job. Dio Cassius wrote that after the crewmen had tried in vain to put out the flames with buckets of water, they resorted to trying to smother the flames 'with their mantles and even with corpses' or to cutting off the burning parts of the ship and with the aid of grappling hooks to try to board the enemy ships. Those unable to jump to safety perished in the flames.

As Publicola on Antony's right countered Agrippa's attempts to outflank him, he began to lose contact with the centre, turning at right angles to the line. This left a gap, and seeing the opportunity, Cleopatra's squadron hoisted sail and made for it. Catching the wind, they soon picked up pace, travelling too fast to manoeuvre and engage with the enemy and soon too fast to be caught by Agrippa's ships that were not carrying sail. Seeing Cleopatra's squadron breaking free Antony hastily transferred by rowing boat from his 'ten' flagship to a smaller quinquereme and took off under sail in pursuit, followed by any of his other ships that were able. The rest of the fleet, about two-thirds, heavily engaged in battle as it was, was left behind. It was another of Antony's apparently impetuous actions that played into the hands of Octavian's apologists, who gleefully depicted Antony as fleeing the scene as the battle continued to rage. Some seventy or eighty of his ships may have got away, but many others were left sunk or destroyed, with perhaps over 5,000 casualties. Not all the ships were lost, some surrendered and others managed to make it back to the safety of the Gulf, Sosius' ship amongst them. Agrippa let them go, the damage had already been done. Sosius was captured later and brought before Octavian who pardoned him at the request of Lucius Arruntius.

As Antony fled, his abandoned legions no longer had anyone to fight for. They had fought for a leader and sponsor, not a cause. Short of supplies and with little chance of escape they turned themselves over to Octavian, who could afford to be generous. This left Canidius, bereft of troops, no option but to look after his own best interests and flee and Antony with no army accept the marines on board his remaining ships. That Antony so readily fled the battle on the tails of Cleopatra has remained a puzzle. By committing himself to the fleet rather than the army he effectively lost any hope of success on land. If he had remained with the legions there was always a chance he could have conjured up a victory from a rear-guard action. The fact that the fleet was carrying sail makes it seem most likely that his intention was merely to break out and not to engage with Agrippa and it may have been premeditated that a path was to be cleared for Cleopatra to allow her to escape, a manoeuvre that was executed with some skill. But if the rest of the fleet was meant to follow, the operation was bungled and all order was lost. For the manoeuvre to work it had to have been coordinated, and it could be that, as Dio Cassius argued, Cleopatra lost her nerve and went too soon, with a demoralising effect on Antony. The charge that Antony changed to a faster ship to run from the scene is also unlikely because quinquiremes were slow. His flagship had probably been caught up in the battle and unable to escape, as unfortunately were so many of his other ships, so he had little option if he was to fight on. But for Octavian it was another propaganda coup. Cleopatra could be shown as the perfidious Eastern queen, ready to save her skin at her lover's expense, with Antony left as the lovesick dupe trailing desperately after her at the cost of his reputation and with no regard for his men. Even if this was an exaggeration, Antony had not acted in the best traditions of Roman leadership. In the past he had shown personal courage and loyalty, but he had not done so now, leaving his men to die as he saved himself and his queen. And if it was a gamble, it had not been a very calculated one, because in one moment he had not only lost the battle, but the war.

Suetonius' terse summing up of Octavian's victory was this, 'Presently he defeated Antony in a sea-battle off Actium, where the fighting went on so long that he spent the whole night aboard his flagship', which implies that the fleet fought on after Antony's desertion and the mopping up operation took some time. Antony caught up with Cleopatra, and in Plutarch's account, boarded her ship. There was no moment of joyful reunion, for he avoided her, sitting alone in the prow with his head in his hands until forced to spring into action by an enemy bireme closing in. He ordered the ship around to face down the enemy ship captained by a Spartan, Eurykles, who was out to avenge the death of his father at the hands of Antony. In the skirmish Eurykles missed Antony's ship, but managed to damage two other ships, leaving Antony to return to his position on the prow, head in hands for the next three days.

The couple then parted company at Paraitonion (Mursa Matruh), Antony heading for the former Ptolemaic city of Cyrene (in modern Libya) leaving Cleopatra to return to Egypt, unbowed as if she had won a victory. Cyrene had become a Roman province in 74BC and Antony hoped that the governor, Lucius Pinarius Scarpus, could provide him with some troops, only to find Pinarius and his four legions had gone over to Octavian. By now Antony was becoming desperate, even suicidal, but Cleopatra was not one for giving up. If she could not win in the West, she pinned her hopes on securing the East, only to find that one by one the client-kingdoms, including Cilicia and Judea, were deserting their cause. As they became increasingly isolated the pair made matters worse by retreating into the palace in Alexandria, where they indulged in a doom-laden round of pleasure seeking. They formed a 'Society of Partners in Death' and slid into the life that would fuel the legend of the tragic romance. Cleopatra though was too savvy to lose her wits completely to drink and debauchery. Realising that Antony was no longer fit to lead a military campaign, she began to consider her options. She also maintained her identification with Egypt, so that when the people were said to have offered to rise up and fight for her, she declined saying she did not want to cause their suffering.

Octavian took his time in pursuit, happy to appear the generous victor to the communities through which he passed and to receive their displays of loyalty. He advanced slowly by way of Syria and it was a year before he reached the gates of Alexandria, having had to divert back to Rome in order to deal with a crisis over the taxes raised to pay for the war. The hiatus was a chance to indulge in some final diplomacy. Antony sent envoys to ask if he could be allowed to retire as a private citizen in Athens, or if necessary he would kill himself to ensure the safety of Cleopatra, but he received no reply. Cleopatra's concern was for her children. She hoped that Octavian might legitimize them and crown one of them in her place, the most likely candidate being Caesarion who was sixteen and had come of age. For his part, Octavian's main concern was to get hold of her treasury and he demanded that she disarm and hand over Antony. With negotiations going nowhere, Octavian invaded Egypt in 30BC and in a last vain attempt Antony stirred himself and tried to galvanize some resistance against a pincer movement of troops advancing east from Cyrene and Octavian's army west from Pelusion on the Nile delta. Antony's forces were easily swept aside at Paraitonion, but with his back against the wall Antony recovered some of his old fighting spirit. He led a brilliant cavalry attack as Octavian camped near the Hippodrome at the edge of Alexandria, but it was all too late. The fleet surrendered and his men deserted him, and, so the story went, also the god Dionysus to whom he had dedicated himself.

As Antony was preparing for one last stand he heard the news that Cleopatra had sealed herself in her newly-built mausoleum where her treasure was stored and killed herself. Distraught Antony decided to follow suit, but he bungled his own suicide attempt. As Cleopatra had closed herself in the mausoleum, it is to be assumed that she intended to die there, but in fact she was still alive and he was taken to her, where he died in her arms. With his rival out of the way, the only thing left for Octavian to complete his victory was the parading of Cleopatra and her children through the streets of Rome, a humiliation to which she was not prepared to concede. Cleopatra was taken to the palace where she pleaded with Octavian, but to no avail. In the knowledge that Egypt was to be annexed, she was left with no option in her mind but to contrive to kill herself with the bite of an asp. Horace saw this as an act of bravery, for rather than be a queen brought to slavery in 'Triumph-shackles', she turned to death and 'grasped the asps and did not feel the pains'. Propertius was less complimentary, saying that Rome was finally rid of 'that whore, incestuous queen of Canopus [Alexandria]'. Octavian, not one to leave any loose ends, consolidated his position by executing Caesarion and Antyllus, Antony's son by his third wife, Fulvia. He was now left lord of the world; it had taken him fourteen years to eliminate his rivals.

Caesar Augustus victorious, 1st century AD, in the Vatican Museum.
(*Photo: Till Niermann, CC BY-SA 3.0*)

Octavian returned to Rome through Syria, erasing the memory of Antony and erecting memorials. In Athens, bronze statues of Antony and Cleopatra near the Parthenon that had replaced a previous victory monument were in turn torn down and replaced by a dedication to the hero of Actium, Marcus Agrippa. With victory came the creation of the myth. Rather than the eulogies going to Agrippa, we see Virgil's heroic Octavian on the prow of his ship. Dio Cassius portrayed Octavian fighting against the odds and exhorting his troops as he sailed his ship between the lines. In 29BC, overlooking the bay of Actium, near the hill where he had had his base camp, Octavian founded the city of Nikopolis ('victory city'), the largest ancient ruined city in Greece. Here in a victory monument he put on display in a series of niches 35 rams taken from ships in Antony's captured fleet. Although the bronze rams were melted down in the later years of the Empire, it is from the size of the niches that the archaeologist Dr Zachos has been able to estimate the size of Antony's largest vessels. When Octavian returned to Rome he made the most of his victories. Livy tells us 'he returned to the city to celebrate three triumphs: one over Illyricum, a second for the victory at Actium, and a third over Cleopatra; this was the end of the civil wars, in their twenty-second year'.

For Octavian's supporters, a new 'age of gold' had been ushered in and with Egypt's treasure at his disposal he was able to finance his ambitious government and building programmes. Back in Rome his gradual accrual of powers to himself meant there would be no return to the Republic, and he took direct control of a number of the major provinces, including Egypt. In 27BC he was awarded the titles *Augustus* and *Princeps*. He was now first citizen and would be henceforth known as Caesar Augustus. He also took the title *Imperator* and began a policy of territorial expansion. Rome would no longer be a Republic but an Empire, and in order to maintain stability, and the continuation of his *Pax Augusta* (later the *Pax Romana*, which lasted for around 200 years), he initiated a line of succession, bringing in the era of the Caesars that began with his own Julio-Claudian dynasty.

Chapter Four

Lepanto, 1571

Defeat for the Ottoman fleet by an alliance of
Catholic forces ends the threat of Turkish domination
in the Mediterranean

There has never been such a disastrous war in an Islamic land nor all
the seas of the world since Noah created ships.
    [İbrahim Peçevi (1572–1650) *Tarih-i Peçevi* (Pecevi's History)]

On 6 September 1566, Suleiman the Magnificent died whilst on campaign
in Hungary at the venerable age of 71. He had reigned as Sultan for nearly
forty-six years and during that time he had reformed and expanded the
Ottoman Empire, leading his armies in Europe to the Austrian border and
in Asia to the Persian Gulf, his navies into the Indian Ocean and Red Sea
and taken control of the north African littoral. Any further westward
advance in Europe had been thwarted by the Habsburg Archduke Ferdinand I of Austria at the Siege of Vienna in 1529, and in the Mediterranean
Ferdinand's brother Charles V, King of Spain and Holy Roman Emperor,
had proved an equally implacable enemy and obstacle to mastery of the
Sea. So when Suleiman died, his son Selim II, the 'Sot', had unfinished
business to attend to and a reputation to establish in the shadow of his
illustrious father. Further, it was the duty of every Sultan to continue the
tradition of military conquest and the Janissaries, the elite army corps,
would not be satisfied without it.

    A year before Suleiman's death Pius V had been enthroned as Pope
in Rome. Pius, who was as fervent as his taken name implied, had taken
over the papacy at a time when Christendom was under threat from the
East and Reformation movements were undermining Catholicism in the
West; and he had little desire for compromise. Full of ascetic zeal, he was
as happy to excommunicate Queen Elizabeth I and support Philip II of
Spain, Charles' son, in his attempts to bring England back into the Papal
fold as to initiate a crusade against the Turks. Ottoman armies were still

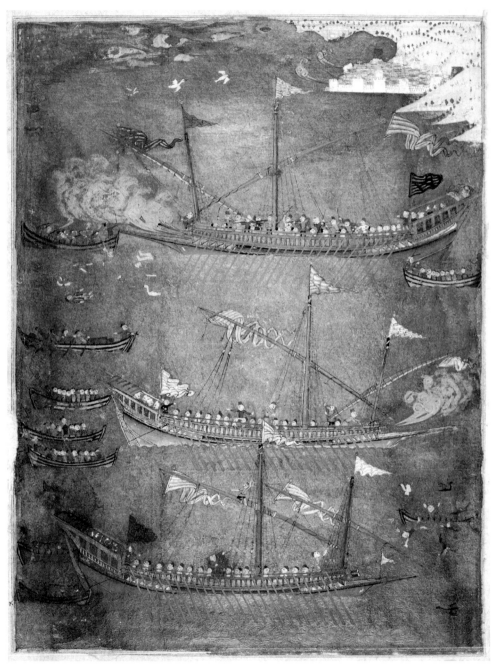

Zaporozhian Cossacks in chaika boats attacking Turkish galleys in the Black Sea, c.1636, Sloane 3584 manuscript, British Library. (*Public domain*)

rightly feared throughout Europe and Asia and thought to be nigh on invincible, but there were signs that perhaps they were approaching the limits of their reach. Although Suleiman's failure to take Vienna had been a setback, the Turks still held eastern Europe in their grip, and it would remain so for many generations to come. At sea their fleet, under the guidance of Hayreddin Barbarossa, had defeated Pope Paul III's 'Holy League' at the Battle of Preveza (1538), but they had failed to go on and take the strategic prize of Malta (1565). Barbarossa, a native of Lesbos from a family of Muslim converts, was the most renowned of the sailors absorbed into the Turkish system. His career as a corsair, raiding as far as Spain, had already earned him the position of Sultan of Algiers before he was co-opted by Selim I, Suleiman's father, to command the Ottoman navy. With Barbarossa as Grand Admiral, the Turks gained both a formidable fleet and Algeria and by the time of his death in 1546, he had increased their north African domains (taking Tunisia), made the Aegean a Turkish sea, and given the Ottoman Sultan dominance throughout the Mediterranean, spreading fear of invasion in every port along the coasts.

Philip II was not only King of Spain: he had a brief spell as King of England and Ireland by marriage to Queen Mary I (until her death in 1558); through his mother, King of Portugal; as a result of Spanish conquests in Italy, King of Naples and Sicily; and as Holy Roman Emperor, Duke of Milan and ruler of the Seventeen Provinces of the Netherlands. As such he was the only monarch who could match the Ottomans for material resources. With the gold and riches of the New World, Philip had the wealth required to build the ships and pay the escalating costs of modern warfare, whereas the old Italian maritime powers of Venice and Genoa were no longer so blessed. In the centre of the Mediterranean they were squeezed between the Spanish who controlled access to the Atlantic and the Ottomans who controlled the trade routes to the Orient and it was to their small Levantine enclaves that the new Sultan Selim the Sot first turned his attention. He realised that a major confrontation with Spain, dominant in the west, would not be to his immediate advantage. Closer to home, he could achieve the victory he craved by removing Venetian control from Cyprus and Crete in his own back yard. His first foray was through diplomatic channels, but eventually, on 28 March 1570, the Ottoman emissary delivered a blunt ultimatum to the Venetian authorities demanding that they hand over Cyprus to the Sultan or take the consequences of 'cruel war' everywhere and the loss of their 'treasure', which the Turks would seize. In the West where Selim was depicted as a pleasure-seeking debauchee, he was said to want Cyprus because he liked the wine, yet this was no whim but the culmination of a strategy. The Ottomans had done their homework; the attack on Cyprus had been two years in preparation.

As Sultan Selim was eyeing up Venetian territories in the east, an opportunity arose to stir up trouble for Philip at home. Spain had only become completely Christian, at least nominally, as recently as 1499 when the Emirate of Granada capitulated to the joint rulers, Ferdinand of Aragon and Isabella of Castile. The former Moorish Muslim population, known as Moriscos, were reluctant converts who had already risen up against the harsh enforcement of their new faith. In 1568 they rebelled again and this time they received aid and reinforcements from the Berbers of north Africa and the Turks. Unsurprisingly the Spanish were fearful this could be the precursor to another Islamic incursion into the Iberian Peninsula and Ottoman dominance in the western Mediterranean. The tortuous Reconquista of the Iberian Peninsula from the Moors had taken nearly 800 years and left the Spanish with a crusader mentality, a view not necessarily shared by their neighbours. Philip may have seen himself as a defender of Catholicism against protestant and infidel alike, but incessant conflict between the European monarchies had meant that they could never form a united front against Ottoman aggression. France preferred an alliance with the infidel in order to continue its long running conflict with Spain, and both were keen to exploit the weakness of the Italian states.

It was in this climate of apprehension and distrust that the Venetians had already made overtures to the Spanish court with the tentative proposal of another Holy League. Even if the French could not be brought on board by the increased threat from Selim, at least the Spanish and Italians might seek common cause. The problem for Spain was the knowledge that the Venetians were likely to drop any notions of fighting for the common good of Christendom if they could strike a deal that maintained their trade with the Turks. With a crisis looming, the zealous Pope Pius V saw his opportunity to step in. Holy Leagues had been formed before under previous Popes, to oust the French from Italy (1496, 1511) and against the Ottoman threat in 1538 and 1560. This time it would be a Catholic crusade, excluding France, to end the prospect of complete Turkish dominance in the eastern Mediterranean. Although Philip was not enamoured by the prospect, under the Pope's powers of persuasion, backed up by his financial and military commitment, he saw an opportunity to counter Ottoman aggression in Spain by taking the fight to Cyprus. This was the very ploy the Turkish strategy had discounted, believing that Philip would have thought himself too far away to act on behalf of the beleaguered island. In the knowledge that help might be forthcoming the Venetians rejected the Turkish ultimatum and two days later a fleet of galleys was already on its way from Spain to Italy under the command of the experienced Genoese admiral Giovanni Andrea (*Gianandrea*) Doria. Doria was the great-nephew of Andrea Doria, the commander of the previous ill-fated allied fleet at Preveza. He too had suffered at the hands of the Ottomans at the Battle of Djerba off Tunisia in 1560, when the previous Holy Alliance fleet under his command had been soundly defeated. Luckily for the Christians, the Ottomans had once again not pushed home their victory, but taken with a number of other defeats inflicted on them by the Ottomans, his appointment did not instil confidence amongst the Venetians. The distrust was mutual.

Each detachment of the alliance was under its own commander. The Venetian baton of command fell to Girolamo Zane, and at the end of March 1570 he took an advance detachment of their fleet out of the lagoon to meet with the Spanish. Overall command of the alliance was given to Marcantonio Colonna, the Pope's choice. It was a diplomatic appointment rather than a military one as Colonna, an Italian aristocrat from the Papal States, was no seaman; his experience was as a cavalry commander in the service of Philip. Philip accepted the Pope's nominee, but he was sure he instructed Doria to use his better seafaring knowledge and judgement to advise Colonna on the proper course of action when necessary. In reality, Philip did not want to lose another fleet of costly Spanish galleys after the losses of Preveza and Djerba. If possible he preferred to make a show rather than to actually engage in battle on behalf of the Venetians and their far-flung colony. Doria too was taking a risk; twelve of the galleys were his own property rented out to Philip.

While the Spanish had spent a fortune over the years rebuilding their navies, Venice was less well endowed. They had managed to stay at peace for thirty years and now they had to frantically build and re-commission ships to come up to strength. A further problem was lack of manpower. When Zane put in to Zara (Zadar) in Dalmatia to await the arrival of Doria and Colonna his crews were hit by typhus. After two months he moved his ships on to Corfu, but matters did not improve and rowers recruited from the Greek islands to fill the gaps also fell sick or died. Months of inactivity began to ebb at the morale of his men, so, in frustration at the late arrival of his allies, in July Zane moved on again towards Crete. Philip's continued reluctance to fully commit to a Holy League had delayed Doria in southern Italy. Without positive instructions, he interpreted the king's wishes by proceeding as slowly and unenthusiastically as possible. He eventually met up with Colonna's Papal fleet at Otranto and together they set forth for Crete on 22 August, almost five months after the enterprise to save Cyprus had begun.

Unlike the Christians, the Ottomans were organised and well prepared and their enemy's lack of commitment and delays played into their hands. They had already made their move against Cyprus a month earlier when, on 1 July, Admiral Piyale Pasha, the victor of Djerba, had landed between 60,000 and 80,000 cavalry and janissaries unopposed with the twin objective of taking Nicosia and Famagusta. Although both cities were fortified in the latest fashion, Nicosia's walls were still not completed, and both were undermanned and ill equipped. Furthermore, military command of the island had been left by default to the inadequate Nicolo Dandolo in Nicosia, while the more able general, Astorre Baglione was stationed with the civil governor of the island, Marco Antonio Bragadin, at Famagusta. Dandolo was cautious and autocratic and his lack of enterprise cost the Venetians dear. Unwilling to engage with the enemy he further compounded his tactical errors by failing to act on instructions from the Venetian Senate to free the Greek serfs in order to win their good will. As was often the case, the Greeks, at least initially, found the prospect of a Turkish master preferable to a Venetian one and when the villagers proved all too willing to submit to the Turkish advance, violent retribution by Dandolo only exacerbated the situation. In three weeks the Turkish commander Lala Mustapha Pasha and his troops were at the gates of Nicosia. Both sides were fully aware that only five years previously at the Siege of Malta the Knights of St John and the Maltese had held the Turks at bay for five months until an allied Christian rescue force arrived to inflict a humiliating defeat on the Ottoman forces and Mustapha was not prepared for history to repeat itself. This time he would be more fortunate, as the brave efforts of many of the city's garrison were undermined by the inadequacies of their commander. The final assault came on 9 September followed by the slaughter and enslavement of the inhabitants and the despatch of Dandolo's head in a dish to Bragadin at Famagusta. Paphos, Limasol and Larnaka then fell in quick succession and by 18 September the Turks had surrounded Famagusta.

As their Christian brothers were being slaughtered at the hands of the feared Turks, the allies' forces dithered on Crete. The Spanish and Papal fleets had finally rendezvoused with Zane at Souda Bay on 30 August, Colonna blaming Doria for wasting time on needless diversions, and despite the Venetian losses of around 20,000 men to disease, they had managed to muster a larger fleet than their opponents. What they had not been able to muster was unity and arguments soon flared as how to proceed. Doria's distrust of the Venetians lead him to accuse them, rightly, of being underprepared, and he refused to go any further without payment for losses up front. Colonna had to use his diplomatic skills to achieve a compromise, proposing that rather than relieving Cyprus straight away they would attack the Turks in the rear at Rhodes instead. Eventually agreement was reached and the fleet weighed anchor on 17 September. In the meantime, the Ottomans, who were well informed of their enemy's movements, were carrying on their campaign on Cyprus in the knowledge that relief was not immediately on its way. It was on 21 September, as the commanders of the allied fleet were sheltering from a storm off the Turkish coast, that they learnt that Nicosia had fallen twelve days earlier. In dismay they decided to turn back and the fleet, decimated by disease and losses to storms, limped home. The fall of Nicosia and the impending loss of the island caused consternation in Italy. In Venice the blame for failure was put at the door of Girolamo Zane, and he ended his days in prison; for the Pope, it was Doria who was at fault, but Philip promoted him to general.

The fiasco of the campaign put the formal makeup of the League under threat, with the participants disagreeing on how the financial costs were to be shared or the terms of reference. Philip was still keen to receive Papal subsidies, but as his ambition was to be defender of the Catholic world and a crusader against all infidels, including Protestants, Spain's priorities, with its sphere of interest west of Sicily, were at odds with those of Venice in the east. For Philip, defence of the western Mediterranean and the retaking of Tunis were more important than Cyprus and, if the Ottomans reduced Venetian power it would be to his advantage. For the Venetians, resolving their difficult relationship with the Turks was paramount. They were uninterested in Tunis and Philip's self-aggrandisement, only in protecting their assets. The Venetians were so anxious to do so that they were secretly continuing a diplomatic effort in Constantinople with the Grand Vizier, Sokollu Mehmed Pasha. Sokollu, a political rival of Lala Mustapha and Piyale Pasha, was against Selim's campaign and he felt that a form of rapprochement could be reached with Venice over Cyprus without going to war. To add to the confusion of strategies and motives, Spain and Venice were only in complete agreement in their strong antipathy to the Pope's ultimate vision of a crusade to recapture the Holy Land.

At Famagusta, Lala Mustapha was up against sterner resistance than at Nicosia. Led by the organisational skill of Bragadin and the military knowledge of Baglione, the garrison and populace came together as they had not done under Dandolo. Bragadin was as prepared as Dandolo had not been, and even though they were outnumbered ten to one, through good management of resources, morale and discipline were maintained in the face of every intimidation Mustapha could think of, including the parading of severed heads and captives before the city walls. As the siege dragged on through the winter, a daring hit and run raid in January 1571 by Marco Querini jolted the opposing forces into action. Marco Querini, Venice's new naval commander in Crete, made an unseasonal foray with a fleet of twelve galleys and four high-sided sailing ships in support of the defenders of Famagusta. The Ottoman navy had been depleted over the winter and timing his expedition to coincide with the start of Ramadan, he took them by surprise. Querini first lured some Turkish ships out of the harbour into the open where he was able to destroy three of them before landing reinforcements for the garrison, and apparently some captured Muslim pilgrims. He then left to harass the enemy along the coast.

This success encouraged Baglione and Bragadin to attempt an ambush. Feigning that a large number of the garrison had left with the Venetian ships, they encouraged Mustapha to make an all-out attack against, what he thought, were undefended walls. These two events were to have serious consequences. When the Sultan heard that large numbers of his troops had been mown down by canon and arquebus fire, the survivors put to the sword in a follow up cavalry charge, and the safety of the pilgrimage routes to Mecca violated, he was furious. Vizier Sokollu replaced his rival Piyale Pasha with Müezzinzade Ali Pasha as *kapudan* of the fleet. The less experienced Ali Pasha, who had previously served as governor of Egypt, was a favourite of the Sultan and married to one of his daughters. He was also another rival of Sokollu. Having been given the responsibility of restoring Turkish pride, if Ali's appointment failed it has been conjectured that Sokollu would be the beneficiary. Whatever the internal political intrigues of the Ottoman government, the first priority was to pre-empt any further Venetian actions and Ali Pasha was quickly despatched with reinforcements earlier than had been planned.

The immediate task was to watch Crete, and a force was sent there in February, before Ali made for Cyprus with unusual instructions: 'find and immediately attack the infidels' fleet in order to save the honour of our religion and the state'. This was contrary to the normal Turkish view of the primary role of the fleet, which was to transport and support troops as they had successfully done at the Siege of Rhodes, and less successfully at Malta. That Selim would have sent such a rash directive is possible, but the malign machinations of Sokollu have also been suspected as being behind it. Reinforced and with a vast army of 100,000 men at his disposal, Mustapha could afford to take his time. Tunnellers were put to work in the soft soil digging trenches up to the walls of Famagusta. Everyone knew now the days of the city were numbered. Inexorably the food supplies inside dwindled and in mid-April Baglione let 5,000 local non-combatants – children, the old and the infirm – leave the city, and in turn Mustapha shrewdly showed clemency in allowing them to return to their villages. The brave resistance continued on until the end of July when eventually, with virtually all supplies finished, the remaining population exhausted, the walls crumbling from continuous heavy bombardment and the efforts of the miners, and no relief from Venice materialising, Bragadin and Baglione were forced to bow to the inevitable. Having consoled themselves that they had done their duty to the last they raised the white flag.

To start with the surrender progressed well enough and reasonable terms were agreed, but then the strains of the siege began to tell on both sides when a show of noble defiance or arrogance on the Venetian side went down badly with the Ottomans. Mustapha Pasha was already angry enough at the time it had taken to bring Famagusta to its knees at the cost of half his army. On 5 August 1571, just as the formalities were reaching their close and Bragadin and his survivors prepared to sail to freedom, the fate of the fifty Muslim pilgrims was raised. Despite the pleas of the Venetians that Querini had taken most of them with him and the few who were left had escaped, Mustapha believed that Bragadin had had them tortured and slaughtered after the peace treaty was signed, breaking the terms of the agreement.

Any courtesy was now scrapped. The Venetians were immediately arrested and Bragadin put on the rack. Baglione protested that Mustapha had broken his faith, but in vain; he was executed along with the other commanders, his head displayed to the army and added to the pile of 350 heads outside the pasha's tent. While the remaining 20,000 Christians were peremptorily being slaughtered, Bragadin's stubborn arrogance earned him special treatment, to die as slowly as possible. First his ears and nose were cut off, then he was kept alive for a further twelve days while his wounds festered and after which he was paraded through the streets and forced to carry sacks of earth along the city walls, kissing the ground each time he passed the pasha. His stubbornness unabashed, Bragadin refused attempts to convert him to Islam, and in the eyes of the Venetians accepted his martyrdom with the knowledge he would be saved by his faith saying, 'My body is yours. Torture it as you will.' Tied to a chair he was hoisted up a galley's mast to witness the non-arrival of the promised relieving Christian fleet and then ducked in the sea to the jeers of the on-lookers. The final humiliation was to be tied naked to an ancient column in the square outside the church of St Nicholas, later converted to a mosque, and flayed alive. By the time his torturer reached his waist he was dead. This was not enough for his tormentors, who proceeded to stuff his skin with straw and dress what was left of the courageous Bragadin in a commander's uniform to be paraded through the streets of Famagusta on a donkey. Bragadin's dummy was then taken on a tour through the Levant before arriving at Constantinople for the delectation of the Sultan. Lala Mustapha's rival, Sokollu was not pleased by the gift. He anticipated that it would only stiffen the resolve of the Venetians and undermine his diplomatic efforts to split the Christian alliance. He was right. The Venetians would be outraged.

Mustapha's mocking of the absence of rescuing ships on the horizon as the defenders of Famagusta suffered their final humiliation was justified. Although the Venetians had quickly re-equipped their fleet after the losses of the previous year, the squabbling of the Christian allies and the reluctance of Philip to fully engage had fatally delayed the efforts to form a united front against the Ottomans. It was only by 25 May that finally Pope Pius was able to confirm the formal make up of his dreamt of Holy League. In addition to the commitment of galleys from the Papal States under Doria and Colonna, there were those drawn from Spain and Philip's territories in Italy, the Republics of Venice and Genoa, the Knights of Malta, the Grand Duchy of Tuscany, the Duchy of Savoy, the Duchy of Urbino and the Duchy of Parma. The Portuguese were absent because of their campaign in Morocco, and their own difficulties with the Turks in the Red Sea and Indian Ocean left them with no ships to spare. As a compromise to the various parties Philip proposed that overall command of the fleet be given to Don Juan of Austria, his younger illegitimate half-brother, with the Pope's general Marcantonio Colonna as his lieutenant. The wisdom of this was that Don Juan was seen as an outsider and neutral. Paradoxically, as Philip prepared for war, the eastern Austrian branch of the Holy Roman Empire under his more pragmatic cousin, Maximillian II, maintained its truce with the Ottomans. When, on 23 August, Don Juan at last arrived in Messina from Barcelona with the Spanish squadron he was greeted by scenes of jubilation accompanied by a reception of much pomp and ceremony. Unknown to everyone it was already too late to save Famagusta.

Don Juan had inherited a volatile situation. No one trusted the Venetians and the men of the various contingents were at each other's throats, often literally, with fights breaking out among them. Added to the mutual hostility was unease over the lack of pay, and Don Juan wisely quickly set about settling matters. At 24 he was already an experienced soldier with a dashing reputation earned by commanding thirty galleys for Philip against the Barbary corsairs and putting down the Morisco rebellion. His seniors had picked him for his leadership qualities, but they did not regard him as a free agent. Primarily a soldier rather than a naval commander, he was soon receiving fulsome advice from all quarters. On the one hand the Papal supporters and the Venetians were urging him on, while Doria had instructions from the ever-cautious Philip, who was the main funder of the expedition, to keep him in check and the Spanish fleet out of trouble. For the Spanish, failure while appearing to be willing was the better outcome as long as it preserved their fleet.

In contrast to the Christian alliance's continued vacillations, again the Ottomans had their plans prepared well in advance. To counter the Christian threat, the Sultan had not only sent Ali Pasha in March to settle the situation in Cyprus, but a second fleet had been despatched in May from Constantinople under the second Vizier, Pertev Pasha, and before Famagusta had fallen the two fleets had already combined and begun harassing Crete. Meanwhile the third Vizier, Ahmed Pasha, was marching a land army towards the Adriatic coast and Uluch Ali Reis (Occhiali), the Pasha of Algiers, was sailing from Tripoli to join forces. The plan was to take more than just Cyprus, but to strike at the Venetians' possessions in the Adriatic, perhaps even taking Venice itself. As Sokollu had informed the Venetians, the Turkish ambition was to extend their dominion as far as Rome.

It was not until mid-September that all the ships of the Holy League's contributing parties had arrived and the fleet was prepared to sail. A typical galley was powered by around 200 oarsmen or *galleoti* (galley slaves) and carried between 100 and 130 soldiers; the Spanish held around 150 soldiers, but the Venetian galleys were reportedly considerably understrength. Don Juan found favour with the Venetians when he offered their commander Sebastiano Venier extra men (2,000 Germans, 1,500 Spaniards and 1,500 Italians) plus money and supplies for their up to twenty transports to make up for their shortages. The 75-year-old Venier swallowed his pride and accepted in the end, taking, apart from the Germans, between 3,000 and

4,000 men, depending on the Venetian account or the Don's. The contingents' flagships, or *lanternas*, were larger vessels, having around thirty pairs of oars with seven rowers per oar as opposed to twenty-five with five rowers. In addition, there was an element of the fleet that would play an important role in the outcome of the expedition. The Venetian shipwrights had hastily converted ten merchant galleys into warships known as galleasses. Although slower and more cumbersome than the war galleys they had the advantage of more space, allowing the mounting of extra guns and the firing of broadsides, and extra height from which to dominate the enemy. When Colonna had been criticised for their use in pursuing the Ottoman fleet he responded that the 'galleasses were like fortresses towering over and firing down on the enemy'.

The majority of ships came from Venice, 108 galleys, six galleasses, and two other vessels carrying 5,000 fighting men. Philip provided the majority of the troops, around 18,000 plus eighty-one galleys, twenty ships and there were some privately owned galleys in Spanish service. The other smaller contingents included twenty-seven Genoese galleys, twelve Papal galleys with 1,500 troops, five galleys from the Order of St Stephen and the Grand duchy of Tuscany, three from the Duke of Savoy and four from the Knights of Malta. At last, early on 16 September, Don Juan was able to write one last letter to one of his advisors, Don Garcia de Toledo, telling him that he was about to sail out from Messina that very day to engage the enemy with a total of 208 galleys, six galleasses and 24 support ships manned by around 40,000 oarsmen and sailors and carrying between 26,000 and 28,000 paid infantry, including 4,000 'gentlemen adventurers'. Spanish, Italian (2,500) and German (5,000) troops were spread between the ships. Even though he was in command of such a large armada, he knew from his intelligence sources that in all likelihood his fleet would be outnumbered by the Ottomans.

Four days before their departure he had mustered the allied commanders aboard his flagship to hammer out a plan. Don Juan proposed two options, to seek out the enemy and attack, or (Don Garcia's advice) to wait for the enemy to come to them. Despite behind the scenes French attempts to broker a peace between Venice and the Sultan, the Pope's representatives and the Venetians were for immediate attack, while unsurprisingly Doria and the Spanish continued to urge caution. Don Juan was not one to be cautious, and contrary to his Spanish colleagues he advocated going after the enemy with victory in mind. Option one was carried unanimously after the Spanish gave way under pressure. The order of battle was then agreed, on or before 14 September, and it would be kept to assiduously. The strategy first was to make for Gomenizza (Igoumenitsa, then only a small harbour on the Greek mainland across the strait from Corfu) from where they could flush out the enemy.

On the evening of 16 September, once the crews and soldiers had received the sacrament and the papal ambassador given his blessing, the largest Christian armada of the 16th century pulled out of the harbour amid public celebration. As they passed the mole, a further blessing was bestowed on the array of fighting ships by the papal nuncio. The numbers, which are never exactly precise, may have increased slightly to 209 galleys accompanied by the perhaps twenty-seven large support ships with a flotilla of numerous 'small vessels' in attendance. On board the Spanish galley *Marquesa* was Miguel de Cervantes, the future author of *Don Quixote*. He had enlisted as a soldier in the *Infanteria de Marina*, the Spanish Marines. Among the other 'adventurers' was the English pirate and mercenary Sir Thomas Stukeley, in command of three ships, Aurelio Scetti, a Florentine musician who had spent twelve years on the galleys for murdering his wife and a number of Greek volunteers hoping that the enterprise might offer an opportunity for a general uprising in the Peloponnese against the Turkish occupation. Most unlikely of all was Maria la Bailadora aboard Don Juan's flagship *Real*, a flamenco dancer who had disguised herself as a soldier to be with her lover.

When they reached open water, Don Juan reviewed his fleet and made preliminary tests of their formation. Each commander was given his orders as to their positions in the line of battle. Once properly under way, Venier began to complain that the fleet was not making good enough speed. On 19 September, Don Juan stopped to take on a small number of troops and supplies at Cotrone at the southern tip of Italy, before he took advantage of a spell of good weather to press on, and by the 25th they had reached the north-eastern tip of Corfu. They were not sailing blind. Don Juan had sent Orazio Orsini di Bomarzo and Gil de Andrada, a Knight of St John, ahead with four swift galleys to gain intelligence. The two gathered reports that the Ottoman fleet numbered around 280 warships and that the enemy were aware of the numbers of their opponent's armada. The Christians learnt that while they had been taking their time to get organised, the Ottoman fleet had spent the summer ravaging Venetian shore positions on Crete and the island of Cerigo (Kythera) before making for the Adriatic. There they had attacked Corfu before heading on to Preveza, perhaps indicating that they were about to disperse for the winter.

Two photograhs showing a replica of Don Juan of Austria's flagship, the *Galera Real*, in Barcelona Maritime Museum. *(Photos: David Merret and Richard Mortel, CC BY 2.0)*

In fact, the Turks, having indeed conducted a successful campaign along the Adriatic coast, capturing forts and raiding, were returning to their base at Lepanto, modern Nafpaktos, in the Gulf of Corinth. Ali Pasha knew full well that the Christian fleet was on its way, for his own spies had been busy. He knew of Don Juan's intended destination, and, after audaciously infiltrating Messina harbour to assess the number of the League's ships, they had obtained a copy of his battle plan. Rumours that the Turks were afraid of the League's strength and wanted to avoid battle, in contradiction of the Sultan's orders, were unfounded. Ali Pasha was none too worried, and puzzled as to why Don Juan would want to commit to battle while so heavily outnumbered. Unfortunately for the Ottoman commander, the audacity of his spies, Kara Hodja and Kara Djali (Deli), was not matched by the quality of their information. They had under-estimated the number of Christian galleys by a whole Venetian squadron leading Ali to believe the enemy had a fleet of only 140 ships. In his view, with winter approaching it was probably too late to engage in open hostilities and the well-known disunity of the Christians would probably mean that they would fall apart at the first opportunity and be forced to retreat. So, as his ships were in need of repair and with his men exhausted, a return to base had seemed the best option.

On 26 September, the Holy League reached the anchorage at Corfu city where they learned first-hand of the devastation of the island by Turkish troops. Frustrated at not being able to take the citadel, they had taken out their fury on the local population and their sacred places. These wanton acts of destruction duly inflamed the crusading passions of the Venetians when it came time to discuss the plan of campaign. The Spanish as usual advised caution, proposing a face-saving raid on the nearby coast where the Venetians could retake the castles of Sopoto (Sopot, modern Borsh in Albania) and Margarition (modern Margariti in Greece) that they had briefly held during a local revolt against Ottoman rule, and then, with winter approaching, retreat. But, armed with his own equally suspect intelligence, Don Juan and the Venetians, supported by the Pope, were all for the original plan, to seek and destroy the enemy. Released Venetian prisoners and local Greek fishermen had informed Don Juan in turn that the Turks had only 180 galleys and were short of troops, so surely a Christian victory was guaranteed. These same fishermen had informed the Turks that an Ottoman victory was equally assured. Too late Philip wrote to Don Juan urging him to retreat to Sicily for the winter and start out again next year; the die was already cast. Don Juan pushed on to anchor in the bay of Gomenizza. On 29 September the news arrived that the Ottoman fleet was at Lepanto.

As anticipated by Ali Pasha, in the following days tensions among the Christians flared up again and almost scuppered the whole expedition. On 2 October, Don Juan, ever eager to maintain battle readiness, assigned Doria to inspect Venier's flagship; Venier took this as an insult. Later in the day, matters took a more serious turn when a quarrel broke out between the captain of a Venetian galley, Andrea Calergi, a Greek from Crete, and Muzio Alticozzi di Cortona, an Italian captain in the service of Spain. After a number of men were killed and wounded on both sides, Venier took swift retribution by hanging four of the Spaniards. Don Juan was furious, and it was only through the considered counsel of Colonna that he merely demoted Venier rather than resorting to the extreme measures advocated by some of the generals. Venier would maintain his position in the line of battle, but his second in command Agostino Barbarigo would take his place in the councils of war.

The following day the fleet weighed anchor and set out towards Lepanto, Don Juan being of the opinion that fighting the Turk was preferable to fighting each other. It was on their arrival on 4 October at the northern tip of the Venetian held island of Cephalonia, that the Christians finally heard the devastating news; Famagusta had fallen, and with it all hope of saving Cyprus. It was a crushing blow that furthered the Venetians' desire for revenge, but rationally put the purpose of the expedition in doubt. Although the courageous martyrdom of Bragadin might have stiffened their resolve, the Venetians knew that their allies did not necessarily share their enthusiasm for battle. At another council of war, the prospect of resorting to a punitive raid on nearby Turkish held territory was raised again, but Don Juan remained steadfast. The fleet slowly continued on its journey south in squally autumn weather, until three days later the weather cleared as they neared the small islands at the approaches to the Gulf of Patras known to the Italians as the Curtzolari and in modern Greek as the Ekhinades. Rumours that a portion of the Ottoman fleet might be at sea meant Don Juan had ensured everything was battle ready and the men alert, so as dawn came up on a fine Sunday morning his eager-eyed lookouts posted on the islands and in the ships' masts quickly spotted approaching enemy ships, but it was the whole Ottoman fleet, their masts as thick as a forest. The tricky problem of luring the Turks out from their safe haven had been made redundant, astonishingly they had come out to do battle in open water without any need for coercion.

At harbour in Lepanto the Turks held the advantage. Given that their ships were in need of repair and many of their seasonal troops had left for the winter, they could have left the onus on the Christians to make a move. To reach Lepanto, the armada had to first pass from the Gulf of Patras through the narrow channel known as the Little Dardanelles, guarded on either shore by the twin forts, Rio and Antirio, into the almost land-locked Gulf of Corinth. Lepanto itself was an ancient harbour and dockyard on the north coast of the gulf as it widens just beyond Antirio that had been the Athenians' western base during the Peloponnesian War (431–404BC). Its strategic and defensible site meant it had continued to be a highly desirable prize during the power struggles that followed the demise of the Byzantine Empire. The Venetians managed to acquire the town not by force, but by purchasing it in 1407 from the Albanian warlord Paul Spata. Their improvements to the town's defences enabled it to remain as a Venetian enclave while the surrounding region was overrun by the Ottoman Empire, until its fortress was finally taken in 1499.

The decision to leave the well-tested protection of Lepanto was not lightly taken and the Ottoman leadership had their own divisions of opinion on how to proceed. During the final council of war, Ali Pasha was determined that they take the fight to the Christian fleet to gain the glory of a victory that would open up the whole of Mediterranean Europe.

Wiser heads advised caution. With their shortage of men, why give up their safe position. Mehemet Bey, the commander of the Turkish naval base at Negroponte (the Greek island of Euboea) felt that it was unwise to count on Christian disunity in such a critical moment, Uluch Ali thought the risks outweighed the rewards (he had brought twenty-five galleys from Tripoli and meant to return with them), Mahomet Sirocco (Sulik Mehmed Pasha), commander of the Egyptian fleet, thought it best to remain under the protection of Lepanto's fortifications and let the League come to them, and Pertev Pasha, the troop commander, was emphatic that the infantrymen given him for the battle did not inspire his confidence, remembering as he did the decimation of his troops at Malta. Supporting Ali was Hassan Pasha, Barbarossa's son. He played to Ali's low opinion of the League, endorsing the view that their internal rivalries would again be their undoing. In the end, having heard all the counter-arguments, Ali remained adamant that they should take on the enemy, a decision, according to the Turkish chronicler Peçevi, highly influenced by threats on his position and his life from the Sultan in Constantinople.

The opposing commanders-in-chief were soldiers rather than sailors, but Ali Pasha's lack of naval experience would prove the greater handicap. Don Juan had listened to his advisors, particularly Don Garcia de Toledo who had led the relief force that broke the Siege of Malta in 1565. Don Garcia's advice was to learn from Barbarossa's defeat of the previous Holy League under Andrea Doria at Preveza. There, Doria had ordered his large fleet into one squadron, leading to confusion as the ships got in one another's way. Don Garcia's advice was to follow the example of Barbarossa and deploy the fleet in three squadrons with 'those galleys in which you have the greatest confidence' at the extremity of the wings under 'exceptional captains' and to 'ensure that enough sea remains between the squadrons so that they can turn and manoeuvre without impeding one another'. Don Juan wisely listened to his more experienced counsellor, and with the order of battle already decided and practised the League was well prepared; in fact, they had practised their dispositions only three days earlier. Don Juan had also taken the precaution of mixing the make-up of his three divisions, with ships from each participating party spread across the line to counter any disunity amongst the groups. He was to take command from the centre of the main division of sixty-two galleys aboard his flagship, the *Galera Real*, with Venier on the Venetian flagship and Colonna on the papal flagship to his left and right. The Venetian Agostino Barbarigo would lead the left wing (fifty-three galleys), assisted by Marco Querini and Antonio de Canale, and Gianandrea Doria, Philip's admiral, the right wing (fifty-three galleys). Álvaro de Bazán, Marquess of Santa Cruz de Mudela, who had taken part in the recapture of Tunis in 1535 with Andrea Doria, was given command of the rearguard (thirty-eight galleys) with instructions to fill any breaches in the line. The vanguard under Juan de Cardonna was made up of the six Venetian 44-gun galleasses. Don Juan had also listened to Doria, who had suggested removing the rams, which had now become more ornamental than practical, from the prows of the galleys. Once these *espolones* ('spurs') were out of the way it gave the guns on the forecastles a wider and lower field of fire.

The Ottomans had not been as innovative as the Venetians. Galleys were still primarily ramming vessels, with a few guns at the prow, and it was here that the men would gather to board the opposing ship. And they still put their trust in their archers, who could release thirty arrows before an enemy arquebusier could reload. Unlike the Christians, the Ottoman archers were unarmoured and the ships offered little protection against enemy gunfire. The Ottoman fleet, made up of both galleys and the smaller *fustas* or galliots, the fast oar- and sail-powered ships favoured by the corsairs, was thus lighter and built for speed, whereas the heavier Christian ships packed more firepower. Initially the Ottomans were drawn up in two lines in a crescent, the formation designed to avoid attack from the flanks or from behind, the most vulnerable areas of the galley. With such a large fleet this formation proved too difficult to maintain, so Ali Pasha mirrored the formation of the League with himself aboard the *Sultana* at the front of the centre with eighty-seven galleys and his best sixty-two ships in the first line. The galleys were made up of contingents from the Imperial Squadron from Constantinople, which included Hasan Pasha, and those from Rhodes, the Black Sea (Bulgaria and Bithynia on the north coast of Asia Minor), Gallipoli, Negroponte and Tripoli. Mahomet Sirocco, the governor of Alexandria, commanded the right which comprised of sixty galleys from Constantinople, Tripoli, Anatolia and Alexandria, and two galliots also from Alexandria. Uluch Ali took the left (sixty-one galleys, thirty-two galliots) drawn from Constantinople, Algeria, Syria, Anatolia, Albania and Negroponte. The Ottoman rearguard consisted of eight galleys and twenty-two galliots under Amuret Dragut Rais. Mahomet Sirocco was more of a land general than a naval commander and he had taken part in the operation against Famagusta the previous year. Uluch Ali on the other hand was a former Italian galley slave who had been captured by pirates while fishing. After converting to Islam he had turned corsair and quickly gained promotion in the Ottoman

The Battle of Lepanto based on a 1572 etching by Fernando Bertelli attributed to Ignazio Dianti showing the disposition of the two fleets. (*The Vatican Gallery of Maps, public domain*)

fleet, serving as a commander at the Battle of Djerba and the Siege of Malta.

With the Ottoman fleet just 10 miles away, there was no longer any option of retreat for the Holy League, and Don Juan hoisted a green flag and a gun was fired, the signals for battle. As the Christian fleet rounded the islands from the north into the Gulf of Patras it had been sailing into a mild easterly wind, and Don Juan had deployed the majority of his lighter more manoeuvrable galleys on the left, close to the shore. Sailing into the wind made forming the battle lines difficult and slow for the League's ships, especially for the lighter ones, whereas the Ottomans had the wind at their backs. It was imperative for both fleets to keep the lines intact. To do this, vessels had to maintain their position and not lag behind, leaving a gap in the line, or go too fast, as an isolated ship was an easy target, all the while keeping a distance to prevent the clash of oars. Ali Pasha's *Sultana* was to act as his fleet's front marker, with orders that no one should get ahead on pain of death.

The fleets approached one another at walking pace. In the van of the Christian fleet were the six galleasses, two sailing about a quarter of a mile in front of the main body of ships. These slower bulky floating fortresses were being towed forward into position, two before each division, by eight galleys taken from the rearguard. Around mid-morning the wind dropped and changed direction, blowing from the west, a sign interpreted as Divine intervention by the Christians. This not only gave some relief to their oarsmen, but it would allow them more time to grab their weapons as soon as they encountered the enemy. Even at this late stage, the Christian purpose of the expedition was not allowed to be forgotten. Each ship had a priest on board and Mass had been said every day. The Pope had insisted on the discouragement of blasphemy and gambling, no easy task amongst hardened soldiers, sailors and galley slaves, and Don Juan had felt obliged to hang some miscreants at Messina to set an example.

On the verge of battle there was just time for one more Mass for the remission of sins before the prospect of an untimely death, then the drums and trumpets were sounded and the cry went up, 'Victory and long live Jesus Christ'. As the ships shuffled into their final battle formation, Don Juan transferred from the *Galera Real* to a light, racing frigate to pass

Venetian galleass in *A History of Naval Architecture* by John Fincham (1851) from a 1570s painting. (*Public domain*)

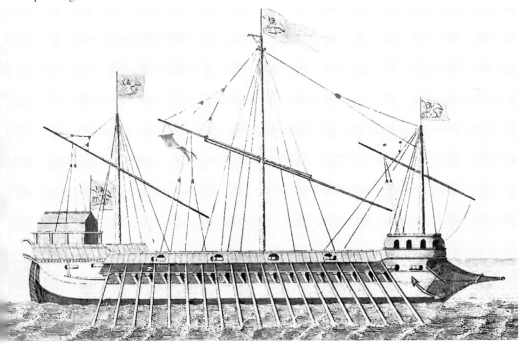

between them and give encouragement. Wearing brilliant armour and carrying a crucifix, he urged the Venetians to revenge Bragadin and the Spanish to do their Christian duty; to the Christian galley slaves he promised freedom (not something entirely in his gift) if they fought well, and he had their chains removed. For the Muslim slaves there was no such offer, in fact they were handcuffed as well as chained in case they mutinied. As he passed the Venetian flagship, Venier saluted him, all animosity forgotten.

The Muslims too were called to prayer by their Imams. With men drawn from so many backgrounds their sense of piety was not uniform; many of the corsairs and the conquered had embraced Islam only out of expediency. Unlike Don Juan, Ali Pasha promised his Christian galley slaves their freedom if he won the day, saying, 'Friends, I expect you today to do your duty by me, in return for what I have done for you. If I win the battle, I promise you your liberty; if the day is yours, God has given it to you'. This was a promise within his power and something his sense of honour would demand. While the oarsmen were straining on their benches to the beat of the drum and the lash of the whip, the slow approach gave the Christian soldiers time to make last minute preparations, sharpening blades and priming guns. On the Ottoman ships the bowmen prepared their bows and dipped their arrows in poison. As they fought barefoot, they smeared oil and butter on the decks making them treacherous for any heavily shod and armoured enemy boarding parties.

Initially, the appearance of the almost stationary galleasses confused the Ottomans. Although they had some notion that they were more heavily armed fore and aft, they were not sure exactly of their purpose, but as they closed it became apparent to Ali that his opponent was going to use them to disrupt his formation by bludgeoning holes in his line. He then put any concerns to one side and as they came within range fired a blank shot across the enemy bows as an invitation to battle. Don Juan replied with a live round. Then Ali unfurled one of the Ottomans' most precious possessions, the 'Banner of the Caliphs', the great green war banner of Islam, embroidered with texts from the Qu'ran and the name of Allah intertwined 28,900 times. With this inspiring signal, the zurnas, the Ottoman trumpets, sounded and the cymbals crashed. The Christians had their response prepared. Crucifixes were raised on every ship and the Pope's sky-blue banner with an image of Christ crucified was raised on the *Galera Real*. Don Juan on his knees received a blessing from a friar and then in a moment of exuberance danced a galliard to the accompaniment of fifes. Cries of victory rang out on both sides accompanied by pleas to the saints or verses from the Qu'ran. The din and the glittering spectacle of the opposing fleets, with the sun dancing off bright armour and colourful banners, as they bore down on one another in the noon-day sun, was enough to strike 'amazement and wonder' into the heart of Girolamo Diedo, a Venetian eye-witness, as well as being a 'terrifying sight'. Any reflection on the wonder of the moment was brought to an abrupt end when, at around 10.30, with the enemy at 150 yards, the Venetian gunners lit their tapers.

The ships were so close and so packed it was impossible to miss. The scene was suddenly filled with gun smoke. Diedo records that three opposing galleys went down in an instant. After the first four galleasses opened fire, the two others were still slightly behind, they turned about to deliver a second blast from the stern. The barrage threw the Ottomans into confusion. Their advance halted as they tacked to avoid the galleasses. Ali ordered the drummers to up the rate so as to pass the floating fortresses as quickly as possible, but broadside on they were raked by arquebus fire to devastating effect. Once beyond the galleasses the Turks were able to open fire on the main Christian line, but they aimed too high. Don Juan in contrast was patient and he waited for them to close, for his plan was to engage at close quarters. With his rams removed his galleys could aim close and low. At the opportune moment each League galley opened fire, sending billowing black smoke downwind into the faces of the Ottoman fleet, obscuring their aim. In no time a third of Ali's ships had already been sunk or crippled.

Ali Pasha's plan had been for his swiftest, shallow-drafted galleys on the right under Mahomet Sirocco, who had local pilots on board with knowledge of Greek waters, to press close to the shallows near the shore and then outflank the Venetian left. It was a risky manoeuvre, and Uluch Ali for one was not in favour of it. If successful, Turkish cavalry units were waiting on the shore to pick up any Venetian survivors who might make for land once their galleys were sunk. Uluch feared the proximity of the shore might be a temptation for the Ottoman crews too. While the Venetian galleasses were causing mayhem to the main body of the Ottoman fleet, Mahomet Sirocco slipped away towards the shore, and seven of his galleys having navigated the shallows he made to turn the flank of Barbarigo's squadron and come up from behind. In the confined space with little room to manoeuvre Barbarigo placed his own *lanterna* and those galleys nearest to him to block their way and for an hour suffered a devastating rain of arrows and a pelting from arquebus fire, followed by attempts to board his ship. In an effort to be heard above the din of battle he raised his visor, only to be hit in the eye by an arrow. He was taken below where he died. Barbarigo's nephew, Giovani Contarini, brought his galley to the flagship's assistance, but he too was shot dead. The collapse of the Christian left flank was only averted by the stern resistance of the crews, many of whom came from Dalmatia, Crete and the islands that had been ravaged by the Turks during the summer, plus the swift reinforcement provided by the rearguard that funnelled extra troops onto the embattled galleys from behind.

A decisive moment came when the Christian slaves, unmoved by Ali Pasha's words, broke free and turned on their Ottoman masters. In the ensuing panic matters were made worse when one of the galleasses turned on the Ottoman right. Sirocco's galley was rammed and its rudder sheared off. As it lay waterlogged in the shallows Mahomet Sirocco was identified by his bright robes floating in the water. He was so badly wounded that a Venetian cut off his head as an act of mercy. Following their flagship, the Ottoman right wing had drifted into the shore where they could be penned in. Those Christian captains on the left of centre who could seized the opportunity. According to Diedo, despite the general confusion of battle, they made a concerted manoeuvre, turning to port as one, to surround the Ottoman ships so that they were 'enclosed, as in a harbour'. Uluch's fears proved well grounded. Having put up a stout resistance, the closeness of the shore proved too much and soon the crews were abandoning ship. In the general scramble, ships collided and men were trampled underfoot, while others drowned having thrown themselves into the water. Ali's gamble had failed. The Venetians pursued them with no mercy. Shouting 'Famagusta! Famagusta!' they took to the longboats and killed the survivors on the beach; 'It was an appalling massacre', in Diedo's words. Seeing their chance, the Christian galley slaves on the Venetian ships, who were no more trusting of promises of freedom than those on the Ottoman ships, grabbed their weapons, jumped ship and made for the hills, preferring to take their chance with the Greek bandits.

In the centre, the battle had taken the form of a head-on collision, similar to that depicted in old western movies where the US 7th Cavalry and the Sioux crash headlong into one another. In like fashion, the person and prominence of the leader was of vital importance; if one or other was taken out, it could turn the whole battle. Ali had an impetuous streak, and he had almost from the start sought to confront Don Juan as if face-to-face in a chivalric contest. Don Juan was not one to shy away from such a challenge. Despite fears for his safety from his men, he remained in position on the prow, a conspicuous figure in his bright armour wielding his two-handed sword. The other main protagonists at the centre were clustered around the opposing flagships, and it was these ships the Turks had targeted, so that it would be a battle decided by the elites at the centre. The initial shots from the *Sultana* had hit their mark, taking out the first few rows of oarsmen on the *Real*. The Christians held their fire until point blank range. At first the *Sultana*, having veered slightly, appeared to be heading for Sebastian Venier's Venetian flagship, but Ali Pasha had only one intention, to take on his opposite number.

As the *Sultana* and its escorting ships closed, the Christians let off a devastating salvo, stopping some of the Turkish galleys. According to Onorato Caetana, commander of the papal infantry aboard *La Grifona*, his was the first of the Christian ships to engage with the enemy, taking on the galleys of the ruthless Barbary corsairs Kara Hodja, the 'black priest', a former friar converted to Islam, and Kara Djali. The two flagships crashed bow to bow into one another, the *Sultana* rising above the *Real*. As they did so the opposing troops unleashed volleys of arquebus fire, and the Turkish archers strafed the *Real's* decks with arrows from above so that it bristled like the back of a porcupine. To port, Colonna's papal flagship had been rammed by Pertev Pasha's galley, causing it to spin round and slam into the side of the *Sultana*, while another Christian galley crashed into its stern. Suddenly everything was confusion, with galleys entangled with one another, oars splintered, deafening noise and black smoke.

It was now a matter of hand-to-hand combat. Boarding parties rushed onto opposing ships. From the *Real*, according to legend, one of the first to cross onto the *Sultana*, sword in hand, was Maria la Bailadora, the flamenco dancer. Behind her were a further 800 men from the *Real*, including 400 Sardinian arquebusiers, attempting to board against 200 Turkish arquebusiers and 100 archers on the *Sultana*. As they grappled, they were not only fighting each other but fighting for space. In the first assault the Muslims were forced back as far as their main mast, where the decks became too slippery with blood and oil for the Spanish to make further progress. In the meantime, reinforcements piled in from other ships and barricades were erected, likening the encounter into a fight in an alley. By now the *Sultana* was surrounded. Venier had rammed the Turkish flagship's port side, but was in turn surrounded by enemy ships and had to be saved by two galleys from the rearguard. On the other side Colonna had repulsed the galley of Mehemet Bey, which had Ali Pasha's 17- and 13-year-old sons on aboard, and on *La Grifona*, Kara Hodja was killed by a shot from an arquebus as he led his boarding party. The disciplined Spanish pikemen then so successfully beat back the attempts of the other boarders that they took the enemy ships. This time the Christian slaves, free of their shackles, courageously joined the cause, vowing to die or earn their freedom.

The barrage from the galleasses had left Ali Pasha out of control of his line, which was no longer acting as one, but as individual squadrons charging around like cavalry units in a land battle. This allowed the Christian forces to penetrate the remnants of the Ottoman battle line in various places and to surround and defeat the isolated ships. On board the *Sultana*, the Turks had responded by pushing the Spanish back to their own ship and the fight would go back and forth for over an hour. Don Juan, who remained a conspicuous figure in the thick of the action, received a wound in the leg from a dagger. From his adjoining galley, Venier, too old to wield a sword like his commander and suffering from bad feet, had taken to the fight in his slippers, loosing off a fusillade of crossbow bolts from his adjoining galley. The *Sultana* was becoming increasingly isolated. Colonna on one side, Venier on the other, raked the ship with fire from guns and bows. The constant reinforcement from the rearguard and the superior firepower of the Christians would eventually prove too much for the Turks.

On the *Sultana* the Turks had been pushed back again behind their barricade in a last ditch effort, with Ali Pasha shooting off arrows for all his worth. How the Ottoman *kapudan pasha* died is uncertain. It is probable that he could have been merely hacked to bits in the general mêlée, but it was also said that uncharacteristically he had died by his own hand in an attempt to flee; or more colourfully that he was despatched by an arquebus shot to the head, after which his head was removed by a zealous Spanish soldier who raised it up on a pike to shouts of 'Victory!' When the head was taken to Don Juan, the Christian commander was said to have been disgusted that his adversary had been treated with such disrespect and ordered it thrown into the sea. The sight of the Holy League's flag being run up the *Sultana's* mast, and the knowledge that the Banner of the Caliphs had been captured led to a collapse in Turkish morale, and those who could not flee, surrendered. Ali's sons, who had tried in vain to come to the aid of their father, were taken with Mehemet Bey's flagship. As resistance at the centre began to crumble Pertev Pasha's burning galley, which had had its rudder blown away, was boarded by Colonna's men. Pertev had already made a discreet retreat aboard a small *fusta* as his oarsmen cried out 'Don't shoot, we're Christians'.

Matters had not been so clear-cut on the left. Here Uluch Ali was proving a hard match for Doria. Doria's lack of enthusiasm for the fight

was well known and it appeared to Don Juan that his squadron was drifting too far out to sea. To counter that he sent a message summoning him
back to the fight. It is likely this was an unfair assumption, as Doria's
concern was not to be outflanked by Uluch Ali's superior numbers. If
Uluch Ali could get round he could achieve what Mahomet Sirocco had
failed to do, attack the League's centre from behind. To do this Uluch was
drifting further south to detach the Christian right from the centre and
create a gap to slip through. As the gap opened, some Venetian galleys
feared treachery on the Genoese commander's part and turned back,
further fragmenting his line. Uluch Ali was a master seaman of whom it
was said he could ride his galley like a horse, and at a signal a section of his
squadron turned about to seize the opportunity to head for the gap and
out manoeuvre Doria on the inside. Coming up on the League's centre
from the stern, Uluch's galleys and galliots now had the wind behind them
and they could take on the enemy in the kind of broken mêlée that suited
them; outnumbering enemy ships that had become detached and isolated,
the ideal targets. Uluch's corsairs fell on the Venetian, Sicilian and the
much-hated Maltese Knights of St John with a vengeance and carnage
followed. The Knights fought bravely but the Ottoman archers released a
hailstorm of arrows onto the decks leaving piles of bodies pierced like
pincushions. Uluch Ali took six galleys himself, including the Maltese
flagship. The small Maltese flotilla was commanded by Pietro Giustiniani,
Prior of Messina, and even though he had been wounded by five arrows,
he was the last man alive when the flagship was taken. The Sicilian galleys
that tried to come to the rescue suffered a similar fate, with everyone on
board massacred, and there were no survivors either on the Genoese flagship, five of the Venetian galleys, or the flagship of Savoy. When the
galleys were boarded the fighting was hard and bloody. Among the
numerous acts of valour shown by the beleaguered Christians was that of
the crew of one galley who, when they realised the game was up, blew up
the ship, taking the surrounding enemy vessels with them.

Uluch Ali's dashing assault had come too late. As he made for the heart
of the battle, his prizes in tow, the Ottoman centre was already collapsing
and he found himself pressed by Doria's regrouped squadron on one side
and the galleys of Don Juan, Venier and Colonna turning to face him on
the other. Uluch decided that there was no use fighting for a lost cause, so
he cut his prizes loose, with Pietro Giustiniani still aboard the Maltese
flagship, making sure to take the distinctive and huge flag of the Knights
of St John, red with a white cross, as a trophy to Selim for display in
Constantinople. Then he slipped away with fourteen of his galleys. The

battle was all but over and it only remained for the last of the Turks' brave resistance to be mopped up. Many Muslims fought on to the finish, resorting to throwing oranges and lemons at the enemy when they ran out of ammunition or arrows, only to have them thrown disdainfully back at them. The devastation was immense, with wreckage and bodies strewn over 8 miles. The engagement had lasted four hours and the scene was now one of burning ships sinking below the waves and men struggling in a sea red with blood, so apocalyptic and strange that Diedo wrote, 'it's as if men were extracted from their bodies and transported to another world'. But the Christian soldiers were not moved to pity by the cries of mercy from the enemy wounded and dying, but finished them off with arquebus or pike before turning to looting their ships. There were so many corpses and so much debris in the water that when the Christian galleys tried to make for safe anchorage they found it hard to leave, even abandoning Christians to drown, and it was only when a storm got up that the remains were dispersed. The battle had left 40,000 men dead, 25,000 of which were Ottoman, and nearly 100 ships destroyed. The League had captured a further 137 enemy ships and a mere 3,500 prisoners, and liberated 12,000 Christian slaves. Slaughter at this rate would not be repeated until the battle of Loos in 1915.

For the Ottomans, Uluch Ali had come out of the contest with honour and the following year he was given command of a new Ottoman fleet. In the immediate aftermath, the Turks played down the significance of what was a crushing defeat, and indeed they went on to take Cyprus and consolidate their position in the eastern Mediterranean. But never again would they threaten the west or control the sea as before. As for Miguel de Cervantes, after heroically ignoring a fever to take part in the battle he was wounded by shot from an arquebus twice, in the chest and in the left hand so that he lost its use, 'for', as he said later, 'the greater glory of the right'. He had fortunately survived the encounter with honour and was able to live off the glory, like all the best tellers of tales, recording it, as Tobias Smollett tells us in a short biography that precedes his translation of *Don Quixote* (1755), 'on diverse occasions: and, indeed it is very natural to suppose his imagination would dwell upon such an adventure, as the favourite incident of his life'. As Cervantes said of his wounds in the Prologue to Book II of *Don Quixote*, he hoped they would not bring indignation on the part of the reader for they were not acquired in 'some tavern brawl' but during 'the most glorious occasion that past or present centuries have beheld or which future ages hope to see'.

Chapter Five

Aboukir Bay, 1798

Nelson's victory at the Battle of the Nile thwarts
Napoleon's plan to take Egypt and weaken Britain by
threatening its interests in the East

In the early afternoon of Wednesday, 1 August 1798, Midshipman George Elliot was perched on the fore royal (the highest) yardarm of HMS *Goliath* scouring the horizon for the French ships that had been eluding them during weeks of searching. He did not know it yet, but they were in fact not far away, lying at anchor in Aboukir Bay, east of Alexandria. It was George's fourteenth birthday and he was already a seasoned campaigner having served at the Battle of Cape St Vincent (1797) under Admiral Sir John Jervis. Jervis had been made Earl St Vincent in honour of his decisive victory over a Spanish fleet almost double the size of his own, but the battle had also been notable for the exploits of a young Commodore named Horatio Nelson. In the midst of the action, Nelson had taken the *San Nicholas* by leading a boarding party, the first time such an exploit had been accomplished by an officer of his rank since 1513. By his speed of action and courage Nelson had become an international celebrity, but his desire to be at the heart of the action had its downside. At 41, Nelson had already lost the use of an eye and arm in battle, the arm only the year before during an attempted amphibious assault on Santa Cruz de Tenerife in the Canary Islands.

HMS *Goliath* and HMS *Zealous* were scouting ahead of the small fleet under Nelson's command that had been charged with tracking down Napoleon and his army after they had left Toulon for an unknown destination. The meteoric rise through the ranks of the young artillery officer, Napoleon Bonaparte, had altered the course of an alliance of monarchies' (the First Coalition) war with Revolutionary France. Napoleon was instrumental in taking back Toulon (1793), France's main Mediterranean naval base, from the counter-revolutionaries supported by Britain, forcing the British navy to seek a base elsewhere. In response to this, the Royal Navy blockaded Toulon while they sought for alliances with potentially friendly Mediterranean states. Corsican dissatisfaction with French occupation offered one such opportunity and it was during the assault on Calvi in 1794, that Nelson lost the sight of his right eye. After Napoleon was called away from Toulon to successfully quell a Royalist revolt in Paris, he was promoted to Commander of the Interior and of the Army in Italy. With an army at his disposal, Napoleon's answer to the blockade was to outflank it by invading Italy. After Spain changed sides in 1796, and subsequently the more obvious threat to Britain's security coming directly from across the Channel, Admiral Jervis had decided it was no longer tenable to keep a naval presence in the Mediterranean. The withdrawal from Corsica and the retreat to Gibraltar meant for the first time there would be no British ships plying the waters beyond the Strait since the reign of the Stuarts.

The British absence had lasted two years, but now Nelson and his ships were back. Although eleven years older than Napoleon, Nelson had also been promoted quickly. He was made Rear Admiral after Cape St Vincent, and the following year given the role of Commander-in-Chief of an independent Mediterranean Squadron. The appointment was not universally welcomed. Some of his senior officers at Cape St Vincent felt they had been passed over, particularly Sir John Orde, who was so put out he went so far as to challenge the 62-year old Jervis to a duel, an action he was dissuaded from carrying through. To Nelson's credit, he had done more than just make a significant contribution to Jervis' victory. He had distinguished himself on a number of occasions through his personal leadership and bravery, a significant factor in his popularity with his men who saw him taking the same risks as themselves. During a difficult period for the navy when conditions on board ship had not kept pace with the times, and crews had already shown their displeasure by mutinying at Spithead, Nelson's approach to on-board conduct and discipline had proved a crucial element in restoring morale within the fleet. Jervis' faith in Nelson had been established towards the end of the previous Mediterranean operations when the Admiral had entrusted him with a free role. Because of this experience, Nelson believed his appointment was down to his extensive knowledge of Italy and the Italian coast.

The need for the British navy to re-enter the Mediterranean had been prompted by intelligence of a build-up of French forces at Toulon. Napoleon had threatened an invasion of England for some time, but the Royal Navy's blockades of the Atlantic ports under French control had so far stifled any attempt. It was a different story in the Mediterranean. With the British out of the way the French were left free to roam at will.

Napoleon's victorious armies had swept the Austrians from northern Italy, bringing the First Coalition against Revolutionary France to an end, and the signing of the treaty of Campo Formio (1797) left Britain standing alone. Hapsburg territories (including most of modern Belgium) were transferred to French control and the Republic of Venice and its maritime empire shared – its possessions in the Ionian Sea, including Corfu, going to France and those along the Adriatic coast to neutral Austria. At this stage, France's long-standing alliance with the Ottoman Empire was still in force, which meant that the eastern Mediterranean and the north African coast were in friendly hands. Britain had no bases east of Gibraltar and its only potential allies were the united Kingdoms of Naples and Sicily (the Kingdom of the Two Sicilies), both hostile to Napoleon, the neutral Kingdom of Sardinia, and Malta, under the Knights of St John and the protection of the Tsar of Russia.

Nelson's immediate task had been to find out Napoleon's intentions. The first fear was that he was about to launch his invasion from the Mediterranean, but it was also possible that he might make a strike towards Russia through the Black Sea, or even have his eye on the Sultan's territories in Ottoman controlled Greece or Egypt. So it was that in the gathering dusk of the evening of 9 May 1798, Nelson's flagship *Vanguard* and a small squadron slipped, hopefully unobtrusively, out of Gibraltar and through the Strait into hostile waters. Accompanying the *Vanguard*, captained by Edward Berry, were two other 74-gun ships-of-the-line, the *Orion* under Nelson's second in command James Saumarez, a veteran of Cape St Vincent, and the *Alexander* under Alexander Ball, plus the frigates *Emerald* and *Terpsichore* and a captured French sloop, *Bonne Citoyenne*. In his eagerness to make contact with the French, Nelson left before the two other frigates allocated to him, *Flora* and *Caroline*, were able to join the squadron. They were left orders to rendezvous on latitude 42° 20′ N in the Golfe de Lyon on the approaches to Toulon.

The expedition got off to a poor start. The rendezvous failed to be met and then on Sunday, 20 May, a severe storm scattered his fleet. It was the flagship that suffered most in the gale, losing its main-topmast while there were still men in the rigging – luckily only one man went overboard and drowned and another was killed in the fall – and two other masts damaged and left hanging over the sides. The storm lasted until the Tuesday, when the *Alexander* came to the rescue. Captain Ball took the *Vanguard* under tow and they put into Caloforte off southwest Sardinia for repairs, a necessity that tested the neutrality of a local government none too eager to be seen giving succour to the British. For the moment, Nelson's stealthy incursion into the Mediterranean had given him a brief advantage, allowing him to surprise some enemy ships, capture them and interrogate the crews. Unfortunately, little useful information had been gleaned. During the *Vanguard*'s period out of action, Saumarez had more luck. He found out from the crew of a small Spanish ship seized by the *Orion* that when Nelson's ships had been fighting against the storm, Napoleon had slipped out of Toulon on 19 May with thirteen ships-of-the-line, the one figure everyone is agreed on. The estimates of the rest of Napoleon's armada vary between seven and forty-two frigates and 300 or more transports. The large number of transports was needed to carry his army of 30,000 infantry, 2,800 cavalrymen plus horses, two companies of sappers and miners, sixty field guns and forty siege guns. In command was Vice-Admiral François-Paul Brueys d'Aigalliers, Comte de Brueys, an aristocratic 45-year-old with eight years' experience in the Mediterranean.

While Nelson was holed up on the southwest side of Sardinia, Brueys was guiding the French fleet swiftly southward around the island's opposite northeast corner. With the help of the men of the *Alexander* and the *Orion*, in four days Nelson was back at sea and retracing his steps towards Toulon to pick up the rest of his scattered ships. Before he could locate his cruisers he was joined by Captain Hardy aboard an 18-gun French built brig, *La Mutine*, bringing news of his fleet and reinforcements. His ships had met up with Captain Hope aboard a frigate, *Alcmene*, sent out by Jervis, who under the impression that Nelson had returned to Gibraltar, had taken it upon himself to continue the search for Napoleon, further scattering the ships. Nelson was non-too-pleased to find he had lost most of his fleet in such a manner, nevertheless it was not all bad news; they were to be joined by an elite force under Captain Thomas Troubridge. Having been appraised of Napoleon's departure from Toulon, Jervis' new orders were that the mission was no longer one of shadowing the French, but one of seek and destroy.

To aid Nelson in his mission, Jervis had sent ten 74-gun third-rate ships of the line, the ships regarded as the best for their combination of power and speed. These reinforcements reunited Nelson with more of his former comrades. Troubridge aboard the *Culloden* had been at Cape St Vincent and Tenerife, Samuel Hood of the *Zealous* at Tenerife, and an American, Ralph Miller, of the *Theseus* had been Nelson's flag captain at Cape St Vincent, Cadiz and Tenerife. Another American, Benjamin Hallowell, captained the *Swiftsure* and a good-humoured Irishman, Henry Darby, captain of the *Bellerophon*, was second in seniority to Troubridge. That the *Bellerophon* was unaffected by the mutinies of 1797 was credited to Darby's

Portrait of the French admiral, François Paul de Brueys d'Aigaliers, painted before 1895 by an unknown artist, Museum of Versailles. *(Public domain)*

particular relationship with his crew, a fifth of who were Irish. Davidge Gould of the *Audacious* and Thomas Foley of the *Goliath* had also seen service alongside Nelson. The three other ships-of-the-line were the *Minotaur*, *Defence*, and *Majestic*. The numbers were made up by the fourth-rate 50-gun *Leander*, captained by Thomas Thompson who had also served under Nelson and Troubridge at Tenerife. The newcomers brought Nelson's complement up to fourteen ships-of-the-line and a brig. The ships and crew came highly recommended by Jervis, being 'in excellent order' and 'well officered, manned and appointed'. The 74-gunners were manned by around 600 men and boys, and there were even some wives on board. The only weakness in the fleet was the lack of cruisers, which at this time referred to smaller more mobile vessels, usually frigates, used to scout and act as protection for the main fleet. Originally Jervis had assigned nine cruisers to Nelson; during the storm three of the frigates had become detached and then joined up with the *Alcmene* to go their own way, two never managed to rendezvous and the other frigates, *Seahorse* and *Thalia* arrived too late to play any significant role. This left Nelson handi-capped in what turned out to be weeks of hide and seek with the French fleet. As he did not want to risk his capital ships getting separated, he kept them in close order, which left the sloop *Mutine* to do the scouting legwork that would have been performed by the cruisers.

Betraying a lingering worry that an invasion was still possible, the last instructions from Jervis were to keep Napoleon in the Mediterranean. In the event Napoleon's plan was not to invade Britain, and it has been argued that such a project was so unfeasible that he never intended to, only ever using it as a diversionary tactic. He had in fact become bored with Europe, describing it to his secretary Louis Antoine Fauvelet de Bourrienne as 'a molehill' where his 'glory was already past'; only the Orient would now suffice to slake his ambition. So with Europe in a period of relative calm, he saw this as an opportune moment to upset France's uneasy alliance with Turkey by inciting revolt amongst its Christian subjects in Greece and the Levant and to take Egypt. The latter would strike at Britain's trade routes with India, and could even be a prelude to a conquest of the subcontinent as Bourrienne thought. As Napoleon outlined to the Directory (the French revolutionary government), his strategy was:

> ... to go to Egypt, to establish myself there and found a French Colony ... Then, as soon as I have made England tremble for the safety of India, I shall return to Paris, and give the enemy his death-blow. There is nothing to fear in the meantime. Europe is calm. Austria cannot attack. England is occupied with preparing her defences against invasion, and Turkey will welcome the expulsion of the Mameluke [sic] ...

The Mamluks had been a persistent thorn in the side of the Ottoman Sultans. A warrior class that had originated as slaves in the 8th century, they wielded significant power in the semi-autonomous province of Egypt, and Napoleon was hoping he could use this as an excuse for what in fact would be an invasion. His secret objective received the blessing of a Directory all too happy to keep such an ambitious general as far away as possible. Napoleon's ambition went beyond mere military objectives; he had scientific aspirations too. Travelling along with the army was a large contingent of civilians with the purpose of forming the nucleus of a new *Academy Egypt*, an endeavour designed to enhance his prestige back home.

The French admiral's main advantage over Nelson was that he knew his destination, whereas Nelson would be in the difficult situation of constantly trying to second-guess Napoleon's objective. Nelson calculated that as the French had sailed with a north-westerly wind they were not trying to break out of the Mediterranean but were heading further in. This left a vast expanse of sea to cover to find them. In addition, without cruisers Nelson had the predicament of how to engage with the enemy if he came across them in open waters. The capital ships could take their opposite numbers in line of battle, but without support he had no way of dealing with the transports. He decided to split his fleet into three, two squadrons to take on the escorts and one to do its best with the transports. He was under no illusion that, if the French expedition was as large as reported, with so few resources the best outcome to be hoped for was to scatter it rather than destroy it. The first of the possible targets to eliminate were Naples and Sicily, the Kingdom of the Two Sicilies.

On 8 June, Nelson passed the northern tip of Corsica heading south towards Naples. The French had two and a half weeks start. When he arrived in Naples and then Sicily, he found no invading French army, so at least he was able to take on some supplies. What he did find was a 'Ministry of their Sicilian Majesties' less than enthusiastic in the support it was prepared to offer; certainly no ships, something he thought shortsighted if they wanted British aid in saving them from the French. He did receive useful information though. The enemy fleet, originally split into two divisions, had rendezvoused off Sicily and was heading for Malta. Control of Malta would provide an important stepping-stone for operations in the eastern Mediterranean, but he thought it unlikely to be the final objective. The idea had already been floated that Napoleon might take advantage of unrest in Egypt to get access to the Red Sea, and then team up with the anti-British Sultan of Mysore, Tipu Sahib, who was in conflict with the East India Company. By 15 June, it was becoming more of a reality when Nelson wrote to the First Sea Lord, Lord George Spencer, 'If they pass Sicily I believe they are going on their scheme of possessing Alexandria and getting troops to India.' On reaching Messina, at the head of the strait between Sicily and Italy, Nelson learned that Malta had already fallen on 12 June after a three-day siege, so he hastily set off in the hope he could catch the French before they moved on. Napoleon had tarried in Malta for a week, reorganizing the life of the islanders in accordance with revolutionary concepts, while not overlooking the opportunity to loot treasure from its palaces and churches. Unfortunately for Nelson, Napoleon did not dally long enough. He had already left by the time Nelson received his latest news update at Cape Passero, Sicily's southern tip.

The news was confusing. There were rumours that Napoleon was heading back towards Sicily. Nelson again had to weigh up the options. Why secure and garrison Malta, with its fine harbour at Valetta, if only to turn back against the winds with a large and cumbersome fleet? And in doing so there would have been a good chance the two opposing fleets should have made contact. Nelson decided on balance to go with his calculated guess that Egypt was the armada's destination. It was a risky gamble. He was potentially sacrificing the safety of the Two Sicilies by taking his ships into relatively unknown waters on the hunch he was protecting India. With the summer north-westerlies at their backs his squadron made good time. They reached Alexandria on 28 June, having covered 800 miles in six days, only to find there was no sign of the French and the local Turkish authorities relaxed in the notion they were in no danger. As the largest port in the eastern Mediterranean, Alexandria had been the obvious choice of harbour to accommodate the French fleet, but now Nelson was wracked with doubt. The enemy had vanished into thin air. On the positive side, if they knew of his presence, they could have been deterred from their objective. Or perhaps they had been heading for Corfu after all. In French possession, the island offered the opportunity to land in Greece or attack Turkey. In desperation Nelson and his ships spend the next three weeks searching the eastern Mediterranean as far as the Turkish coast for any sign of the French before returning to Sicily, where they put in to a not very warm welcome at Syracuse. On 23 July, Nelson wrote to Sir William Hamilton, the British envoy in Naples concerning his reception and to express his only hope that 'I shall still find the French Fleet, and be able to get at them: the event then will be in the hands of Providence, of whose goodness none can doubt'. After sending his 'best respects to Lady Hamilton' he added the PS, 'No Frigates! – to which has been, and may again, be attributed the loss of the French Fleet.' After a six day break to take on supplies the search was resumed.

With weeks turning into months, it was important for morale not to allow the men to get bored. As they crisscrossed the Mediterranean's blue waters in pursuit of their elusive foe, Nelson kept the men in constant readiness for battle, a factor that would pay dividends when the time came for action. Berry, Nelson's Flag Captain aboard the *Vanguard*, wrote in his account of the campaign that the men were 'daily exercised at the great guns and small arms, and that every thing was in the best state of preparation for actual service'. The failure at Alexandria dealt Nelson's own morale a blow, for inability to locate the French fleet would leave him facing potential ruin. The news of his lack of success was already causing anxiety back home. Questions began to be asked as to his suitability and there was criticism in the British press, even Admiral Goodall, a friend and admirer who had served with Nelson during the blockade of Toulon, wondered if 'the French fleet has passed under his nose'. The fear was that Napoleon had set him up on a wild goose chase as a decoy. Two days out from Syracuse, the British squadron put in at the Bay of Coron (Koroni), at the southern tip of the western Peloponnese, where Nelson learned to his dismay that his prediction had been correct all along. Napoleon was at Alexandria, having ironically arrived only hours after the British had left. By sheer luck the coast had been left clear for the French troops to disembark under cover of darkness and begin their invasion. Nelson had outpaced the French and on 22 June the two fleets had passed by so close that Napoleon was able to hear the distant sounds of the British signalling to one another by gunshot. Captain Thompson on the *Leander* had even spotted six enemy frigates south of Malta but without scout ships Nelson decided not to give chase, reluctant to separate his force on what may have been a fool's errand. Unknown to Nelson the ships were the tail end of Napoleon's fleet sailing in the same direction slightly to the south and east. As Alfred Mahan put it:

> This remarkable miscarriage, happening to a man of so much energy and intuition, was due primarily to his want of small lookout ships; and secondly, to Bonaparte's using the simple, yet at sea sufficient, ruse of taking an indirect instead of a direct course to his object.

Napoleon had taken a dogleg approach to Alexandria, going by way of the coast of Crete. On 27 June he had received information from a frigate that Nelson's fourteen ships had been sighted off Naples ten days earlier. By then Nelson was already ahead, so Napoleon decided to make landfall 70 miles west of Alexandria. A frigate was sent to reconnoitre and only when he heard that Nelson had arrived and then departed did he make his own entry to the port on 1 July, disembarking his troops that same evening to make sure of their safety.

The worry for Nelson now was that the French fleet may have left Egypt, perhaps heading for Corfu, taking any hope of engaging it in battle, and leaving him with no choice but to enforce a time-consuming blockade of the disembarked French army. Under full sail his ships raced towards Alexandria, coming close enough on 31 July for Nelson to send the *Alexander* and *Swiftsure* ahead to reconnoitre. Once again the initial news was dispiriting. The French flag was flying over the castle. In addition, unknown to the British, Napoleon had already defeated the Egyptian Mamluk army at the Battle of the Pyramids on 21 July, entered Cairo two days later and in effect conquered Egypt. Apart from the transports, only two ships-of-the-line and six frigates were safely in the harbour; the rest of the fleet was gone. Nelson felt that the fleet would not have abandoned the transports, so as he and his captains gathered to discuss their options, in one last effort to ensure that the French fleet was not somewhere close by, Nelson sent the *Zealous* and the *Goliath* to scout the coast eastwards towards Aboukir Bay, an anchorage known to be deep enough to take the French warships. It was around two in the afternoon that the *Goliath* rounded the headland that obscured the bay and young George Elliot's telescope fixed on the French fleet lying at anchor. Eager to report the news before the *Zealous*, rather than shout out, George scurried down the rigging to pass it on in person. Unfortunately, in the hurry to send the message, a signalling cable snagged or broke, so it was 14.45 before the *Zealous* ran up the flags that read, 'Sixteen sail of the line at anchor bearing East by South'. The first day of August was the same day that Octavian, later Augustus Caesar, had entered Alexandria in triumph in 30BC.

Although Alexandria afforded a large harbour, it was not thought deep enough for the French flagship, the 118-gun *Océan*-class *L'Orient*. The *Océan*-class ships were three-deckers, in comparison to the third-rate two-deck ships-of-the-line favoured by the British, and the largest type of warship at the time. Napoleon had offered Brueys the option of taking the fleet to Corfu, but as Nelson had hoped, the French admiral felt duty bound to protect the transports and offer support to the army. To do this he had taken up a defensive position at Aboukir. The sandy bay, which is about 15 miles (25km) east of Alexandria, stretches for over a further 15 miles from Aboukir point to the western mouth of the Nile at Rosetta. Lying 2.5 miles off the point is Aboukir Island, once connected to the mainland but now tentatively linked by the shallows that are characteristic of the bay. For protection Brueys had placed an inadequately-light battery on the island in addition to occupying the small castle at the point. The shoals around the island extend a further mile and a quarter out to sea, forcing vessels to give it a wide birth as they enter from the west. The point and island offered shelter in summer from the prevailing north-westerly winds, but the shoals that continued around the bay necessitated Brueys anchoring his fleet in line 3 miles from the beach beyond the four-fathom (24ft/7.2m) mark, within which it would be too shallow for his ships-of-the-line.

The line of thirteen warships lay on a slightly curved north-north-western axis following the line of the bay, with the leading ship facing into the wind anchored in five fathoms of water somewhat over a mile south-east of the Island. Brueys had placed his flagship at the centre of the line of ships, each about two-thirds of a cable's length apart (400ft/123m). Also on board *L'Orient* were the captain of the fleet, Rear Admiral Honoré Ganteaume, and Commodore Luc-Julien-Joseph Casabianca, the captain of the ship. Either end of the *Orient* were two 80-gun ships, the *Franklin*, under his second in command Rear Admiral the Count Armand Blanquet du Chayla, and the *Tonnant*. Rear Admiral Pierre-Charles Villeneuve in another 80-gunner, the *Guillaume Tell*, commanded the rear line. The remaining nine ships in the formation were 74-gunners. Closer in to the shore and guarding the landward flank of his capital ships Brueys had placed his four frigates. In addition, among the shoals were a number of brigs, bomb vessels and gunboats.

The news that the French fleet had finally been sighted was met with jubilation by the British crews and both joy and relief by the Admiral. With the wind maintaining a favourable direction, and despite dusk drawing near, Nelson's first instinct was to attack. Adored by his men and admired by his captains, his individual brand of leadership had been forged on close personal relationships with his subordinates. As admiral this meant creating an atmosphere of trust and personal responsibility. Nelson led from the front and expected his captains to do the same. All his captains would have known him at least by reputation; that he would have shouted 'Death or glory!' as he boarded the *San Nicholas* at Cape St Vincent, and that he cared little for neat tactical victories, only for the total defeat of the enemy. Jervis had blessed him with an elite group of officers, many of whom knew each other, and Nelson would talk tactics with them in friendly discussion, often informally over dinner, during which he laid forth his plans and expectations. According to Captain Berry it was Nelson's practice to bring:

> ... his Captains on board the Vanguard, where he would fully develop to them his own ideas of the different and best modes of Attack, and such plans as he proposed to execute upon falling in with the Enemy, whatever their position or situation might be, by day or by night. There was no possible position in which they could be found, that he did not take into his calculation, and for the most advantageous attack of which, he had not digested and arranged the best possible disposition of the Force which he commanded. With the masterly ideas of their Admiral, therefore, on the subject of Naval Tactics, every one of the Captains of his Squadron was most thoroughly acquainted; and upon surveying the situation of the Enemy, they could ascertain with precision what were the ideas and intentions of their Commander, without the aid of any further instructions ...

This did not mean he had all the captains together at once. Often it was in small groups or one-to-one, and most often the senior commanders. Berry gives the impression that with each captain fully apprised of the Admiral's wishes few signals were required, which saved time and allowed the captains to concentrate on the conduct of their own ship. In fact, Nelson did carry on the normal procedure of signalling, but in the knowledge his overall intentions were understood. The camaraderie Nelson engendered created a tight group that he dubbed his 'Band of Brothers' quoting Shakespeare's speech by Henry V to the outnumbered English troops before Agincourt:

> We few, we happy few, we band of brothers'.
> For he today that sheds his blood with me
> Shall be my brother ...

Having decided not to wait till dawn, Nelson gathered his ships together; *Alexander* and *Swiftsure* were in pursuit of an enemy ship to the south and the *Culloden* was towing a prize with a valuable cargo of wine, the rest of the fleet was scattered over 3 miles. At 15.00 the signal to prepare for action was sent. Answering the drum tattoo, the crews cleared the decks for action, sluicing them with water to prevent fire, gritting them to prevent slipping and placing fire buckets at strategic points. Then the gun-crews took up their positions, the gun-ports opened, three tons of metal and wood were wheeled into position and lashed secure, and the powder, shot and cartridges brought up from the magazine. Carpenters and surgeons stood by at their positions to mend the expected injuries to ship and men as best they could. Nelson believed in the advantages of surprise and decisive action and that the British cause was best served in close-quarter combat where their superior gunmanship would tell. Trusting in his crews' ability to carry out his orders no matter what, he was happy to engage the enemy at night. He ordered four lanterns to be fixed to the top of the mizzen (rear) mast to distinguish friend from foe.

The British ships had not gone unnoticed by the French, but Brueys was confident that the British would wait until dawn before making a move. He had drawn up his fleet in what he believed was a textbook defensive formation, copied from Admiral Samuel Hood (not to be confused with the captain of the *Zealous*) at the Battle of St Kitts in 1782 during the American Revolutionary War. While at anchor Hood had repulsed a larger French fleet in which Brueys was serving as a young officer. As his ships were protected in the front by the shore batteries and the dangerous shoals of Aboukir Island and on the port side by the shoals stretching out from the shore, it is probable that he expected the British to sweep around the bay forcing any attack to come from the rear. And with hundreds of his men out foraging on shore or manning the batteries, Brueys was happier to wait till next day to engage with the enemy, perhaps even at sea where his superior numbers would be an advantage. Nelson had no such thoughts, he was anticipating an action fought at anchor and at night and at 16.22 ordered that every ship should be prepared to anchor from the stern. His captains knew from this that he was asking them to anchor alongside their opposite number and fight from there. To accomplish such a tricky manoeuvre a team of sailors had to drag the 20-ton anchor cable from the bow to the stern, and then sailing before the wind, the ship would come to sudden stop when the anchor was dropped. If all went well the ship would hold its course so that, if the anchor was dropped at the correct moment, it was in the right place to remain broadside to the enemy without swinging. There were springs attached to the cable that allowed adjustments to be made if needed. Simultaneously to the anchor being dropped, the topmen in the rigging had to furl the sails before rushing down to man the guns. All of this would have to be done in darkness and under fire.

At 17.00 Nelson signalled his intention to attack at close quarters the slightly weaker van and centre of the French line, followed at 17.30 by the instruction for the squadron to form up in line of battle in the most convenient manner, with the *Vanguard* at the centre. Taking into consideration the wind direction it would be difficult for the French ships at the rear to come to the aid of those at the front of the line, so by concentrating his forces there he could nullify their superiority in numbers and firepower. Apart from having some larger ships, the French also tended to use heavier guns, including 36-pounders rather than the standard British 32-pounder. More important than size of ship or shot was the expertise of the gunners, and the experienced British crews consistently outgunned their Spanish and French opponents. With superior guns and powder and having honed their skills at sea rather than being cooped up in port, the battle-hardened British sailors were more disciplined, well drilled and tactically aware. Whereas the French preferred to fight at long range aiming at the masts and rigging to disable the enemy, wasting considerable shot in the process, the British had developed the more destructive ploy of engaging at close-range, punching holes into the enemy's hull and decimating their guns and gun-crew. In comparison, Brueys had complained that his ships were in poor condition and, although not lacking in courage, 'Our crews are weak, both in number and quality.' The Revolution had had a severe impact on the French navy, stripping out the officer class and leaving it short of good leadership. With a smaller merchant marine, the French did not have as large a pool of mariners to draw from as the British and their gunners were often army gunners rather than professional naval gunners. In addition, even though the French fleet had between 8,000 and 9,000 men at Aboukir, each capital ship was around 200 seamen short of its ideal complement.

The British ships were so eager to engage the enemy it became a race to see who would arrive first. As they rounded Aboukir Island a French brig, *Alerte*, appeared in an attempt to lure them onto the shoals. The ships held their discipline but Nelson was aware that they could easily run aground and asked for assistance from Captain Hood aboard the *Zealous* who was slightly closer in. Hood was taking soundings with a lead line and found the depth to be 11 fathoms. He offered to keep ahead, sounding as he went in order to mark the safe passage.

Luckily, as they were heading into unknown waters, it was Foley aboard the *Goliath* who was leading the pack, for he was in possession of an accurate stolen French chart, the *Petite Atlas Maritime*, published in 1764. Although Brueys had thought he had positioned his ships well, he had not done so well enough, because as Foley rounded the island he noticed that there was a gap between the leading French ship, the *Guerrier*, and the shoals to its port side which was wide enough to allow the *Goliath* to pass and attack from the shore side. Foley guessed correctly that as the French would expect any attack to come from starboard they would not have their

Battle of the Nile, Augt. 1st 1798 (1816) engraving by Thomas Sutherland (1785–1838) showing the British fleet in battle order bearing down on the French line at anchor, National Maritime Museum, Greenwich. *(Public domain)*

portside guns at the ready. Passing the futile efforts of the shore battery and avoiding the opening salvoes of the French ships, Foley took the initiative in true Nelson fashion and slipped between the shore and the *Guerrier*, raking its side with shot before, having over-run his intended position, anchoring at the stern opposite the second ship in line, the *Conquérant*. Close behind, Hood quickly followed his example, taking the *Zealous* around the head of the French line, raking the *Guerrier* as it went, and bringing the *Zealous* to anchor at the stern within a pistol shot off the French ship's port bow in Foley's intended place. The path of the *Audacious* is of some dispute: it either followed around the *Zealous*, anchoring between it and the *Goliath* from where it could fire on the stern of the *Guerrier* and on the *Conquérant*, or passed between the *Guerrier* and *Conquérant*, which may have been lying too far apart and were not cabled together as they should have been.

Nelson's second in command, Sir James Saumarez, took the *Orion* on a wide sweep perilously close to the shallows to by-pass the leading three British ships and anchor opposite the fifth and sixth ships in the French line, the *Peuple Souverain* and the 80-gun *Franklin*. He took out the 36-gun frigate *Sérieuse* on his starboard side with a devastating double-shotted broadside as he went. The *Sérieuse* had made the mistake of firing first, as it was a convention at the time that ships of the line did not engage with frigates if there were ships of their own size available.

Captain Miller audaciously preferred to manoeuvre his ship *Theseus* through the narrow gap left between the *Zealous* and the enemy ships. He observed that as usual 'their shot sweep just over us, and knowing well that at such a moment Frenchmen would not have coolness enough to change their elevation' it allowed the *Theseus* to pass close by the French ship. As the British crews cheered one another on, Miller then:

> ... closed them suddenly, and, running under the arch of their shot, reserved my fire, every gun being loaded with two and some with three round shot, until I had the Guerrier's masts in a line, and her jib-boom about 6 feet clear of our rigging: we then opened with such effect, that a second breath could not be drawn before the main- and mizzen-mast were also gone.

Having taken out the *Guerrier's* remaining masts, Miller passed on the outside of the *Goliath* to take up position opposite the third and fourth French ships, the *Spartiate* and *Aquilon*. When he spotted a British ship on the *Spartiate*'s other flank he moved the *Theseus* on in fear of inflicting friendly fire and directed his attention to the mainmast of the *Aquilon*.

According to Berry's account, it had been around sunset when the *Goliath* made its attack. The onslaught was so ferocious, less than quarter of an hour elapsed between the foremast of the *Guerrier* going overboard, to general cheers from the British fleet, until, and as the sun sank below the horizon, the mainmast and mizzenmast disappeared as well. In a further 15 minutes the *Conquérant* and *Spartiate* had also lost most of their masts, and by '... about seven o'clock total darkness had come on; but the whole hemisphere was, with intervals, illuminated by the fire of the hostile fleets'. Despite being ravaged by cannonball and musket fire, the crew of the *Guerrier* fought on for another three hours, before surrendering after numerous requests by Hood. During the battle a boat from the *Theseus* picked up thirty survivors from the *Sérieuse* that was now lying below water in the sandy bed of the shallows. The *Conquérant* proved weak opposition; being old, lightly gunned and lightly manned it was soon put out of action with significant loss of life.

Foley's inspired manoeuvre, perhaps based either on his chart or his seaman's knowledge that the French would have left enough draught for the ships at anchor to swing towards the shore if the wind was in an easterly direction, created the opportunity to catch the French in a crossfire. With five British ships having taken the inshore station, Nelson decided it was time to take on the French on their starboard side, so keeping to the original plan he anchored the *Vanguard* on the opposite side of the *Spartiate*. For once Miller had made a poor call by claiming he moved the *Theseus* further down the line to avoid firing on the (unknown to him) flagship, and thereby losing the advantage. If, as has been suggested, he was deferring to his superior to give him the prize of taking the *Spartiate*, he left Nelson a tough challenge. The *Spartiate* was brand-new, only launched the previous year, and captained by Maxime Julien Émeriau de Beauverger, who had fought at St Kitts with Brueys. Despite all his experience, Émeriau would have been hard pressed if Miller had remained at his post, as he had insufficient crew on board to man the guns on both sides, but when the *Theseus* moved on he was able to deploy all his men on the starboard guns. A fierce exchange of fire ensued. The guns of the *Spartiate*, reinforced by those of the *Aquilon*, inflicted serious damage on the *Vanguard* causing sixty casualties in ten minutes. Only when the *Minotaur*, which had taken up its own position ahead of the *Vanguard*, opened fire on both the *Spartiate* and the *Aquilon* did the situation ease. The poor *Aquilon* was now caught in the intended crossfire between the *Theseus* and the *Minotaur*. The *Defence* in turn overlapped the *Vanguard* and *Minotaur* to take on the *Aquilon* and the *Peuple Souverain*. By 20.30, the *Aquilon's* mainmast and mizzenmast were down and its captain Antoine René Thévenard had died after having both his legs blown off.

Half an hour later, following a fierce contest the *Spartiate* surrendered. Attacked from all sides after the *Audacious* joined in, she had been reduced to a wreck, holed below the waterline, with sixty-four of her crew dead and 150 injured, including the Captain, who had been wounded twice. Berry ordered Lieutenant Galwey to board her with a troop of marines and he duly returned with Émeriau's sword, which Berry presented to Nelson below decks. The victory had been costly for the *Vanguard* too. It had suffered 105 casualties, one of which was the Admiral. Nelson had been wounded in the forehead by a piece of shrapnel and temporarily blinded by a flap of skin that had dropped over his one good eye. Concussed, and with blood everywhere he believed he was dying, but still took his turn to wait in the queue to be attended to. So convinced he was that he was at death's door, Nelson was desperate to convey his thanks to Captain Louis of the *Minotaur* for saving the *Vanguard* and then he said to Berry, 'I am killed. Remember me to my wife.' Nelson's wound proved to be not too serious, but it still put him out of action for a while. Not that it mattered; the course of the battle was now beyond his control, and in Berry's opinion almost won despite the French flagship and the rear of their line being intact.

Aboard *l'Orient*, Admiral Brueys had been caught completely by surprise. When the British ships had been sighted he had been slow to react. Still in discussion with his captains, he had decided unconvincingly in the end to stay put on the assumption nothing would happen before dawn. Even when it was obvious they were under attack there was little response; the French only opened fire when the British were almost on top of them. Then he belatedly ordered his ships to close up and put chains between them, a command not universally complied with. Brueys' first action had been to frantically recall as many of his men on land duties as he could and send for reinforcements from Alexandria. In response a few thousand men were mustered and rushed towards the scene of the battle, but too late to influence the course of events. It was just after sunset when the *Bellerophon* came alongside and *l'Orient* was forced into serious action. The *Majestic* followed, pressing on ahead towards the 80-gun *Tonnant*. The *Culloden* had been the most far-flung of Nelson's ships, but Captain Troubridge had made such good time that he had overtaken both the *Alexander* and the *Swiftsure*. In his eagerness to make up even more time he then took the *Culloden* too close to the shoals rounding Aboukir Island; he was to spend the rest of the night, assisted by the *Mutine*, desperately trying to get his warship off the sands. When the additional help of the *Leander* proved ineffective, Troubridge realised his endeavours were futile and he told Captain Thompson to join the fray.

Troubridge's misfortune, which left the squadron further outnumbered, proved useful to the others still rounding the point. The grounded *Culloden* acted as a lightship marking which areas to avoid. Using the flashes of the guns as beacons, *Swiftsure* and *Alexander* joined the battle at 20.00, taking up position fore and aft of *l'Orient*. An hour later Thompson arrived. He knew he could not match the French ships for firepower, so he slipped the 50-gun *Leander* in the un-cabled gap left between the stern of the *Peuple Souverain* and the bow of the *Franklin* so as to be able to rake both of them. Some of his shot went over or through the *Franklin* to land on *l'Orient* behind. It was only at this point that Nelson's full complement, apart from the unfortunate *Culloden*, were engaged with the enemy. The loss of the *Culloden* was a significant blow to Nelson, depriving him of one of his ablest and closest captains.

Even in a darkness illuminated only by the flash of gunfire and the burning ships, it was soon apparent that the van of the French fleet was being annihilated. By 20.30, the *Peuple Souverain*, under fire from both the *Defence* and earlier from the *Orion* on its port side, had lost its fore and main masts and its hull was severely damaged; after a further two and a half hours its guns fell silent, and, its cable cut, it drifted out of position and would eventually run aground. With the *Peuple Souverain* gone, the *Orion* and *Defence* could turn their full attention on to the 80-gun *Franklin*. The hardest task was to take on the heavy artillery of the largest ships at the heart of the French line. It was here that the *Bellerophon* and *Majestic* were exposed to the opposition's maximum firepower. Outgunned, to stand any chance of success they had to be perfectly positioned. Unfortunately for Captain Darby, he overshot his intended position leaving the *Bellerophon* broadside to broadside with the 120-gun *l'Orient* almost twice her length. The *Majestic* also mistimed its approach, sailed past the *Tonnant* and came bow-to-bow with the next in line, the *Heureux*, with which it became entangled. The *Bellerophon* suffered badly from *l'Orient's* heavy barrage, made worse by still being under fire from the 80-gun *Franklin*. As a result, after half an hour, severely damaged and with two masts gone and sails cut to ribbons, Darby, who had received a severe head wound, ordered the ship's cables to be cut so as to get out of the line of fire.

As the entangled *Majestic* could not bring her guns to bear she took a severe beating from both the *Heureux* and the *Tonnant*. Early on in the engagement, Captain George Westcott had been killed by a musket ball to the throat, leaving Robert Cuthbert in command. Cuthbert exercised such skill in extricating the *Majestic* from its situation and attempting to take on the *Heureux* and *Mercure* that he was promoted to acting commander by Nelson after the battle. Cuthbert attempted to place the *Majestic* between the *Heureux* and *Le Mercure* but they had followed Brueys' order to put a cable between them. The *Majestic* continued to take a pounding, losing its mainmast and mizzenmast, but defended so resolutely that when Captain Jean-Pierre Étienne ordered his men to board her, they refused. The price of being unable to carry out the required anchoring manoeuvre with precision cost the *Bellerophon* and the *Majestic* dear. The ships suffered the heaviest of the British casualties. The *Bellerophon* drifted off to the east away from the main battle, but not completely out of harm's way, being fired on by the *Généreux* towards the end of the French line as she passed by.

It was now that the fresh arrivals, *Swiftsure*, *Alexander* and *Leander*, were to play a significant role at the heart of the battle, while the French rear line remained mystifyingly uninvolved. The inactivity of the frigates *Justice* and *Diane*, the *Généreux* and the 80-gun *Guillaume Tell* meant that Brueys lost any advantage through superior numbers. As it took up position, the *Swiftsure* had come across a dismasted ship with no light or colours leaving the scene. Captain Hallowell, on the verge of ordering a broadside, luckily hailed the ship first. His caution was repaid when the immediate reply came, '*Bellerophon*, going out of action disabled.' In the confusion of smoke and darkness and without knowing his exact location Hallowell had anchored the *Swiftsure* in the spot the *Bellerophon* had recently vacated.

The destruction of the French van now allowed the British ships to double up on the enemy's largest vessels. The *Franklin* was soon being hounded by the *Leander*, *Defence*, *Orion* and *Swiftsure*, and once *l'Orient* had dispensed with the *Bellerophon*, it found itself beset by both the *Swiftsure* and the *Alexander*. Hallowell and his men showed commendable composure and discipline as they held their fire until the opportune moment. In the meantime, Captain Ball had manoeuvred the *Alexander* between the stern of the *l'Orient* and the bow of the *Tonnant*, firing broadsides from a point where his ship was out of reach of his opponents' guns while being able to continue to rain down a continuous barrage on to them.

Being the largest ship afloat was of little use to *l'Orient* if there were not enough men to man the guns. Only the heaviest guns were brought into action, and in desperation, as the enemy swarmed around like wasps, any endeavour to change position to get her guns to bear was hampered by being too tightly moored. Under relentless fire the French flagship took many casualties. In one account Brueys was badly wounded in the head and arm and was taken down from the poop deck to the main deck, in another version, told by survivors to a midshipman on the *Swiftsure*, it was after losing both his legs that he was seated, with tourniquets on the stumps, in an armchair on the deck. Whatever his injuries it was a futile gesture; he was almost cut in two by a cannonball to the stomach and, despite still insisting to stay at his post, died fifteen minutes later. It was around 21.00, as the *Leander* arrived and the *Spartiate* surrendered, that fire broke out at the stern of the French flagship, perhaps from a combustible thrown from the *Alexander* through one of the cabin windows. The fire quickly took hold. With the fire buckets overturned, attempts to extinguish the flames were further hampered by the debris on deck that had buried the fire pump and axes. Containers of paint or oil left on deck after repainting only made matters worse and in fifteen minutes the fire was obviously out of control. Seeing the chaos, the gunners on the *Swiftsure* aimed their round-shot and grapeshot at the blazing areas to keep the fire-crews at bay. While some valiantly stayed by their guns, many that could began to jump overboard.

When Nelson heard *l'Orient* was ablaze he came back up on deck to witness the great ship's last moments. As soon as it became apparent that fire would consume the ship's magazine, all the ships close by began to look to their own safety, cutting their cables and putting as much distance as possible between them and the blazing wreck. The *Swiftsure* had been hit below the waterline and was badly damaged, so Captain Hallowell calculated that his ship's best chance of survival, being so close to *l'Orient*, was to hold its position and let the force of the explosion pass overhead. He kept his broadsides up until the last minute, then as the firing ceased for a moment as everyone waited for the inevitable, he ordered the gun ports and hatchways closed and for the rigging and decks to be dowsed with water. Suddenly a deafening explosion lit up the night sky, followed by an eerie silence. In Berry's words:

> The light thrown by the fire of L'Orient upon the surrounding objects enabled us to perceive with more certainty the situation of the two Fleets, the Colours of both being clearly distinguishable. The cannonading was partially kept up to leeward of the Centre till about ten o'clock, when L'Orient blew up with a most tremendous explosion. An awful pause and death-like silence for about three minutes ensued, when the wreck of the masts, yards, &c. &c. which had been carried to a vast height, fell down into the water and on board the

surrounding Ships. A port fire from L'Orient fell into the main royal of the Alexander, the fire occasioned by which was however extinguished in about two minutes, by the active exertions of Capt. Ball.

The *Franklin* too suffered collateral damage from the large amounts of falling debris and when fires broke out there was an explosion in the arms locker.

After a brief shocked lull, the gunfire resumed. The explosion was so fierce it caused alarm in Alexandria, where it was heard by Napoleon's bivouacked troops, and the light illuminated the crowds of local onlookers watching the battle from the shore. Although there had been a mad scramble in the last moments to escape the flames, many still perished, among them the ship's captain, Commodore Casabianca with his young son. Rear Admiral Ganteaume was one of the lucky ones. He managed to find a small boat that took him to the safety of one of the smaller vessels and on to Alexandria. Nelson ordered his men to put out boats to pick up survivors and his fellow captains followed suit, but their efforts only gleaned seventy traumatised survivors from a full complement that would have numbered over 1,000. The numbers of dead are disputed. According to the captain of the frigate *Diane*, Denis Decrès, the French were able to save over 700 men. Along with the dead, *l'Orient* took with it to the sea bottom 5 million francs in gold and 1 million in silver plate taken from the Knights Hospitaller in Malta.

The destruction of the flagship notionally put Rear Admiral Blanquet aboard the *Franklin* in command of the fleet, and it was the *Franklin*'s guns that resumed the fight. In fact, Blanquet and his second in command Captain Maurice Gillet were both badly wounded and below decks, so the ship was in the hands of Commander Martinet. The disappearance of *l'Orient* left the *Franklin* totally surrounded and 'within pistol shot'. Martinet continued the resistance until 23.30, when, after being reduced to a complete wreck and with 400 casualties, Blanquet was forced to strike his colours and surrender to officers from the *Defence*.

Following the brave example of his admiral, the commander of the *Tonnant*, Commodore Aristide Aubert Du Petit Thouars stayed at his post despite having lost both legs and an arm. He was still urging his men not to surrender as he bled to death. Although the van and the centre of the French fleet were lost, its total annihilation was not complete. Behind the *Tonnant*, the *Heureux* and the *Mercure* had also cut their cables and were drifting to the south. Around midnight, the exhausted crews took a rest, and there was a lull in the firing. As dawn broke Nelson had recovered

The Destruction of L'Orient at the Battle of the Nile (1827) by George Arnold, National Maritime Museum, Greenwich. The *Franklin* is to the extreme left. *(Public domain)*

enough to urge his captains to turn their attention on the French rear, a command not easily followed. Many of his ships were severely damaged and under repair, a situation not seized on by those very French ships to the rear that had been out of the fight so far. Rear Admiral Villeneuve, their commander, was criticised afterwards for his reluctance to leave his position towards the tail of the line and to commit to the fight. His excuse was that the *Guillaume Tell* was lying against the wind and his vision was obscured by smoke from the battle.

The *Majestic*, *Theseus* and *Alexander* answered Nelson's exhortation and they were quickly reinforced by the *Leander* and *Goliath*. Their efforts dismasted the *Tonnant*, forcing it to run aground and finally to surrender the next day. The *Heureux*, the *Mercure* and the frigate *Artémise* also ran onto the sands as they tried to escape. The British ships continued their bombardment, and after taking a pounding the *Artémise* struck its colours. Before the ship could be taken though, the men jumped overboard and made for the shore having, to the annoyance of the British, already started a fire that caused the magazine to explode.

Of the enemy ships of the line the *Guillaume Tell* and the *Généreux* were the only ones left in any condition to take advantage of the offshore breeze and escape. Villeneuve, who had been reinforced by 300 men from Alexandria, decided that this was now the wisest thing to do. Taking the two remaining frigates with them in line of battle, the two capital ships made for the open sea. The *Zealous* gave them a parting broadside as they passed and the French returned the fire, aiming high as usual and only damaging the upper rigging. Nelson initially wanted to give chase, but he realised he did not have the ships available in good enough condition to do so. What remained to be done was a mopping up operation as the last of the French ships surrendered. During the French retreat, the *Zealous* intervened to prevent the frigate *Justice* boarding the *Bellerophon*, which was anchored and under repair. The final ship of the line, the *Timoléon*, was unable to join the others, having run aground after its rudder and masts had been damaged by friendly fire from the *Généreux*. Captain Louis-Léonce Trullet shouted to his commander as the *Guillaume Tell* passed that he would resist as long as possible and, true to his word, the *Timoléon* obstinately held on until the following noon. Overnight and during the morning Trullet evacuated his men, and then in the final act of the conflict he set fire to his ship and it went up in a spectacular explosion.

During the night of 2 August, Nelson had already begun penning a letter to Admiral Jervis: 'My Lord, Almighty God has blessed His Majesty's Arms in the late Battle by a great Victory over the Fleet of the Enemy, who

I attacked at sunset on the 1st August, off the mouth of the Nile'. According to Napoleon's Controller General of Finances, Matthius Poussielgue (the man responsible for the looting of the treasures of Malta), the fighting had continued until three in the morning of the 2nd and then there was a lull until five when:

> ... it continued with as much fury as ever ... until about 2 o'clock in the afternoon and then we saw two of the line and two frigates under a press of sail on a wind, standing towards the eastward: we made out that all were under French colours. No other ships made any movement and firing ceased entirely.

The sight of the four French ships beating the retreat did not impress Napoleon. In his memoires he laid the blame for the defeat firmly at the door of Villeneuve:

> The opinion of both fleets is unanimous. Villeneuve could have turned this into a French victory at any time: he could have done this at eight in the evening; he could have done it at midnight, after the loss of L'Orient; and it was once again in his power at daybreak.

The criticism had some validity in the sense that both fleets were fairly evenly matched, with the French having the advantage of firepower, but they lacked Nelson's decisiveness and the British qualities of initiative and superior seamanship. As Nelson wrote to Lord Howe afterwards, 'I had the happiness to command a band of brothers, therefore, night was to my advantage.' Nelson had revolutionised naval tactics, but the French captains were still playing by the old rules of engagement. Villeneuve stuck rigorously to his position regardless of the state of the battle or the bravery shown by his comrades, and to successfully sail against the wind to outflank the British attack was probably beyond the capability of his sailors. Napoleon also blamed Brueys for the disposition of his ships and the fact they were anchored and not at sea. This was in fact a misrepresentation, because he had ordered Brueys to stay close to protect his transport ships. In addition, it was Napoleon who had depleted the navy's complement by putting the sailors on land duties.

When the *Timoléon* exploded the battle was effectively over, and the British had not lost a ship. They had captured six serviceable front-line vessels, destroyed seven, and taken over 3,300 prisoners, 800 of whom were wounded. The French wounded were sent under truce to Alexandria to be looked after by their own doctors. With too many prisoners to deal with the majority were shipped ashore on parole on condition they would not take up arms against the British, something it was realised would be too much to be hoped for. Only the senior officers and those deemed to be of value were kept. Maltese, Genoese and Spanish sailors from the French fleet offered their services to the British, expressing 'the greatest happiness at thus being freed, as they themselves said, from the tyranny and cruelty of the French' (Berry). The French had suffered severe casualties in a lopsided engagement. The *Minotaur*, which inflicted most of the *Aquilon's* 300 casualties, took only 87 in return. Nelson estimated that the British had suffered 895 casualties, the most on the *Bellerophon*, the *Majestic*, and the *Vanguard*, while the *Zealous* had the least at a mere eight. From conversations with the French captains, Saumarez estimated that nearly 3,000 French crewmen had been killed on their ships. Some of the others lucky enough to make it to shore had only survived to perish at the hands of the local Arabs. Most of the British dead were wrapped in hammocks or sailcloth, weighed down by cannon balls and buried at sea, but those that died of their wounds were buried on Aboukir Island, which became known as Nelson Island. Their graves were discovered in 2000 by Italian archaeologist Dr Paolo Gallo, who was able only to positively identify one body, that of Commander James Russell. When the graves became endangered by sea erosion, thirty bodies were reburied at Chatby Commonwealth War Cemetery in Alexandria in 2005.

From all the casualties it was the fate of Captain Casabianca and his young son, Giocante, that became the stuff of legend. What actually happened is uncertain; in one account they both died after jumping overboard just before *l'Orient* exploded, in another, Giocante lost his leg and his father refused to leave him, but it was the popular myth immortalised in the lines of *Casabianca* by Felicia Dorothea Hemans (1793–1835) that took hold of the public's imagination. The opening lines of the poem became some of the most well known in English verse and the staple of many a classroom lesson:

> The boy stood on the burning deck
> Whence all but he had fled;
> The flame that lit the battle's wreck
> Shone round him o'er the dead

In Hemans' account, Giocante stoically remains at his post waiting for his father, who unknown to him, is already dead, only to die when the magazine exploded. The moment of the French flagship's destruction became one of the most painted subjects in naval history. As a *memento* of the battle and a reminder to the hero-worshipped Nelson of his own mortality, Captain Hallowell got *Swiftsure*'s carpenter to make a coffin out of a recovered section of *l'Orient*'s mainmast which he presented to the admiral. He suggested that Nelson might like the idea of being buried in one of his own trophies. Nelson kept the coffin standing in his cabin, and when the time came, he was buried in it.

It was as complete a victory as Nelson could have hoped for. He summed it up thus: 'Victory is not a name strong enough for such a scene.' It was the greatest victory yet achieved by the British navy, and one that left it in control of the Mediterranean. Without naval support Napoleon and his army were marooned in Egypt. It only remained to leave Captain Hood in charge of enough ships to maintain a blockade: the *Zealous*, the *Goliath* and the *Swiftsure*, plus two late arrivals, the frigates sent by Jervis.

In a final twist to the tale, of the two ships that Nelson dispatched to take the news of his victory to England, the *Leander* was intercepted off Crete by the *Généreux*. Even though the *Leander* was undermanned and had only fifty-one serviceable guns it still took six hours before it surrendered. It was only when the humble *Mutine* put in to Naples that the world knew of the devastating British victory; news that would have a profound impact on those wishing to stand against Napoleon's European imperialistic ambitions, particularly in Italy.

Sultan Selim III declared war on France, which allowed the Tsar to send his Black Sea fleet into the Mediterranean, and then Austria joined the coalition. The French lost their Ionian possessions, including Corfu, first to the Russians and then to the British. After a siege lasting two years the British took Malta, a prize possession that was to have as much future significance as Gibraltar. On hearing the news, St Vincent wrote to Nelson (27 Sept.) from Cadiz, 'God be praised, and you and your gallant band rewarded by a grateful country for the greatest achievement the history of the world can produce.' The news then travelled overland, only reaching England on 2 October, where it was greeted with the ringing of church bells, the firing of cannons, and illuminations in London. Fear of invasion was over. For Emma, Lady Hamilton, the news was more personal. On being told, she fainted, the first public indication of where her feelings lay. When Nelson returned to Naples in September she nursed him. During his convalescence they fell in love, and embarked on a notorious affair.

Brueys' acquiescence to Napoleon's wish to keep the fleet at Alexandria instead of retiring to Corfu, his preferred option, had played into Nelson's hands, and on sighting the French fleet Nelson had remarked, 'Before this time tomorrow, I shall have gained a peerage, or Westminster Abbey', and

Rear-Admiral Sir Horatio Nelson (1799) wearing the Turkish military decoration, a diamond chelengk, in his hat given to him by the Sultan Selim III. Oil on canvas by Lemuel Francis Abbott (1760–1806), National Maritime Museum, Geenwhich. *(Public domain)*

so it proved. Instead of the humiliation that he might have faced had the French fleet once again eluded him, Nelson was elevated to the peerage. Everyone claimed with hindsight the credit for having sent him into the Mediterranean, including King George and Lord Minto, the father of the young Midshipman George Elliot, who both sang his praises in parliament. Although most of his critics were silenced by his victory, there were still some dissident voices complaining that he had allowed Napoleon to disembark and conquer Egypt unmolested. As a result, Nelson was not made a Viscount as he deserved, but Baron Nelson of the Nile and Burnham Thorpe. Napoleon was forced to stay in the Middle East for a year, trying to further his ambitions with his beleaguered army, but after defeat at Acre he was forced to return to France, leaving his army behind. Despite his Egyptian setback Napoleon remained popular in France, and on his return he was able to manipulate the political situation to make himself *de facto* emperor. Seven years after the Battle of the Nile, Nelson and Villeneuve would meet again as commanders of the opposing fleets at the Battle of Trafalgar (1805). Nelson achieved another victory and a hero's death, Villeneuve, another defeat. Rather than face Napoleon's ire once more, Villeneuve committed suicide.

Chapter Six

Navarino, 1827

A European coalition united by the cause of Greek liberty defeats the Turkish navy to create an independent Greek state and further weaken the grip of the Ottoman Empire in Europe

Early on a bright Saturday morning in October 1827, a combined fleet of British, French and Russian warships was slowly manoeuvring into line a few miles out from the entrance to Navarino Bay in the western Peloponnese. In the van were the British ships under Admiral Codrington, who, as the senior ranking officer, it had been agreed should assume overall command. Some 5 miles to the rear were the French and Russians. Bottled up inside the bay, a large Ottoman fleet made up of Egyptian, Turkish and Tunisian vessels lay at anchor. What was to happen next hung delicately in the balance and to a large extent would be determined by events out of the immediate control of the supreme commanders.

Although officially the fleets were not at war, the ships of the western allies were intent on entering the bay at the ready. Charles McPherson, a sailor aboard the British frigate *Genoa* recalled that the 'tubs were filled with shot and everything else prepared'. The men were at battle stations, and at six bells in the forenoon watch (11.00) they mustered into position encouraged by their officers; Lieutenant Broke with the words:

> Now, my men, you see we are going into the harbour today. I know you'll be right glad of it; at least, I suppose you would be as much against cruising off here all winter as I am. So, I say, let's in today, and fight it out like British seamen, and if we fall, why there's an end to our cruise. I hope, when the guns are to man, you'll all be at your stations.

Many of the men had been up most of the night, so if they could they took the opportunity to grab some sleep between the guns as the ships advanced towards an unknown outcome.

Navarino (1827) by Ambroise Louis Garneray (1783–1857) looking out from the Turkish gun-battery on the island of Sphakteria across the Bay of Navarino towards Neokastro (the New Fortress) on its hill above the town with the horseshoe formation of the Turco-Egyptian fleet clearly depicted under fire from the western allies. *(Public domain)*

If the two fleets were not at war, the question was, why were they so primed for action, for the Ottomans, led by Ibrahim Pasha of Egypt, too were at the ready. The European allies, as was to become more common practice in recent times, were acting as mediators in a bloody conflict between Greek revolutionaries or freedom fighters and their Turkish overlords. The Greeks had raised their banner of liberty on 25 March 1821 in a bid to gain independence from the Ottoman Empire, and with their supporters had swiftly taken control of much of the Peloponnese. In the following euphoria a revolutionary government was installed in Nafplion, but its continuing survival was heavily dependent on aid and money from abroad. If the mood of the people throughout Europe and America might be moving in favour of ideas of national liberation encouraged by the French Revolution, their governments were more cautious, and the nascent Greek government had to put all its diplomatic efforts into achieving official international recognition as the revolt dragged on. In a mismatch of resources with the Turks, the Greeks had one advantage, their skill as sailors. The rebels' initial success had been largely due to their makeshift navy, whose efforts had prevented the Turks from reinforcing their troops from the sea. Initially caught on the back-foot and bottled up in their few remaining strongholds, when the Turks finally reacted, they did so in strength and with ruthless ferocity. To quell the revolt, in 1822 Sultan Mahmud II turned to his semi-autonomous Egyptian vassal, Mehmed (Muhammad) Ali Pasha. Mehmed Ali and his son Ibrahim had spent the years since Napoleon's invasion reforming and modernizing Egypt with the help of European expertise, and as a result he possessed a modern, disciplined army and navy, trained in the main by French officers. Mehmed and Ibrahim were also ambitious and the Sultan was wary of their growing power. As an inducement for them to commit to helping the Ottoman cause, the Sultan offered the Pashliks of Crete to Mehmed and the Morea (the Peloponnese) to Ibrahim if they would re-conquer the Empire's lost territories.

Crete had never been totally lost to the Turks but it still took two years for Mehmed's Egyptian troops to finally bring the island to heel. With Crete subdued, the Sultan's plan was to use it as a stepping-stone to bring the Greek islands back under control and to invade the Peloponnese. In the meantime, an army coming overland from the north would have the Greeks squeezed within a pincer movement. The Sultan's plans were delayed when the Greek navy managed to thwart the Turks' attempts to take the important islands of Samos, Spetses and Hydra, stalling their invasion of the Peloponnese and forcing the Turkish fleet to withdraw to

Bodrum, where they waited to be joined by an Egyptian fleet out from Alexandria. Ibrahim had decided to concentrate his efforts on the Peloponnese and a vast armada of 400 ships, including 54 warships and transports carrying 14,000 infantry, 2,000 cavalry and 500 artillerymen plus their 150 cannon, the largest seen in the eastern Mediterranean since Napoleon's invasion, set off for its rendezvous.

The planned invasion got no further when a Greek fleet of up to 75 ships engaged 100 of the Ottoman fighting ships in open water off Cape Gerondas close to the island of Leros. Using their favourite weapon, the fireship, the Greeks managed to destroy six enemy warships, but at considerable cost. Nevertheless, the Turks were obliged to delay again and winter in Crete until, in February 1825 on French advice Ibrahim decided it would be to his advantage not to wait for the calms of summer that suited the lighter Greek ships but to launch his invasion now.

On the 23rd and 24th Ibrahim landed the advance party of his army at the Turkish-held former Venetian stronghold of Modon (Methoni). Having taken his opponents by surprise he was soon making good the Turkish losses, aided in part by civil war and dissention between the Greek factions. He set about ravishing the countryside, securing Turkish positions and besieging Greek strongholds. The harbour and forts at Navarino were taken in early 1825 and followed by Argos within striking distance of Nafplion. In the meantime, the Turkish army under Reshid Pasha had advanced on Missolonghi, where the poet Lord Byron had died (1824), from the north. After a prolonged siege the town eventually fell in 1826 after it was starved into submission with Ibrahim's aid. Next June Reshid was in Athens, the last major stronghold in central Greece. After six years of brutal warfare the Greek revolt was floundering.

While many Philhellenes across Europe and America had been galvanised by Byron's death and the devastation of the Morea to continue the fight for Greek liberty, their governments were still sitting on the fence, wary of their rivals and the consequences of intervention on the international balance of power and the established order. Without official foreign backing, the revolt looked doomed. However, reports that Ibrahim intended to make the Peloponnese into a wasteland and then people it with immigrants from Egypt, coupled with the courage of the beleaguered fighters, played into the Philhellenes' hands and enough public support was mobilized to finally persuade the British, French and Russian governments to act. The Russians were already committed to helping their Christian Orthodox brethren, and perhaps gain a little territory at Turkish expense for themselves, and with the sympathetic George Canning replacing

Castlereagh as Britain's Foreign Secretary the policy of non-intervention brokered by Prince Metternich, his Austrian counterpart, at the conclusion of the Napoleonic War began to unravel. To pre-empt Russian unilateral action, in July 1827, Canning, now Prime Minister, persuaded France and Russia to sign the Treaty of London whereby the three powers agreed to induce an armistice between the belligerents and start peace negotiations. The terms of the Treaty urged the Sultan to recognize the independence of Greece while remaining its supreme ruler. The Porte, the Ottoman government in Constantinople, was understandably unwilling to make such concessions from a winning position, while the hard-pressed Greek provisional government at Nafplion was happier to accept the terms.

As the diplomatic posturing got underway, the Greek government were quite willing to talk, but this did not put an end to the fighting, which continued, in part encouraged by Western volunteers leading groups of irregulars. Particularly responsible were Sir Richard Church and Lord Thomas Cochrane, an army and a naval commander, who had so wholeheartedly thrown themselves into the Greek cause that although they were theoretically acting on behalf of the government they were independently waging their own war against the Turks. Their activities led to the Turks protesting that they could not negotiate while hostilities were continuing. Back in Egypt, Mehmed Pasha was tiring of the lack of progress in bringing the war to a conclusion and vacillating in his commitment to the Sultan. Thrust into this volatile situation with the task of keeping the peace and promoting the peace negotiations was the recently-appointed Commander-in-chief of the British Mediterranean Fleet, Vice-Admiral Sir Edward Codrington. How the Treaty was to be enforced had been left unclear, so in the knowledge that the Turks were reluctant to accept mediation, the British government had issued a clarification to Codrington setting out a specific course of action for him to pursue going forward:

> In the event anticipated of the refusal of the Porte to admit the mediation and to consent to an armistice, you will then, in the first place, have to enter on friendly relations with the Greeks, and next to intercept every supply sent by sea of men, arms, destined against Greece and coming either from Turkey or Africa in general.

Further instructions from Canning emphasised that the desire of the Allies was to enforce the armistice without recourse to military intervention, but in the event of all other means being exhausted, Codrington was free to resort to military force. It was with the purpose of maintaining the armistice that Codrington had arrived with a squadron of ships at Navarino in October 1827 in the wake of a large fleet of Ottoman reinforcements.

Codrington was a bluff, highly experienced navy man. He had joined at the age of 14 and gone on to distinguish himself as captain of HMS *Orion* at the Battle of Trafalgar under Nelson over twenty years previously. Courageous in action, he was conscientious and naturally cautious in his planning, and his devotion to his officers and crew was rewarded with their loyalty. It might be thought that his direct manner, which had brought him into conflict with his superiors when speaking up on behalf of his men, would make him unsuitable for the delicate role of mediator and leader of an uneasy alliance. Even if he was not a natural diplomat, Codrington took his task seriously, scrupulously attempting to maintain an air of impartiality and acting out his peacekeeping orders, as he saw them, in good faith; but his membership of the London Philhellenic Committee reveals where his true sympathies lay. His fellow admirals were not necessarily so restrained in their judgement. Also veterans of the Napoleonic wars, as were many of the lesser ranks on both sides, the admirals were united in their sympathy to the Greek cause. Marie Henri Daniel Gauthier, Comte de Rigny, had fought with courage against the British during the blockades of Cherbourg and Le Havre in 1811, and the commander of the Russian fleet, Count Lodewijk van Heiden, was a Dutchman who had offered his services to the Tsar's navy during the complicated period of shifting alliances that pitted him against the French and then with the French against the British. With the recent history of the allies so fresh in the minds of many of the participants, it was only to be expected that Codrington had misgivings about how collaboration between such recent enemies might be effected. Even Ibrahim Pasha had fought during the recent wars, taking on the British in Alexandria in 1807 and forcing them to retreat out of Egypt.

Unlike Codrington, who had not served in the Mediterranean for over forty years and had only just over six months to get acquainted with the region, de Rigny had been sailing these waters for the last five years and was experienced in local sensibilities and on good terms with the Egyptians. With a tactful, easy-going nature, he was prepared to take things as they came, even by force if necessary. The two commanders were initially wary of one another and with the overall command of the fleet falling to Codrington there was naturally some unease on the part of de Rigny at first. They had first met in Smyrna at the beginning of August after Codrington had completed a familiarisation tour starting out from the

British base at Malta that took in Nafplion, where he was required to restore some order between rival political factions. It was there that he had learned of the Treaty of London and he travelled on to Smyrna to receive instructions from Stratford Canning, cousin of George and the British Ambassador in Constantinople. Although Codrington and de Rigny both wanted to alleviate Greek suffering, they also found common cause in the need to stamp out indiscriminate piracy, something the Greek sailors were engaged in to supplement their meagre livelihoods. Because the Treaty had been drawn up by politicians far from the events unfolding on the ground, it was vague enough to offer some differences of interpretation, but both were of the view it would eventually lead to Greek independence. Austria's non-signatory of the Treaty left possible areas of disagreement as to how to deal with its neutrality, especially as in reality the Austrian captains tended to interpret the terms of their neutrality in favour of the Turks.

It was as the British and French admirals were getting acquainted in Smyrna that they received the news that Mehmed Ali Pasha had had another change of heart and a large Turco-Egyptian fleet of around a hundred ships had left Alexandria on 5 August to support to Ibrahim's campaign in the Peloponnese. Under the command of Ibrahim's brother-in-law Moharrem Bey, the Egyptian fleet of three frigates, nine corvettes, four brigs and six sloops had been supplemented by an Imperial squadron from Constantinople under Tahir Pasha comprising of two ships-of-the-line, five frigates and nine corvettes, and a Tunisian squadron of three frigates, a brig, six fireships and forty transports manned in all by 30,000 sailors, carrying 3,500 guns and over 4,500 men including 600 Albanian irregulars. Five of the warships had been built in France, and assisting the Turks were six former French naval officers under the leadership of Captain Jean-Marie Letellier, all of whom had served under Napoleon. In Mehmed's words to his son, 'It is not the sort of fleet you have seen hitherto. It is now a brilliant fleet in the modern style, and such as has never been seen before in the Muslim world.' Ibrahim would assume overall command of the fleet as well as the land army when it arrived in the Peloponnese and it would be with Ibrahim that the allied commanders would have to deal.

Prime Minister Canning had warned Mehmed Pasha not to get further involved in the conflict on the side of Turkey as it might provoke a 'hostile collision' despite the best endeavours to avoid it. Disregarding Canning's attempted intervention, the fleet arrived at Navarino Bay on 7 September. The bay offered a deep natural harbour just over 3 miles (5km) long by nearly 2 miles (3km) wide, protected along its length from the open sea by the small thin island of Sphakteria, leaving access to the bay by two narrow channels to the north and the south. The shallow northern channel is narrowed further by the presence of a sandbank that prohibits the passage of larger vessels. The southern wider channel, flanked by rocks, is just over half a mile (1,000m) wide, leaving enough room to pass through safely. Within the enclosed area of the bay, slightly to the north of the centre, lies the tiny island of Chelonisi. The town, which sits by a promontory at the southern end, is known by its ancient name of Pylos today and is mainly remembered as the home of the legendary wise King Nestor who supplied ships in support of the Greek cause in the Trojan War. A fort built in 425BC by the Athenians during the Peloponnesian War on the northern promontory became the site of a castle after the Frankish conquest in the 13th century, and the settlement became known as Navarin in French or Navarino in Italian. The fortress and harbour then changed hands several times, having been fought over by the Venetians and Genoese, been held by the Spanish Navarrese Company and again by Venice before falling into the hands of the Turks in 1501 who used it as a base for piracy and their naval operations in the Ionian and Adriatic seas. In the aftermath of the Battle of Lepanto, Turkish naval vessels were scuttled near the northern entrance making access hazardous, so in 1572 the Turks replaced the Frankish castle, now known as the Old Castle (Palaiokastro), with a new fortress (Neokastro) to guard the wider southern entrance. Navarino continued to be a desired possession and during the Morean War of 1685 Neokastro fell to the Venetians before coming back under Ottoman rule when the Turks retook the Peloponnese in 1715. Navarino was then made the centre of a new Sanjak of the Morea and resumed its role as a base for the Ottoman navy. During the early success of their uprising, the Greeks took Neokastro, slaughtering the garrison before the Turks were able to react and attempts to send reinforcements were kept at bay by the Greek navy. Navarino fell back into Turkish hands in 1825 only when Ibrahim launched his brutal counter-offensive.

At first, the departure of the Turco-Egyptian fleet from Alexandria drew a different response from the two allied admirals. At this stage, as neither of their squadrons was as yet at full strength and the Russians were still on their way from the Baltic to join the allies, they were heavily out-numbered. As soon as Codrington learned that the ships had arrived at Navarino where Ibrahim was camped, he left Nafplion and four days later he had positioned his squadron outside the Bay with the intent of bottling up the Ottoman fleet where it could do no harm. In contrast de Rigny,

The Battle of Sphakteria and Seige of Navarino during the Greek War of Independence (1825), by Panagiotis Zographos. The painting shows the Ottoman attack under Ibrahim Pasha of the island of Sphakteria in the centre, with Palaiokastro (the Old Castle) on the right and Neokastro on the left guarding access to the Bay of Navarino. *(Public domain)*

reading Ibrahim's intended strategy correctly, had decided to cruise off Kythera in the hope that the Turks would break out from Navarino and make for Hydra in an attempt to knock out the Greek navy's main base, and he could then engage them at sea. In reality, neither the French nor British, with only 28 fighting ships between them, were really in a position to push for an encounter. Furthermore, the diplomatic message from home was to continue to encourage negotiation, even though the deployment of the Ottoman fleet in the Peloponnese was seen as an infringement of the terms of the Treaty that the powers had laid out.

Contact having been made between Codrington and Ibrahim, the niceties of diplomacy through intermediaries began to prove difficult for men more used to action rather than talking. Codrington's negotiating position was made more difficult by his awareness of the continued activities of Cochrane and Church. This meant he had to try to keep them on a leash while at the same time holding Ibrahim back from any retaliation. Ibrahim protested, again with some justification, that he was being asked to uphold a ceasefire and engage in talks as the Greeks carried on operations regardless. Indeed, at that very moment Church was eyeing up Patras and Cochrane planning a revolt behind Turkish lines in Epirus, beyond the agreed combat zone. If Ibrahim was to pull back, the Turks wanted guarantees, but as things stood they felt they were free to interpret matters in their own interest. So, on 21 September, while the talks continued and despite the warnings against any hostile action, a part of the Turco-Egyptian fleet slipped out of Navarino, apparently making for Hydra as de Rigny had anticipated. Codrington was now forced in the circumstances to prepare for a possible battle even though he was heavily outnumbered. Luckily for the British, it was then that de Rigny and the French squadron made a timely appearance at Navarino, putting a halt to the Turks' plans. The more aggressive de Rigny added his own warnings to the Turks with the result that Ibrahim now felt it prudent to invite Codrington and de Rigny for a face-to-face meeting on 25 September.

The face-to-face conference took place in Ibrahim's tent outside the town walls from where, seated on his sofa, he had a fine view of the bay. The meeting was carried out within an atmosphere of the utmost politeness and protocol. Important matters were only to be discussed after coffee and the smoking of a *chibouque*, a Turkish tobacco pipe with a ten-foot long stem. When it was time to get down to business, Codrington and de Rigny frankly pointed out to Ibrahim that under the terms of the Treaty it was their duty to intercept any reinforcements being sent to him for use against Greece. In return, Ibrahim politely pointed out that he was

Destroying a warship by use of a fireship during the Greek War of Independence as portrayed in *The Burning of a Turkish Frigate* by Konstantinos Volanakis (1837–1907). *(Public domain)*

a soldier and under orders from the Sultan to attack Hydra. The admirals acknowledged his own sense of duty but warned him that if he put to sea they would be forced to act, and it would be an 'act of madness that the Sultan could not applaud' for him to engage with them as the destruction of his fleet would surely follow. They added that although his obstinacy would offer them the opportunity as military men to distinguish themselves, their priority was the maintenance of good relations between their respective countries. Ibrahim in response declared that as his government had not foreseen such a situation of confrontation between the two fleets, he promised he would suspend operations until he received further instruction from Constantinople. The admirals on their part said that the Greeks had accepted the mediation of the Allies and Codrington would put a stop to the activities of Church and Cochrane.

Unfortunately for Codrington, his pleas and warnings fell on deaf ears, for Cochrane continued to ignore the terms of the armistice by cruising off Epirus in an attempt to encouraging the local Albanians and Greeks to rise up, and Church was at that moment marching from Corinth on Patras. This action caused Ibrahim to request that he be allowed to send reinforcements, but when Codrington refused he thought it wise to let the matter lie for the moment, even if he felt Codrington was being unfair. Ibrahim stated later that he was not intending to break his word, only to supply the garrison at Patras with food.

With Ibrahim forced to sit tight and await further instructions from Constantinople, something that was calculated to take till 15 October at the earliest, Codrington and de Rigny believed they had averted any chance of hostilities for the time being. They allowed the Turkish warships that had left the harbour back in, ceased the blockade and parted company, de Rigny for Kythera leaving Codrington in the vicinity of Navarino to keep an eye on things. Both took the opportunity to carry out repairs on their ships, but Ibrahim was not happy with his enforced inactivity. His discontent was exacerbated by pressure from the 'neutral' Austrians for him to resist the advances of the Allies and counter the attacks of the Greek rebels. Ibrahim felt his hands were tied; the Greeks continued to do what they liked and despite his protests Codrington would not allow him to intervene. To add to his sense of injustice, on the night of 29 September, the pioneering Captain Frank Hastings, a subordinate of Cochrane's, had secured a victory in his formidable steamship the *Karteria*. Aided by a Greek brig and two gunships he sank nine Turkish ships in the Bay of Salona (modern Amfissa) in the Gulf of Corinth in an engagement known as the Battle of Itea. The *Karteria*, which used innovatory red-hot cannon balls, was a vision of the future, the first steam ship to see action in battle. Itea proved to be the last straw for Ibrahim and during the first night of October a fleet of seven frigates, nine corvettes and two brigs accompanied by twenty-one transport ships, four of them Austrian, set sail out of Navarino for the Gulf of Corinth with the objective of saving Patras and dealing with Hastings, Cochrane and Church.

Codrington tailed the fleet through the passage between Zakynthos and the mainland, concluding that their efficient manoeuvring meant they were under the supervision of the Frenchman Captain Letellier, another Trafalgar veteran. At dawn his faster ships had overtaken the fleet and set up a blockade at the entrance to the Gulf of Patras and after a short parley, he persuaded the Turks to return to Navarino. Codrington accompanied the Ottoman ships to stop them from making a dash for Patras harbour, only to encounter further reinforcements that had slipped out of Navarino the other way around Zakynthos, which the British held as a protectorate along with Corfu as part of the United States of the Ionian Islands. The new ships were under the command of Ibrahim, Moharrem Bay and the Turkish Admiral Tahir Pasha. Despite now being outnumbered, Codrington decided to brazen it out and in due course the Turks returned to Navarino. At this point, as he wrote to his wife, he felt the worst was over and there was little chance of any fighting. But if he thought Ibrahim had given up, he was wrong, as that very night, 3 October, Ibrahim was writing to the Porte saying he would try again tomorrow. The Turks did not feel that they had broken the terms of the armistice, in fact they blamed Codrington, and under cover of darkness they slipped off again. This time bad weather played into the British admiral's hands, preventing the Ottoman ships from entry into Patras and scattering their fleet. With Codrington's ships blocking the entrance to the harbour, on 6 October Ibrahim once again tried to persuade him of their case, but Codrington would not budge, and the scattered Turks were forced to retreat back to Navarino. Codrington felt he had scored a bloodless victory.

In the meantime, de Rigny was impatiently chomping at the bit at Kythera, using the repairs to his ships as an opportunity to maintain his watch over Hydra. He was convinced that Ibrahim was itching for action and still had the island in his sights. Paradoxically, Ibrahim's father Mehmed Ali felt the same about the Allies. The Russian commander Heiden, who had finally entered the Mediterranean in August, was also eager to join the fray, so as the tension ratcheted up it was probably Ibrahim who was the least bellicose. As a man of his word, he did not want to be the one who broke the truce. He had also been made aware by the

Ibrahim Pasha attacks Messolonghi, by Giuseppe Pietro Mazzola (1748–1838).
(*National Gallery of Messolonghi, public domain*)

actions of Codrington of the superior seamanship of the British. Beside which, he and Mehmed had their own ulterior motives not to alienate the British and French if possible. Mehmed knew that ultimately he was on a collision course with the Sultan and they hoped to be able to utilize European knowhow in their forthcoming conflict with the Turks. So as matters were hanging in the balance in Greece, Mehmed had shifted position yet again and was writing to the Ottoman government urging a path of conciliation with the Greeks through their Austrian mediators. It was a dangerous message to convey to the Sultan, as it was something he did not want to hear. At the same time, recent events had led Ibrahim to the conviction that the Allies were on the side of the Greeks, and consequently he began preparing a defensive position within Navarino Bay. As he awaited his instructions from Constantinople and pondered the unappealing consequences of taking on the Allies at sea, Ibrahim decided there was nothing to stop him taking action on land. With that in mind, a force was sent off on the direction of Kalamata to renew his devastation of the Peloponnese.

On 13 October, the Russians finally arrived to rendezvous with the British south of Zakynthos, followed closely by the French, bringing the three squadrons together for the first time. Codrington met Heiden and de Rigny aboard his flagship the *Asia*, but not together. Insisting that he needed to head for Zakynthos for provisions, de Rigny excused himself before the Russian admiral came on board. The Allies were by no means fully ready for action and their combined force was still outnumbered by the Turco-Egyptian fleet. Although Heiden's complement was complete, comprising his flagship, the *Azov*, three other ships-of-the-line (*Gangout*, *Ezekiel* and *Alexander Nevsky*) and four frigates (*Constantine*, *Povernoy*, *Elena* and *Castor*), the British lacked two ships-of-the-line, the *Genoa* and *Albion*, both undergoing repairs at Malta, while Captain Hamilton in the frigate *Cambrian* had been sent off to track Ibrahim's progress to Kalamata and ensure the safety of the Greek population. There were only four French ships present, two ships-of-the-line, *Trident* and *Breslau*, and two frigates, *Sirène* and *Amide*.

Codrington informed his fellow commanders of his latest orders and intelligence from Constantinople and the three were in general agreement that pressure should be put on the squadrons of Ibrahim's fleet to return to their respective home ports. De Rigny acknowledged this might entail the Allies' entering Navarino bay, so he would be obliged to abandon his surveillance of Hydra. He returned the next day from Zakynthos just as the third French ship-of-the-line, *Scipion*, joined the fleet from Kythera having been refitted with a new mast. Once the Allies had taken up position outside Navarino, de Rigny made contact with the *renagadoes*, the French naval officers employed by Ibrahim to help in the preparation of his defensive line. Through them de Rigny may have been able to gain inside knowledge as to the Turks' activities and then it only remained to persuade them not to fight their fellow countrymen. With their work done all left Navarino on 17 October aboard an Austrian ship, except for Letellier, who was sick.

Codrington met Heiden aboard his flagship on 16 October, where he was made aware of Heiden's opinion that the Tsar had probably already declared war. Heiden and Codrington got on well, but for his part Codrington continued to stick by his orders, insisting that war was not inevitable. Even so his patience was running out. His squadron was nearing battle ready, with every man at his post, and the talk amongst the ratings was, as Charles McPherson of the *Genoa* put it, of 'the impending conflict'. On 18 October the three admirals met aboard Codrington's flagship *Asia*. The Allies were faced with a dilemma, and it was forcing their hand. They could continue the blockade through the winter – this would be difficult, expensive and ineffective in curtailing Ibrahim's activities on land – they could move into the bay in the hope that their mere presence would impede the enemy fleet and bring about a change of heart on his part, something they thought unlikely, or they could enter the Bay to actively impress on Ibrahim that he must obey the treaty.

The admirals unanimously chose the latter course. For Codrington it was the only option that could bring a halt to Ibrahim's 'brutal war of extermination' and end the suffering of the Greek population. Both de Rigny and Heiden were of the opinion this would inevitably lead to bloodshed, but Codrington still misread the Turkish mind. He assumed Ibrahim would see the futility of the situation and relent, not under-standing the overriding Ottoman sense of honour and fatalism. To safe-guard themselves from criticism the three drew up a protocol outlining their reasons for taking independent action in view of the vague nature of their instructions.

The next day the *Genoa* and *Albion* arrived from Malta accompanied by the brig *Mosquito* bringing the fleet nearly up to full strength. In the mean-time, Captain Hamilton had reported in person that Ibrahim's troops were carrying out a brutal scorched earth policy that was reducing the population of Messenia to starvation. Codrington sent Hamilton back to Kalamata, accompanied by the sloop *Philomel* and the Russian frigate *Constantine* to add weight. Hamilton's mission was to contact the Greeks and make whatever effort to protect them from the 'barbarities' of Ibrahim's army, and to push the Ottomans back within the confines of Navarino. At the same time, he sent a letter signed by the three admirals to Ibrahim, who he assumed was in Navarino, via Colonel Craddock aboard the cruiser *Dartmouth*. The letter accused Ibrahim once again of violating the armistice, something that Ibrahim would defiantly have rejected if he had seen it, but he was actually at Modon preparing to lead his army in person. It was now too late to deter Ibrahim and the various ships returned to the fleet. Whatever Ibrahim's misgivings about taking on the Allied fleet, the mood in Constantinople was not conciliatory and instructions had been sent to him the same day to continue with the plan to attack Hydra regardless of the consequences. Events were rapidly moving towards an inevitable showdown.

By now the die was cast and Admiral Codrington gathered his senior commanders together aboard the *Asia* to give them their operational orders, orders based on sound intelligence. He was well informed on the size of Ibrahim's fleet and its disposition, backed up by the topographical survey written by Captain Leake that would be published in his *Travels in the Morea* in 1830, and the local knowledge of Greek pilots and fishermen.

In addition, as a keen historian, his reading included Thucydides' account of the Peloponnesian War and the description of the encounter that took place at Navarino during which a combined Athenian naval and military force overcame the Spartans encamped on Sphakteria island. Thucydides gave a detailed topographical description and the problems the Athenians encountered with the weather. Captain Leake too reported that the exposed area outside the southern entrance was problematic to maintaining a position, especially during winter. Codrington noted that the Athenians had sailed around the island through the passage by ancient Pylos, an option no longer practical due to the increased size of the ships. There was a similarity with the present situation, as the Turks had a gun battery guarding the bay on the island. The Spartan fleet was also drawn up in the confined space of the bay blocking both entrances, and it was here that the Athenians took them on, after failing to entice them into open waters.

Unlike the Spartans, the Ottomans only had to guard the southern entrance. Almost daily reconnaissance reports meant that Codrington was aware that their fleet numbered just over a hundred ships, forty of which were non-combatant. Letellier had positioned the warships at anchor in order of battle; a horseshoe facing the entrance to the bay with the island of Sphakteria on the right, the tiny island of Chelonisi behind the centre of the crescent and Neokastro at the left. It had taken over three days for the French naval advisors to get the fleet into position and as they were no longer present, matters were left in the less experienced hands of the Ottoman captains. To break the formation would be difficult, and with Ibrahim away the responsibility of taking decisive action, either to withdraw or to embark on an offensive course, possibly for Hydra, would be beyond the safe remit of the admirals. Their only course was to wait.

The exact number and size of the combined Ottoman warships is a matter of some debate, ranging from sixty-five to an effective strength of around thirty-six. According to the anonymous *Précis de la Bataille Navale de Navarin* (Paris, 1829) compiled from the recollections of the French officers present, the Turco-Egyptian fleet consisted of three 74-gun ships-of-the-line, twenty frigates, thirty-two corvettes, seven brigs or sloops and five fireships, drawn up in three lines, the ships-of-the-line and the more powerful frigates at the front about two cables apart (about 600ft/183m), with the frigates and corvettes in the second line placed so as they could fire between the gaps, reinforced at the rear by a last line of smaller ships. The horseshoe was protected at the flanks by the fireships, three to the right and two to the left. For further protection, the left flank was over-looked by the fortress of Neokastro, while the right flank was within range of a gun battery on Sphakteria. The secretary to the Kapudan Bey, the Ottoman Vice-Admiral, assessed the size of the Turco-Egyptian force differently: two Turkish 84-gun battleships, one 76-gun ship, fifteen 48-gun frigates, eighteen corvettes, and four brigs, supported by the Egyptians' four double-banked 64-gun frigates, eight corvettes of between 18 and 24 guns, eight brigs, and five fire-vessels; sixty-five vessels in total under sail.

In the absence of Ibrahim, the left wing of the horseshoe was under the command of Moharrem Bey in the French-built 60-gun frigate, *Guerrière*, renamed *Murchid-i-Djihad* (*Warrior*). Heading the line to the fore of *Guerrière* were the frigates, Hassan Bey's 64-gun *Ihsana* (*Ihsanya*), followed by the 56-gun *Souria* and two 44-gunners. Behind *Guerrière* to the north came the two battleships, the 84-gun *Ghiuh Rewan*, flagship of the Imperial Admiral Tahir Pasha, and the 74-gun *Fahti Bahri*, which was said to be in poor condition and not well manned, but surprisingly this was the ship chosen to carry the flag of the Kapudan Bey. These were followed by the 64-gun double-decked frigate *Leone* (*Lion*), another 74-gunner *Burj Zafer*, and another double-decked frigate.

Heading the weaker right wing sheltering in the lee of Sphakteria were two 56-gun frigates, one of which was referred to in Western sources as the powerful *Beautiful Sultana*, followed by two Tunisian frigates, two 56-gun Turkish frigates and a smaller Tunisian frigate. Then came another Turkish frigate, commonly reported to be carrying the flag of Tahir Bey, but as the naval historian Roger Anderson argued it is more likely that Tahir was aboard the battleship *Ghiuh Rewan*, as he was able to see Codrigton during the encounter that was to follow. It is probable that the flag was mistaken for that of the Padrona Bey, the Vice-Admiral of the squadron. Two more Turkish 54-gun frigates completed the array. In the centre of the crescent sheltering behind Chelonisi were a number of brigs and sloops guarding thirty armed transport vessels.

The weather during the night of 19 October was poor, so any decisive activity by the Allies was on hold until conditions improved, but by morning the clouds had dispersed and Saturday 20 October dawned fine with a light breeze. By 4.00am the crews were already employed in last minute feverish preparation as the squadrons manoeuvred into formation. The British ships were in the vanguard near the bay's entrance, waiting for the French and Russians to make up ground to join them. The operation took some time. It was 11.35 when the fleet was brought up to number with the addition of some latecomers, the brig *Mastiff*, the cutter *Hind* and the frigate *Glasgow*, which had been sent to hasten the return of the *Cambrian* and the *Constantine* from Kalamata. The allied squadrons were made up of twelve British ships (total 456 guns), eight Russian (490 guns) and seven French (352 guns). The British squadron included Codrington's 84-gun flagship *Asia*, launched in 1824 and captained by another Napoleonic War veteran Edward Curzon, the 76-gun *Genoa* (which had been captured from the French) under Walter Bathurst, and the 74-gun *Albion* under John Acworth Omnanney, supported by the frigates *Glasgow*, *Cambrian* (launched in 1797), *Dartmouth* and the more modern small 28-gun *Talbot*. In addition, there were the sloops *Rose*, *Mosquito*, *Brisk* and *Philomel*, with between eighteen and ten guns each, and the *Hind*. The French were led by Admiral de Rigny's 60-gun *Sirène*, the most modern of their ships commissioned in 1823, followed by the 74-gun *Scipion*, *Trident* and *Breslau*, which had all seen action in the Napoleonic Wars, supported by the 44-gun frigate *Armide* and the schooners *Alcyon* and *Daphné*. In the rear came the Russian squadron, which though fewer in number than the British possessed newer ships with more firepower, that included the one year-old 74-gun flagship *Asov* under Rear-Admiral Heiden, supported by the still-new 74-gun *Gangout*, *Ezekiel* and *Alexander Nevsky*, plus the frigates *Constantine*, *Povernoy*, *Elena* and *Castor*. With twenty-seven ships in all, whatever the reckoning, the Allies were considerably outnumbered by the Ottoman ships, but what was to their advantage was the superior seamanship of their crews.

Once the fleet had been mustered, it set its sails and led by the *Asia* made its way toward the bay's entrance in two lines, with the French to starboard of the British and closest to the town, followed by the Russians to port abreast but slightly behind. They were embarking on a risky strategy, because, with the wind at their backs, retreat would be difficult. At mid-day the crews took one last dinner together and at 1.30 were ordered to prepare for action. Half an hour later the flagship entered the bay to a greeting blank round fired from one of the forts. The ships were passing within easy range of the Turkish gun-batteries and there was every expectation on the British crews' part that they could soon be on the receiving end of a heavy barrage. As the men were drummed to quarters and the guns hurriedly manned and primed with double-shot, such fears were put to rest when they noticed that most of the Turks appeared unperturbed. They seemed to be happily watching the ships enter in a relaxed attitude, leaning on their guns or sitting on the battlements smoking their pipes. At the same moment, according to Codrington's friend and apologist, Sir John Gore, a small boat appeared, dispatched from the *Guerrière*, with a message from Moharrem Bey requesting that the Allied fleet stop its progress. Codrington replied that he came to give the orders not receive them, and proceeded to take the *Asia* close up to the *Guerrière* and the *Fahti Bahri* and dropped anchor. The *Asia* was followed by the *Genoa* and *Albion*, which took up similar positions in line to the north, each within range of a principal enemy warship to starboard, and the *Dartmouth* took up its planned position covering the fireships nearest to the shore. They were all at anchor within five minutes of the *Asia*, by 2.15pm. In the meantime, the Turkish messenger had not returned to Moharrem Bey but had made for the shore, where he conferred with a number of chiefs and ran swiftly to a tent. After a short delay a red flag was raised and another blank fired, a signal for a boat to be sent from the Kapudan Bey south to the next in line, the *Guerrière*, and on to the fireship next to the *Dartmouth*. Charles McPherson on the *Genoa* saw events slightly differently. The messenger, an officer, came from the fortress shore, not from Moharrem Bey, and after barely two minutes' parley aboard the *Asia* returned to shore, threw down his turban and ran to the fortress gate where he was met and immediately the red flag was waved and a gun fired. The British gunners straight away made ready and awaited the order to fire.

Codrington always insisted that his intentions were not hostile; he had even mustered a marine band on the poop deck of the *Asia*. In his communication to the Admiralty written the next day he stated:

> I gave orders that no guns should be fired unless guns were first fired by the Turks; and those orders were strictly observed. The three English ships were accordingly permitted to pass the batteries and to moor, as they did with great rapidity, without any act of open hostility, although there was evident preparation for it in all the Turkish ships ...

As he said afterwards, if he had intended to take on the enemy he would not have sailed into the centre of the horseshoe but have gone around to take them from behind. He had made the assumption from previous experience that a show of force would be enough. In addition, the fleet had not fully entered into the bay – the Russians in fact were still outside – when a disastrous event took place that would precipitate the battle. Who was to blame for the spark that caused the bloody encounter that followed became a matter of grave diplomatic concern. Although many logs were kept at the time, much of the evidence relied on reports written after the event. According to Captain Fellows aboard the *Dartmouth*, whose report was written nearly two months later, he had just taken up position between the fireship and the first frigate when a messenger, presumably the one dispatched from the Kapudan Bey, boarded and apparently began to prepare to set the fireship alight. In response to what he perceived as an immediate threat to the fleet, Captain Fellows sent First Lieutenant Smyth in the *Dartmouth*'s pinnace (a small rowing boat with a sail) to instruct the Turks to desist and leave the boat or move further away towards the shore, promising if they did so no harm would come to them.

As the pinnace made off Fellows called out to Lieutenant Smyth that 'no act of hostility' should be attempted by them 'on any account'. Despite Smyth's attempts to indicate that their intentions were peaceful, as the pinnace came alongside the fireship the coxswain was killed by a musket shot. Smyth repeated that they intended no harm, but more shots rang out, killing or wounding other members of the crew, and it could be seen that the fires were already being lit. Captain Fellows then dispatched Lieutenant Fitzroy in the cutter to tow the pinnace to safety. The cutter itself came under heavy musket fire from a boat carrying the Turks from the burning ship, and Fitzroy was killed. In response, Fellows ordered the marines to lay down covering fire for the retreating vessels.

It was now 2.25 and events were escalating rapidly. An Egyptian corvette, inshore, fired two shots, one of which passed over the *Dartmouth*. The other hit Admiral de Rigny's *Sirène* just as it was in the act of laying anchor nearby, at the eastern point of the Ottoman horseshoe. This was perhaps the decisive act; for now, even if it was not the intention of the Turkish or Egyptian commanders to precipitate some form of aggressive action (in fact Tahir Pasha's orders for the day said that he would 'never raise the signal for combat, but … in case of attack each ship should defend itself individually') there was no turning back from all-out conflict. In turn Codrington felt that if the Ottomans had intended to take on the allies, they would have waited until all the ships were at anchor, engaged in lengthy discussion throughout the day, and then attack at night with fireships. The way events unfolded instead bore all the hallmarks of an accident or misjudgement, and one with dire consequences. As a result, the battle unfolded with no plan or strategy as a chain reaction, individual ships taking on one another as an act of self-preservation or to aid their comrades. Any sense of how the engagement unfolded had to be reconstructed by the protagonists afterwards.

First, the *Dartmouth* returned the enemy fire, but initially de Rigny held back from fear of hitting his British ally. Opposite de Rigny was the Egyptian frigate *Ibsania*. Taking a speaking trumpet, de Rigny hailed the Egyptian saying that if she did not fire he would not, but to no avail. The *Ibsania* replied immediately by firing on both the *Dartmouth* and the *Sirène*. De Rigny now had no choice but to engage, upon which the shore batteries opened up on the *Trident*, the third of the French ships just entering the harbour. A general mêlée ensued on all sides with the *Sirène* the main target. The *Scipion*, the second French ship, had become vulnerable having reduced sail too quickly, and was also soon under fire from the shore as well as from Egyptian frigates on both sides, added to which a fireship quickly attached itself to its bow. As the flames from the fireship, urged on by a strong breeze, spread towards the gun batteries, sailors scorched themselves plunging into the flames in a frantic effort to put them out, or were wounded as the powder kegs went up. To avert disaster, Captain Milius took the drastic action of letting out the anchor-chain holding the ship, and setting the main-sail and top-sail to turn before the wind in an attempt to divert the flames from reaching the forward powder magazine.

The blazing *Scipion* was impeding the passage of the *Trident* and *Breslau*, and although Milius praised the immense bravery of the crew, their salvation came at the hands of a small boat sent out from the *Trident* that managed to tow the fireship away just as he was attempting his manoeuvre. The small boat, not large enough in itself to complete the task, was aided by the *Dartmouth*, the *Rose* and the *Philomel*, who attached tow-ropes to bring the fireship clear, after which it was destroyed by the French schooners *Aleyone* and *Daphné*. That it took so much effort to take care of one fireship was a mark of how dangerous a weapon it could be.

Once it was clear, the *Scipion* and the *Trident* made to lend their support to the *Sirène*, still bludgeoning it out with the *Ibsania*. After an hour and a half of punishment from the combined French guns the *Ibsania*, by now a total wreck, exploded into flames, leaving the French to turn their attention to the fort.

Towards the centre of the eastern wing, the Kapudan Bey aboard the *Fahti Bahri* took the exchange of fire between the Turks and the *Dartmouth* as his immediate cue to open fire on the *Asia*, a response not matched by the *Guerrière*. In fact, despite the battle having begun, Moharrem Bey sent an officer with a message to Codrington saying that he would hold fire and, in reply, Codrington assured him that he would not open fire first. This left the *Asia* free to divert all his attention onto the *Fahti Bahri*, which it had little difficulty in destroying. The lack of unanimity of purpose on the part of the Ottoman commanders was something that would cost the Turco-Egyptian fleet dear. After around three-quarters of an hour, Codrington felt obliged to make sure of the Egyptian commander's continued neutrality. He sent an officer under a flag of truce with a young Greek interpreter, Petros Mikelis, known as Peter Mitchell to his British shipmates, to board the *Guerrière*. Unfortunately for Mikelis, an enemy officer looking out from a porthole for some reason, who may have recognised him, shot him dead. Codrington's report leaves the motive in doubt. As he put it, the deed was done 'with or without his [Moharrem's] orders, I know not'. Although there were other Greeks employed by the allies, like Petros Mikelis particularly as pilots, he achieved the honour of being the only named Greek who died in the decisive battle for Greek liberty. There were Greeks serving on the Ottoman side too, but these were manacled hand and foot, their nameless bodies washed ashore in the days after the battle. The foolhardy shooting of Mikelis had the unfortunate repercussion of precipitating a general outburst of gunfire that brought the *Guerrière* into the battle. Codrington, who had until then been wary that with the ships in such close proximity the allies might be in danger of harming one another, saw any further attempt to broker a ceasefire as futile.

To the fore of the *Asia*, the *Genoa* had drawn up alongside the *Ghiuh Rewan*, where Captain Bathurst had followed Codrington's command to only open fire when fired upon: but to no avail, for now his ship was under a heavy barrage from the Turkish flagship, another ship-of-the-line, and a 60-gun frigate. From the *Ghiuh Rewan*, the tall Codrington was clearly visible in his Admiral's uniform, and Tahir Pasha ordered his snipers to target him. They were successful, and he was wounded several times, but they failed to remove him from his position on deck. His son Henry, who was serving with him as a Midshipman, was severely wounded in the leg by a fragment of iron railing and a musket ball; he only just avoided having it amputated. The *Asia* and the *Genoa* were outnumbered, and the *Genoa* in particular took a pounding. It suffered more fatalities than any other allied ship (26), including Captain Bathurst.

Despite their problems, when a fireship approached the *Asia's* stern members of the *Genoa's* crew manned one of the ship's boats and dragged it out of the way, and then on their way back they still found time to pick up enemy sailors clinging to the wreckage of their destroyed ships. The men may have shown outstanding bravery, but Codrington was not happy with the conduct of Captain Bathurst or his replacement Captain Dickinson after Bathurst was killed. He complained that the *Genoa* had been incorrectly anchored, meaning that it presented its broadside guns to its own ships rather than to the enemy, which it could only fire upon successfully from the stern. Codrington's accusations of misconduct against Captain Dickinson were quashed in a court-marshal two years later.

Of the British ships, the *Albion* had penetrated furthest into the bay, where it was attacked by a Turkish frigate, which it swiftly dealt with, only to be confronted by the three ships-of-the-line. Luckily for the *Albion*, the *Breslau* was near at hand. On his own initiative, Captain de la Bretonnière had taken the *Breslau*, the fourth French ship, into the centre of the enemy horseshoe, beyond the hard-pressed British ships, to fill the gap between the *Albion* and the newly arrived Russian flagship, the *Azov*, which was still manoeuvring into position. Bretonnière's move was recognized by both his allies as decisive and courageous. The *Breslau* went on to help destroy the *Ghiuh Rewan*, three other frigates, and a 74-gun ship-of-the-line, an action acknowledged as playing a vital role in saving the *Asov* and the *Albion* from destruction. Together they completely destroyed the three battleships before the *Breslau* turned its attention to helping the arriving Russian squadron.

The Russians carried out their orders to the letter, taking up their positions with exemplary skill while under fire from the shore battery on Sphakteria and the ships on the Ottoman right flank. The *Asov*, Heiden's flagship, was at the apex of the horseshoe near the *Breslau* and opposite the Tunisian squadron, who at first were reluctant to engage in the fighting. When battle did commence, the *Asov* found itself taking on five opposing battleships, and as a result suffered more casualties than any other allied ship; twenty-four dead and sixty-seven wounded. With the *Breslau* on hand to even up the odds, Heiden saw an opportunity to assist the *Asia* by transferring some of his guns to fire on the *Guerrière*, with the result that the *Guerrière* became a blazing wreck under the combined fire of the Russian and British ships. It had only taken twenty minutes for the Egyptian flagship to be driven ashore in flames, where Moharrem Bey managed to escape unharmed, before it exploded. As the larger enemy ships were put out of action, the allies became painfully aware of the skilful formation designed by Letellier when the smaller ships of the second line were able to open-up through the gaps in the front line, causing great damage, especially to the flagships of the allied admirals.

The *Asov* continued to take the fight to the enemy, dismasting a 60-gun ship, which then ran aground and blew up, and sinking two large frigates and a corvette. It was involved with the burning of the double-decked frigate said to be flying the flag of Tahir Pasha: the loss of life was severe, with 500 of its 600 crew being killed or wounded. On the left flank, to the southwest of the Russian ships, the frigates *Cambrian*, *Glasgow* and *Talbot* and the French frigate *Armide* had been given the task of dealing with the Ottoman right flank and the Sphakteria shore battery. As the *Glasgow* and *Cambrian* were late arrivals, the burden fell on the *Talbot* and *Armide* until they were supported by the Russian frigates. The smaller ships, *Dartmouth*, *Rose* and *Brisk*, with the French schooners *Daphné* and *Aleyone* on the east flank and *Philomel* and *Mosquito* on the west, had been given the job of destroying the fireships. They were so successful in carrying out their instructions that no fireship attack succeeded. Despite its size, the cutter *Hind* took up position with distinction alongside the *Asia*, right under the guns of the *Guerrière*, while in the midst of the mayhem on board the *Mosquito* a young artist named G.P. Reingle painted and illustrated the battle from first-hand observation.

The battle was over by nightfall, around 6.00pm, and throughout the night the sky was illumined by the explosions of the Turkish ships, some fired deliberately as an act of honour, even if there were men still aboard. It was an Ottoman defeat, but none of their ships struck their colours in surrender. The next day, Tahir Pasha boarded the *Asia*, where he received a tirade from Codrington accusing Ibrahim of a breach of faith and the advice to desist from hostilities or else the remaining ships and the fort would be destroyed. Afterwards it became clear that Tahir was in no way sympathetic towards the Egyptian Pasha and years later, as governor of Aidin, the district in which Smyrna was then situated, Tahir befriended Codrington's son and expressed to him his warmest admiration of his father. The battle had been such a one-sided affair that it left the Ottomans totally defeated. The allies lost no ships, although several suffered significant damage, and suffered relatively few casualties: 174 killed and 475 wounded (the British 75 and 197, the French 40 and 141 and the Russians 59 and 137). As at the Battle of the Nile, there were wives aboard the British ships. Charles McPherson tells us that nine petty officers' wives tended the wounded in the 'cockpit' (the area in the aft lower deck where the wounded were taken) of the *Genoa*. On the other hand, the Turco-Egyptian fleet was decimated; sixty ships destroyed with heavy losses, exacerbated by their poor facilities for treating the wounded, many of whom were chained to their posts. The battle was such a mortal blow to Turkish pride that, during the night or the day after, they fatalistically destroyed even those ships not beyond repair. According to Letellier the only fighting ships left afloat the day after were a dismasted frigate, four corvettes, six brigs and four schooners. Codrington estimated that there were 6,000 killed and 4,000 wounded, many of whom were not Turks or Egyptians but impressed Arabs, Greeks, North Africans, Slavs and even some captured British and American sailors.

The battle was fought while the enemy fleet and the larger part of allied ships were at anchor, leaving little room for manoeuvre. This reduced the contest to a slugging match. Only by hauling on the springs attached to the anchors could a ship adjust its position to get out of the line of fire or bring its guns to bear on the enemy. With the ships so close together, the orders given were for the use of double-shot, when two cannon balls were fired from the same gun; less accurate but more destructive at close range. This was sometimes ignored, as the sailors took to throwing everything at the Turks, including grape-shot and canister, even all piled in together. Heiden alone amongst the allied admirals was able to keep his ships together in a compact group, allowing him more control over his command, and with the frigates staying close to their ships-of-the-line they suffered fewer casualties as a result. Codrington had feared there might be animosity between the Russian and French ships, and it is possible that Codrington kept Heiden and de Rigny, who had only recently met, on opposite wings for that reason. There was talk of Russian ships firing on their own side, but with the difficulties of recognition and communication between foreign navies fighting together amid the general confusion it was inevitable that some shots would go astray. Codrington even blamed the *Genoa* for carelessly firing on the *Asia*. In no time the smoke from cannon fire and burning ships had become so thick that, despite the noise of battle, he had to resort to bellowing his orders through a loud hailer because his signals could not be seen. Even at close quarters the opposing ships were barely visible and the gunners on the *Asia* at one point took aim at the masthead of the *Fahti Bahri* as the only discernible target. In the event each squadron did its duty, and in addition to their superior skill and experience, displayed complete togetherness in their actions, coming to one another's aid without hesitation. After the battle, there was agreement between the allied leaders that, unlike the enemy, their men had acted as one, eagerly defending one another against the common enemy. The display of naval virtues and the bravery of the men impressed de Rigny so much that when he wrote to his sister afterwards he wondered at the effect of an 'English squadron and a French squadron side by side firing on the same target – poor target!' He further went on to say that the victory was due to the plan agreed between the three commanders being well executed. In truth, Navarino was one of the least planned battles. The British admired the Russians' precision and discipline, arriving as they did late to the action but to considerable effect, like the Prussian General Blücher at Waterloo. For his part Heiden thought the allied squadrons acted in such harmony that it was as though they came from one nation.

Ibrahim Pasha returned to Navarino on the afternoon of 21 October to witness what was left of his fleet, and the Allies remained for a further four days. He still held most of the Peloponnese but he was cut off from his supply routes, and when 13,000 French veterans landed at Navarino in 1828 Mehmed Ali's enthusiasm for the venture waned. The victory at Navarino signalled the end of the Turkish re-conquest of Greece. The initial reaction within the government circles of Britain, France and Russia was one of delight and Codrington was awarded the Grand Cross of the Order of the Bath by the Lord High Admiral, the Duke of Clarence. But as is often the way with politics, the change of administration that followed the death of Canning in August brought in a new Foreign Secretary, Lord Dudley, and a month after the battle Codrington found he had some questions to answer to the politicians back home in regard to his conduct. At first it was felt that he had overstepped the mark, and then that he had done too little. Codrington was forced to answer his critics in a lengthy report; to explain why he had not remained neutral and then when he stated that the retreating Ibrahim had taken Greek women and children to be sold as slaves in Alexandria, he was castigated for not intervening, even though this would have been against his orders and may have precipitated further hostilities. The next summer, the Duke of Wellington, as Prime Minister, relieved him of his command. Codrington entered parliament himself as member for Devonport, using his position to fight for compensation from the Admiralty for the losses incurred by his men at their own expense. The Admiralty argued that as the nation was not at war, such expenses did not count. Codrington eventually won his case in 1834.

By then Greece, or at least a part of it, was free. Although Navarino did not bring about an immediate capitulation by the Turkish government, it was a turning point in the war, bringing European forces into play on the ground. With the Ottomans' Albanian and Egyptian mercenaries putting up little resistance to the battle hardened French veterans of Napoleon's army, Mehmed ordered his son to return home, leaving the Greeks and their allies to push the remaining Turks out of the peninsula. Sultan Mahmud's provocation of war with Russia in retaliation to Navarino only brought the Tsar's army across the Danube towards Constantinople and

The Battle of Navarino by Ivan Alvazovski (1846) showing the Russian ships in line ahead identifiable by their white flags. The Turkish ships fly the red flags. Marine College St Petersburg. *(Public domain)*

Ottoman capitulation. The 1829 Treaty of Adrianople recognized Greek autonomy, followed in 1830 by the Porte's acceptance of an independent Greek state in the Protocol of London. The Kingdom of Greece was established in 1832. Ibrahim Pasha, for his part, suffered no lasting damage. He succeeded his father in Egypt and took on the Ottomans, as was always their intention, leading his country to independence.

Chapter Seven

Cape Matapan and the Battle for Malta, 1940–42

The struggle for naval supremacy in the Mediterranean turns on the Royal Navy's victory at Cape Matapan and its efforts to save Malta from Axis occupation opening the way for victory in North Africa and the invasion of Italy

In 1935, the Fascist dictator Benito Mussolini began eying up the acquisition of Malta as the missing piece to further his dream of remaking the Mediterranean as Italy's *Mare Nostrum*. Unfortunately, Malta was a British possession and naval base, but as he thought Italy the most powerful of the Mediterranean countries he believed it was its historic right to claim the Inland Sea as its sphere of interest. To do this Mussolini pursued an independent war strategy running in tandem with Nazi Germany. He had already signalled his expansionist dreams by expanding Italian influence in the Adriatic (taking the small independent state of Fiume) and by invading Abyssinia (Ethiopia) from the south through the Italian-occupied territories of Eritrea and Somalia. But achieving dominance at sea was not going to be so easy. The reality was that although the Italians had a large number of vessels, particularly submarines, they did not possess the most powerful navy. They had invested heavily in lightly armoured ships built for speedy hit and run tactics and were well endowed with destroyers and torpedo boats but were lacking in capital ships. The Royal Navy had the advantage of naval radar and was the only fleet in the Sea to have aircraft carriers at its disposal, *Glorious* and *Ark Royal*. Potentially, the Italian airforce (*Regia Aeronautica*) was in a position to exert air superiority, so air support would be vital for the British, whose Mediterranean Fleet was spread between Gibraltar, guarding the 'Western Approaches', by way of Malta and Cyprus to Alexandria, the key to Egypt and the Suez Canal. The British fleet's home base had been Malta, but with Italy only

60 miles away it was well within range of air attack. In October 1939 it was thought prudent in the knowledge of Mussolini's intentions to move the Headquarters from Valetta to Alexandria, under the command of Admiral Andrew Browne Cunningham, known as 'ABC'. It proved a wise decision, for after Italy had entered the war on 10 June 1940, the next morning the bombs began to fall on the small island fortress.

Although a member of the Axis powers since 1936, Italy's entry into the war was not a given. The fascist countries may have been sympathetic to one another, but they did not always act in consort. Italy continued its own foreign policy, invading Albania in April 1939, prior to the German invasion of Poland on 1 September that prompted Britain and France to declare war. Mussolini preferred to wait and see how events would develop before committing himself, and it was only after German forces had blitz-krieged their way through northern France and Paris had fallen that he felt confident enough to join forces with Hitler. After all, Italy had profited from joining the Allied Powers against the Central Powers (Germany and Austro-Hungary) during the First World War. They had been promised territorial gains if victorious, so it might work again to back the winning side. He also knew British resources were already stretched and Malta had been left weakly defended.

Aware of his ambitions, in order to keep Italy out of the war in May the British cabinet had even considered offering Mussolini some Mediterra-nean concessions, including Malta. There was only a garrison of less than 4,000 soldiers on the island. The air defences consisted of about thirty-four heavy and eight light anti-aircraft guns and four Gloster Gladiators, old-fashioned biplane fighters, with just three available pilots. If Malta were to come under siege, there were only about five weeks of food sup-plies for a population of around 300,000. No wonder many Maltese felt they had been abandoned. When Churchill replaced Neville Chamberlain on 10 May as prime minister, British resolve stiffened and it became a matter of urgency to redress the balance. At the same time the Mediter-ranean fleet was bolstered by the arrival of ships from the Australian Navy (RAN) and occupied Poland and Holland, and the presence of the Greek navy.

Mussolini declared war with a promise to 'solve our maritime frontiers' and to 'break the territorial chains that confine us in our sea, because a country . . . is not truly free if it has no access to the ocean'. All the countries of the Mediterranean littoral depended on the sea for trade, but in par-ticular Italy, 86 per cent of whose imports arrived by sea, three-quarters passing through the British controlled checkpoints of Suez or Gibraltar.

For all sides Malta was pivotal in any ambition to control the sea-lanes and achieving naval and air supremacy. If it came under Axis control the British could be thrown out of north Africa. Malta too depended on getting its supplies by sea, and the freedom of the islanders and the survival of the British garrison would depend over the next three years on the ability of Admiral Cunningham's convoys to get through. The *Regia Marina* had its own convoys to guard, taking supplies to its forces in Africa through the Libyan ports of Tripoli, Benghazi and Tobruk. In late June the opposing navies clashed when the British 7th Cruiser Squadron under Vice-Admiral Tovey intercepted an Italian convoy of warships heading for Tripoli with a significant load of arms and men in preparation for the intended invasion of Egypt. During the engagement the slow-moving Italian destroyer *Espero* was sunk after its Captain, Enrico Baroni, decided to delay the enemy to allow the other two destroyers, *Ostro* and *Zeffro*, to make it to Benghazi. The action revealed the deficiencies on both sides, the Italian's lack of experience and old ships and the Royal Navy's shortage of ammunition which stopped Tovey from driving his attack home and meant that two conveys to Malta had to be cancelled.

In the meantime, there was the problem of the French navy. While France and Britain were allies they held the advantage over Italy, but France was capitulating. When the French government realised there was little hope of saving France an armistice was signed with Germany (22 June 1940) whereby the government could retain nominal independence and control of the unoccupied territories known as Vichy France. The armistice suited Hitler, who did not want the French to carry on the fight from their territories in North Africa. Marshal Pétain, the French prime minister, thought that as Britain and France were not officially at war, the French fleet could remain neutral; this was a risk Churchill was not willing to take, well aware that Italy and Germany would not leave such a valuable asset untouched, and if the Vichy government handed the *Marine Nationale* over to Germany the fleet could block access to the Mediterranean from the west. Many French ships around the world heeded the plea from General de Gaulle to join forces with the British or the Free French, others, like those in Plymouth and Portsmouth, were boarded, while in Alexandria Admiral Cunningham and Admiral René-Émile Godfroy, who were on friendly terms, came to an agreement whereby the French ships there would remain neutral for the duration. However, most of France's capital ships remained loyal to the Vichy government and the largest concentration of ships was in the French Mediterranean fleet.

To deal with this problem in the western Mediterranean a new force under Admiral James Somerville was formed with its base in Gibraltar known as Force H. Force H would eventually operate in both the Atlantic and the Mediterranean, but its first task was Operation Catapult, the neutralisation of the French navy's most powerful ships based at Mers-el-Kébir in Algeria. On 3 July, in a controversial move, an ultimatum was handed to the French commander, Admiral Marcel-Bruno Gensoul. Somerville's orders were 'to secure the transfer, surrender or destruction of the French warships . . . so as to ensure they should not fall into German or Italian hands'. The French were given the choice of joining the fight against Germany, sailing for the French West Indies, handing over the ships to the British, to scuttle the ships or to face the consequences if these options were ignored.

Due to what appears to have been the difficulty of establishing clear lines of communication, not all the options were understood by Gensoul. Somehow, during the protracted negotiations he interpreted the British position as unchivalrous and an affront, and in consequence he ordered his fleet to break out of the harbour. In the knowledge that the British cabinet had lost patience with the proceedings, Somerville had little option but to open fire, sinking the battleship *Bretagne*, which exploded with the loss of 977 of its crew. Two other battleships, three destroyers and a number of support vessels were seriously damaged. The battleship *Strasburg*, three destroyers and a gunboat managed to escape. As a confrontation was not the desired outcome, it was an action that both Churchill and Somerville regretted, and Anglo-French relations were seriously damaged for some time: in retaliation the French airforce raided Gibraltar. If the desire had been to take the threat of the French navy out of the equation, the operation had failed because a powerful fleet still remained intact at Toulon. But for the time being, the *Marine Nationale* stuck to its neutrality, leaving the British with only the Italian *Regia Marina* to contend with. If on the other hand the action was intended as a statement of intent, it succeeded. As the Italian foreign minister said the following day, 'For the moment it proves that the fighting spirit of His Majesty's fleet is quite alive, and still has the aggressive ruthlessness of the captains and pirates of the seventeenth century.'

The Italians did not have long to wait to test this statement. The first large naval engagement of the war took place soon after on 9 July. Three days earlier an Italian convoy consisting of a passenger liner and five freighters carrying 2,000 men, 27 tanks, 237 vehicles and 16,000 tons of fuel and supplies had made for Benghazi, supported by two cruisers, a destroyer squadron and six torpedo boats. From their intelligence reports the Italian naval high command, the *Supermarina*, were anticipating a British operation from Malta, so they ordered the 1st and 2nd Fleet to put to sea in support under the overall command of Vice-Admiral Inigio Campioni aboard the heavy cruiser *Pola*. The 1st Fleet included the two battleships, the *Giulio Cesare* and the *Conte di Cavour*, plus six light cruisers and four destroyer squadrons, and the 2nd Fleet was made up of two heavy cruiser squadrons, a light cruiser squadron and three destroyer squadrons.

The British were indeed planning their own convoy operation. Cunningham aboard his flagship, the battleship *Warspite*, had set out from Alexandria with two other battleships, the aircraft carrier *Eagle*, five light cruisers under Vice-Admiral Tovey, and sixteen destroyers, to deliver supplies to Malta and to meet the two convoys delayed by the *Espero* engagement making the return trip. As a diversionary tactic Somerville had taken elements of Force H from Gibraltar on a sortie against Cagliari in Sardinia. On the way out Cunningham's fleet suffered a series of high level Italian bombing attacks, but it was a hard task to achieve accuracy from 12,000ft and only the light cruiser *Gloucester* received one hit, but it proved serious. The bridge was destroyed, killing the captain, six officers and eleven ratings and the steering equipment was damaged, which meant it could only be steered from the emergency station. When Cunningham received news of the Italians' movements he guessed there might be an important convoy heading for Benghazi, so he decided to position his fleet between the convoy and its home base of Taranto in order to force their hand. After the Italian convoy's arrival at Benghazi on 8 July, Admiral Campioni realised that the Force H manoeuvre was a diversion, and with new aerial intelligence he was aware of Cunningham's movements. With the first part of his job done, as Campioni believed Cunningham's plan was to bombard Augusta in Calabria, he decided to set out in search of the British fleet.

The next phase depended on good aerial reconnaissance. Sunderland flying boats from Malta managed to track the Italian 1st Fleet and Fairey Swordfish biplanes launched from the *Eagle* found and attacked the Italian cruisers with no success, but the Italian planes lost the British. When, after hours of searching for one another both admirals were satisfied they had worked out the other's position, they changed course for battle. By mid-afternoon Cunningham had altered his to the northwest heading to place himself between the Italians and Taranto, while Campioni was steaming northeast to engage.

The British fleet was divided into three groups, 10 miles apart: 'Force A' with the 7th Squadron plus a destroyer under Tovey leading the way; 'Force B', Cunningham's flagship *Warspite* and five destroyers taking charge of the centre; and 'Force C' the slower main battle-group under Vice-Admiral Henry Pridham-Wippell with two battleships, eleven destroyers and the *Eagle* bringing up the rear. Because of the shortage of ammunition, Cunningham hoped for a short decisive engagement at close quarters. Campioni approached with his ships in four columns under orders from the *Supermarina* to limit his actions to within range of the bombers so that a co-ordinated strike could be achieved. The Italians' reluctance to commit to a night action meant that he was to return to base at sunset and leave further action to the submarines.

Just before three in the afternoon the British spotted the enemy at a range of nearly 16 miles (25.6km) and it was noted by Cunningham that when the signal 'enemy battle fleet in sight' was flown from the cruiser *Neptune's* halyards, it was the first time this signal had been used in the Mediterranean since the time of Nelson. Soon after, the Italians spotted the British and the fleets began to close rapidly. After Tovey's light cruisers had made a feinting manoeuvre to the north to draw two of the Italian cruisers, the *Abruzzi* and the *Garibaldi*, to give chase, he was ordered by Cunningham to turn around and engage. He did so and the battle began with the Italians opening fire at 15.20 hours at a range of 23,600 yards, nearly 13.5 miles. The cruisers *Neptune*, *Liverpool* and the Australian *Sidney* responded in kind.

The Italians, with their heavier guns, had the advantage of range and they were able to pepper the cruisers with shells almost at will. It was only when the range closed that the British guns were able to reach the enemy, but they failed to hit their mark. The *Abruzzi* and *Garibaldi* were soon joined by Campioni's battleships and heavy cruisers eager to join the fray. After the *Neptune* was hit by a 6-inch shell, damaging its reconnaissance plane and launching gear, Tovey decided to back off. By then Cunningham's battleship *Warspite* had made up ground and opened fire on the *Abruzzi* and *Garibaldi* and the other approaching cruisers. It was now the Italians' turn to back off. Although he was impatient to engage with the enemy, Cunningham did not want to commit himself whilst outnumbered, so he ordered Tovey to hold back and wait for the rest of the fleet to make up ground. Similarly, Vice-Admiral Legnani, the Italian cruiser commander, held back his ships to clear the way for Campioni's battleships and there was a hiatus as the two sides regrouped. The Italians favoured a system of what might be termed in football parlance 'man marking' whereby each ship was allocated an opposite number. It had been observed that during the First World War Battle of Jutland, when more than one ship targeted an enemy, it was impossible to tell which were the rounds fired by which ship, and thus to make adjustments to the aim. It fell to the battleship *Giulio Caesar* to target the *Warspite* and it began the resumption with an opening salvo at 14.50, followed by its fellow battleship, the *Conte di Cavour* firing on its opposite number the *Malaya*. Unaware of this tactic, in return the *Warspite* opened fire on both ships. As some of the British destroyers were grouped behind the *Warspite*, Italian shells that overshot caused damage to the *Hereward* and *Decoy*.

In the meantime, the Italian 2nd Fleet under Vice-Admiral Ricardo Paladini's command was making up ground and a salvo of shells from the heavy cruiser *Trento* were launched at *Warspite* from her maximum range of 28,000 yards. Paladini ordered his other ships to fire on Tovey's light cruisers, and Tovey returned the compliment. As the shells straddled the *Warspite*, forcing it to fall silent while it changed course, the Italians thought they had achieved a success, only for one of the shots from the *Warspite's* last salvo to hit its mark, ploughing into the rear deck of the *Giulio Cesare*. It was one of the longest shots in the history of naval combat, taking thirty-three seconds to complete a journey of 26,000 yards. The 15-inch shell exploded in the aft funnel, setting off ammunition in the 37-mm magazine and sucking fumes into the boiler rooms, putting four of the boilers out of action. With the effective loss of the *Cesare*, Campioni was reluctant to pit his remaining battleship against the enemy's three and ordered his battle line to retire under a smoke screen. This came at an opportune time for Tovey, whose cruisers were again running out of ammunition.

The Italian heavy cruisers of the 2nd Fleet continued to fire, the *Zara* engaging the *Warspite* whenever there were gaps in the smoke and the *Fiume* taking on the *Liverpool*, supported by the *Pola*, the *Gorizia*, the *Bolzano* and the *Trento*, who opened up on Tovey and on the main British cruiser group. The *Neptune* scored a hit on the *Bolzano*, jamming its rudder. Further rounds exploded in the torpedo room and damaged the starboard gun. After freeing its rudder, the *Bolzano* resumed the fight, only having at 16.10 hours, along with the *Trento*, to dodge torpedoes from nine Sword-fish launched from the *Eagle* half an hour earlier. As more Italian destroyers joined in, they charged the British line and the battle became one of exchanging torpedoes with little success while dodging in and out of the smoke. The British formed up behind the *Warspite* and counterattacked.

This situation, torpedo attack and counter, continued until, as Commander Waller aboard the Australian destroyer *Stuart*, flagship of the 10th destroyer flotilla, reported, after dodging around, making their torpedo runs, and being engaged a few salvos at a time, at 16.40 'the enemy was enveloped in a smokescreen, and fire was finally ceased'. It was only then that the Italian bombers turned up and the 12th Destroyer Squadron of the Italian 2nd Fleet made a final attack, zigzagging between the battle lines to seek an opening. By now the smoke was too thick to make aim effective. After a brief attempt to pursue the disappearing Italians, Cunningham resumed course for Malta. The fleet endured several hours of attacks from seventy-two Italian bombers without being hit, but fifty of the bombers managed to target their own ships in error.

The Italians turned for home claiming victory, although the British were to have the last say when the next morning a Swordfish torpedoed the destroyer *Leone Palcado*, sinking it in shallow water off Sicily. The action, known as the Battle of Calabria, had proved indecisive; both sides achieved their aim of escorting their convoys to port and returning relatively unscathed. It was in fact merely the opening salvo in what would become a long war of attrition that would last until 1945. Although in his report written the following January, Cunningham thought the Royal Navy had achieved a 'certain degree of moral ascendency', the engagement had in fact revealed some shortcomings. While the two fleets had been fairly evenly matched, he complained that his ships were too old and he asked for replacements, the Italian ships had proved to be faster and therefore more manoeuvrable and could out-distance the British guns. The Italians on the other hand went away making a show of being a match for the lauded Royal Navy and tactically out playing them, drawing Cunningham, who had been accused by Churchill of 'pussyfooting around', into a trap that unfortunately they were not able to close successfully.

The route to Malta was not the only sea-lane to be guarded. When Romania began to move towards an alliance with the Axis powers (it joined in November) a number of British tankers were forced to leave and head for Egypt. Aware of their movements, the Italians despatched two high-speed light cruisers with air support out of their base on Leros in the Dodecanese islands to attack and board them. Ten days after Calabria, the cruiser *Sidney*, leading a flotilla of five destroyers detailed to sweep for submarines in Greek waters in advance of a convoy from Port Said to Greece, came across the two cruisers, the *Giovanni delle Bande Nere* and the *Bartolomeo Colleoni*. A running battle ensued in the strait between Cape Spada in northwest Crete and the small island of Antikithera. As the Allied ships joined forces, they were able to box in the faster but outnumbered Italian cruisers, whose situation became worse when their air support failed to materialize. After receiving a number of hits from *Sidney* that caused considerable damage, particularly to the rudder, the *Bartolomeo Colleoni* was trapped. It continued to fight on but was finished off by torpedoes from the *Ilex* and the *Hyperion* and sank 6 miles off the cape. With little other option, *Bande Nere* beat a swift retreat, pursued by *Sidney*, *Hero* and *Hasty*, and although damaged it managed to make Benghazi. Too late to save the day the Italian bombers arrived and the destroyer *Havock* was damaged. The *Sidney*, which had also been present at Mers-el-Kébir, had fought three engagements in sixteen days. The encounter highlighted the shortcomings of the Italians' air and naval coordination and the reliance on fast but lightly-armoured ships that were vulnerable at close quarters.

The British had two priorities, to cut off the Italians from their troops in north Africa and to maintain their convoys. Crucial in these objectives was to build up the Maltese force, both to hold the island and to act as an offensive base, and it became Force H's job to secure the western route to the island. To protect Malta from enemy bombers Hawker Hurricanes were transported out on the aged aircraft carrier *Argos* while planes from the *Ark Royal* carried out diversionary attacks on Cagliari. After a successful mission, a further, bigger convoy brought more supplies to Malta, tanks to the army in Egypt, and reinforcements for Cunningham in Alexandria, including a new aircraft carrier, the *Illustrious*. With increased airpower, the *Ark Royal* operating out of Gibraltar and the *Eagle* and the *Illustrious* from Alexandria, the Royal Navy was gradually gaining some element of control, carrying out attacks on Italian bases like Cagliari and Bardia in Libya.

But the situation became complicated in September when a substantial French fleet slipped out of Toulon and made for Dakar in West Africa, taking a task force from Force H out of the Mediterranean in pursuit. The task force was surprised by their refusal to join the Free French and their belligerent response, which forced the Allies to retreat. French bombers then proceeded to bomb Gibraltar and French ships fired on their British counterparts, putting the French navy, although not officially at war with Britain, in the opposition camp. The engagements off Calabria and Spada had left the Italians with no appetite for a direct confrontation, so they turned to leaving their fleet in harbour as a 'fleet of being', or deterrence, while deploying frogmen commando teams and laying mines around Sicily and Malta. The mines had some success, sinking the destroyer *Hostile* and

The Battle of Cape Spada, the *Bartolomeo Colleoni* sinking with the loss of 121 lives after being hit by HMAS *Sydney*, 19 July 1940. A total of 545 men were saved. *(Photo: Arthur Conry, public domain)*

damaging the destroyers *Imperial* and *Gallant*, and, as quickly they were removed, the Italians replaced them. The sparring between the navies continued; the British with their convoys, the *Regio Marina* giving support to their north African convoys in preparation for their planned assault on Egypt, reinforced with two new battleships, the *Littorio* and the *Vittorio Veneto*.

On 28 October the Italian army entered Greece from Albania, bringing the Royal Hellenic Navy officially into the war against the *Regio Marina* and on the side of the Allies. In an unprovoked attack (thought to have been ordered by Mussolini), the Italian submarine *Delfino* had already sunk the cruiser *Helli* in August, before war was declared. The Greek navy would continue the fight alongside the Allies even after Greece was defeated and occupied by Germany. As the Allies already had the use of Greek ports, they were able to keep the Italians out of Greek coastal waters and when necessary bombard the Italian mainland. Convoys were now diverted from Malta to Greece with supplies to support the defence of the country. Given the Italian navy's passive strategy, Cunningham thought now was a good opportunity to take the fight to them. He decided to launch a low-level aerial torpedo attack, code name Operation Judgement, on the Italian fleet while they were at anchor in Taranto harbour. On 11 November, twenty-one Swordfish from *Illustrious* inflicted damage on four of the enemy's six battleships, knocking the *Conte di Cavour* out for the duration, the *Caio Duilio* for six months and the *Littorio* for four. It was the first time such an attack had been attempted and its success did not go unnoticed by the Japanese, who studied it in preparation for their assault on Pearl Harbour. In response the Italians moved their fleet north to Naples, out of carrier range. On the 12th another first for the Royal Navy was notched up when an Italian convoy was successfully attacked at night in the Strait of Otranto.

After the raid on Taranto, Churchill felt moved to enthuse that the balance of power was now in favour of the Allies. Cunningham believed that he had the *Regia Marina* bottled up, but unfortunately he had underestimated their resolve and failed to fully follow through the success of the attack. When Admiral Campioni learned that a major dual convoy operation was planned for Malta, leaving simultaneously from Gibraltar, bringing more Hurricanes, and Alexandria, he set out from Naples with the battleships *Vittorio Veneto* and *Giulio Cesare*, supported by a cruiser division and three destroyer squadrons, to be joined by Rear-Admiral Luigi Sansonetti from Messina with another cruiser division and destroyer squadron. After reaching Malta the two British convoys were to rendez-vous, with some of the transport ships continuing on to Alexandria. When Campioni received news that Somerville's convoy from Gibraltar was passing the Sicilian channel he decided to intercept it. The ensuing inde-cisive encounter off Cape Spartivento was fought at long range. Initially the British were outgunned but when support ships from the Alexandrian squadron arrived on the scene the possibility of an Italian victory was lost. Once again aircraft from the *Ark Royal* proved their worth in keeping Somerville abreast of the enemy's movements.

At the end of 1940 the Allies felt they had the Italians on the retreat. By January 1941, the Greek army had pushed them back across the border and although the Royal Navy had been unable to stop all the convoys reaching north Africa, their lack of supplies contributed to the Italian army's attempted invasion of Egypt being forced back by Field Marshal Wavell. The inability of the *Regia Marina* to deliver a knockout blow on Allied shipping initiated a major reorganization and rethink. Angelo Iachino, who had replaced the unwell Admiral Paladini as commander of the 2nd Fleet, now took over as overall commander of the entire battle-fleet. The Allies too had not scored a decisive victory, but they had achieved sufficient control of the seas to be able to launch attacks on Rhodes and Stampalia (Astypalaia) in the Italian controlled Dodecanese, the port of Valona (Vlora in Albania), air attacks on Naples that damaged the cruisers *Pola* and *Cesare*, forcing the Italians to relocate to Sardinia, and to complete a number of convoys to Malta and then on to the Aegean and Alexandria.

Even so the navy was becoming stretched between its commitment to protect Britain from German invasion, keeping the convoys running and maintaining its role guarding Malta, Egypt and the eastern Mediter-ranean. Initially Hitler had shown little interest in the Mediterranean, but with his efforts to bomb and starve Britain into surrender not going to plan, and what he considered the unimpressive efforts of his southern ally, he decided to switch his attention south. Grand Admiral Raeder had advised Hitler that the Mediterranean was the pivot of the British Empire, and so by January 1941 Luftwaffe Stuka dive-bombers were flying out from bases in Sicily. In two days they inflicted serious damage on *Illustrious*, knocking her out of action for a year, and destroyed the cruiser *South-ampton*. It was suddenly a different order of aerial combat. Just as Cun-ningham felt he was winning the war in the Mediterranean the balance of power had changed. Then in February the hastily assembled *Afrika Korps*

The *Vittorio Veneto* in the final stages of completion in 1940.
(*Naval History and Heritage Command, public domain*)

under *Generalleutnant* Erwin Rommel, having avoided British attempts to intercept them, landed in Tripoli to help the Italians.

The mechanized *Afrika Korps* with its formidable Panzer tanks had been given the task of preventing an Italian collapse but Rommel, the 'desert fox', was not a general to sit back and soon it was the British and Commonwealth troops who were falling back again. The successes of their swift counter-offensive that had crushed the Italian 10th army and claimed the ports of Bardia and Tobruk were quickly reversed as Rommel pressed on east, leaving Tobruk as an isolated Allied enclave. Wavell's forces were further weakened when Churchill decided that the defence of Greece, an ally, must take precedence over the desert campaign. Holding Greece would also put the Romanian oilfields on which the Germans depended, within range of the RAF's bombers. The British were anticipating a German invasion in the Balkans, and in March, Bulgaria renounced its neutrality and joined the Axis powers, thus enabling the Germans to mount an attack on Yugoslavia from the east and on Greece along its north-eastern border. The move had been anticipated, and beginning on 4 March an expeditionary force was to be ferried from Alexandria at three-day intervals. The three divisions of Australian, New Zealand and Polish troops supported by the British 1st Armoured Brigade, some 58,000 men, were to reinforce a Greek army, already heavily committed in Albania, that would soon be fighting superior numbers on two fronts. It was down to the Italian navy to stop this aid reaching Greece. 'Operation Lustre', the convoys taking the Allied force to Piraeus, tied up most of the Royal Navy's resources in the eastern Mediterranean, so much so that the Fleet's War Diary reported that 'any question of offensive action against the enemy had to be ruled aside', while in the meantime Axis forces were pouring into Tripoli. Under German pressure, and with the promise of improved air cover, the new Italian command was persuaded to take a more aggressive policy.

As the first contingents of the Expeditionary Force were reaching the Macedonian border the Italian navy was launching its own major offensive. Following Luftwaffe claims to have damaged two enemy battleships, leaving the British with only one operational, Admiral Iachino felt emboldened to commence 'Operation Goudo', a sweep of the Aegean with a force of heavy cruisers supported by his flagship, *Vittorio Veneto*. He left Naples on 26 March with an escort of four destroyers and was joined the next day by three heavy cruisers of the 3rd Division and a squadron (12th) of three destroyers out of Messina under Vice-Admiral Sansonetti aboard the *Trieste*. At the same time the 1st Division's heavy cruisers *Fiume* and *Pola* under Vice-Admiral Catteneo aboard the *Zara* sailed out from Taranto supported by four destroyers (9th). In addition, they were to be joined by the 7th Division, a flotilla of two light cruisers supported by two destroyers under Vice-Admiral Legnani sailing from Brindisi. After an attack in January by two torpedo boats on a convoy north of Suda Bay had put a large tanker out of the war, the British had diverted from the route into the Aegean via the Kaso (Kasos) Strait to the east of Crete, choosing to go instead by way of the Antikithera Strait to the west of the island. Iachino's plan was to split his force into two, the 1st and 7th Divisions probing north of Crete and the 3rd to sweep to the west of Gavdos island off Crete's southwest coast. If no enemy ships were encountered the force was to rendezvous on the 28th and head for home. Ianicho, who had fretted about the presence of enemy spies in Naples, had not fully divulged his plans to his other commanders to maintain secrecy.

British intelligence was better informed than its German counterpart, having the advantage of the Bletchley Park cryptographers being able to decipher Luftwaffe and Italian Naval Enigma codes. They knew an operation was pending, if not the exact nature of its objective. Sensing a strike into the Aegean or eastern Mediterranean, as a precaution Admiral Cunningham delayed two conveys to leave the field clear for an unencumbered naval action. Following a report from a reconnaissance aircraft from Malta that there were three Italian cruisers and four destroyers heading for Crete, he set out from Alexandria with his battle-fleet (Force A) that evening. The *Warspite* was accompanied, contrary to the Luftwaffe's information, by his two other battleships *Valiant* and *Barham*, supported by the newly-arrived aircraft carrier *Formidable* and nine destroyers. A lighter force (Force B) under Vice-Admiral Pridham-Wippell of four light cruisers and four destroyers, already on convoy duty in the Aegean, were to join his fleet the next day south of Crete. In a show of strength for Axis agents based in Alexandria, a further flotilla of five destroyers (Force C) followed Force A out of the port. Cunningham had even made a display of visiting his golf club with his overnight bag on the afternoon of departure in the knowledge that the Japanese consul general, a keen golfer, would be there. While Cunningham was playing golf, Iachino had become aware that his ships had been spotted and were being tailed. He had lost the element of surprise, but pressed on following information from his own aerial reconnaissance that the British fleet was still in port and intercepts that indicated that Cunningham only had a partial knowledge of the situation. Appraised of the situation the *Supermarina* sent orders to the 1st and 7th Divisions to abort their sweep north of Crete and join with the main force.

At dawn on an overcast day the Italians were approaching Gavdos, the 3rd Division leading the way 10 miles in front of the flagship *Vittorio Veneto* and the 1st and 7th Divisions 15 miles to the northwest. Some 20 miles to the south of Gavdos, Pridham-Wippell's Force B was heading southeast to rendezvous with Force A, still 150 miles south of Crete's eastern extremity. At 6.35 an Ro.43 seaplane launched from the *Vittorio Veneto* spotted Force B heading south 40 miles southwest of Sansonetti's 3rd Division cruisers. This news caused some excitement on aboard the Italian flagship and, with a belief that their luck might have changed, Iachino ordered Sansonetti to make contact and concentrate on the enemy flagship in the hope that it might be lured into range of the *Vittorio Veneto*. At the same time an aircraft from the *Formidable* had reported four enemy cruisers and six destroyers on a south-easterly course. Initially Pridham-Wippell believed these, Sansonetti's destroyers, had been mistaken for his own ships that were of similar size and on the same course and in a similar position. He changed his mind at 7.45 when the cruisers were sighted by lookouts on his flagship *Orion*, approaching from the north.

The Italian heavy cruisers with their 8-inch guns could outgun their opponent's 6-inch weapons, so when they opened fire the British ships were unable to reply. Pridham-Wippell was well aware that he was outgunned and out-ranged, so he immediately turned 60 degrees at full speed to draw the Italians towards Cunningham's force some 90 miles to the southeast. Contrary to Iachino's orders, Sansonetti gave chase at 31 knots, his maximum speed, all the while trying to get the enemy within range, but with no luck. Iachino realised that Sansonetti was probably falling into a trap, so after pursuing the British halfway to Africa without success he was ordered to desist and at 8.55 the Italians suddenly withdrew. Pridham-Wippell then turned about to shadow the Italian movements while keeping out of range. In the meantime, Cunningham had increased the speed of Force A to twenty-two knots to make up ground. In the hazy conditions information was confused, so, unsure of the exact situation, he decided to launch an air strike against the cruisers from the *Formidable*. Iachino was also struggling with contradictory reports. He had received information from Rhodes that there were two enemy battleships and a carrier accompanied by cruisers and destroyers approaching, but he discounted this as being his own ships. But encouragingly, his cryptographers, decoding messages from Pridham-Wippell to Cunningham, informed him that the British were unaware that his battleship was close by.

Iachino decided to take out the British cruisers with a pincer movement, using the *Vittorio Veneto* to cut off their withdrawal. It seemed a good plan, but unfortunately he had miscalculated the exact position of the enemy. When a surprised officer eating a sandwich on the bridge of the *Orion* remarked, 'What's that battleship over there? I thought ours were miles away', Pridham-Wippell signalled Cunningham he was going to investigate. Iachino had sprung his trap too soon and was sailing in the same direction as the British cruisers. When, at 10.55, they challenged the *Vittorio Veneto* to identify itself, it opened up at a range of 16 miles with a salvo from its 15-inch guns to the complete surprise of the British. Pridham-Wippell lost no time in altering course, heading southwest at full speed under cover of smoke. After enduring a number of near misses the British cruisers found themselves again confronted by the Italian cruisers of the 3rd Division. Iachino quickly turned his battleship about in order to catch the enemy cruisers in a crossfire, forcing them to circle around to the south and then southeast toward Cunningham's approaching fleet now about 70 miles away.

In the meantime, Fairey Albacore torpedo bombers from the *Formidable* had arrived on the scene and spotted the *Vittorio Veneto*. At 11.15 they made an attack head on, forcing Iachino to take evasive action. Without air support, the Italian admiral turned the *Veneto* about and, ignoring contradictory intelligence reports, withdrew to the northwest in the belief that the British fleet was 170 miles away. When the *Orion* emerged from its smokescreen, Pridham-Wippell found the horizon clear and set his course to join Force A which in fact was only 45 miles distant. With the ability to also call on Swordfish based in Maleme in Crete and Blenheim bombers in mainland Greece, Cunningham held a crucial advantage over the Italian fleet.

As the Italian flagship and the 3rd Division sailed towards home they were bombarded by Swordfish and Blenheims, plus a second strike from the *Formidable* of three Albacores and two Swordfishes escorted by two Fairey Fulmars, dual purpose carrier-borne reconnaissance and fighter planes. At 3.10 in the afternoon a torpedo from one of the carrier planes damaged the port screws of the *Vittorio Veneto* temporarily bringing it to a halt. Cunningham thought he had achieved a success, but the battleship was able to resume at a speed of 19 knots using its standard screws. In the hope of catching the *Vittorio Veneto*, Cunningham despatched Pridham-Wippell and the faster destroyers to make a search, while air raids on the Italian ships continued for the rest of the afternoon. When he felt it was becoming too late to catch the Italian flagship before dark, he ordered a final raid. At 7.30, as the light began to fade, Swordfish from Maleme and Albacores from the carrier attacked the whole Italian fleet, which had combined around the flagship. The Italians made smoke and with the aid of searchlights put up a heavy anti-aircraft barrage to protect their battleship. Failing to be able to get through to their target, the planes turned their attention on the heavy cruiser *Pola* and it was brought to a stop when a torpedo knocked out five of its boilers.

In the gathering gloom the situation became complex. As he gathered information, Cunningham vaguely knew of the other Italian force lying to the northwest in the same direction as the *Vittorio Veneto*, but his Italian opposite number was less well aware of the situation. He had been warned by the *Supermarina* of an enemy formation 75 miles to the east, but he assumed this was Pridham-Wippell's cruiser squadron. He now made a fateful error. At 8.18, he ordered cruisers and destroyers of the 1st Division to return and assist the *Pola*, thinking they could easily handle the enemy cruisers if necessary. It was a risky judgement, as a number of the ships were low on fuel, with the destroyer *Carduci* having only enough to steam 200 miles at battle speed. As Iachino wrote later, 'I had not the slightest idea that we were being pursued so closely by the British Fleet. [Otherwise] I would have abandoned the *Pola* to her fate'.

At the same time, the *Orion*'s radar had picked up the *Pola*. Lacking radar, none of the Italian ships were equipped for the uncertainties of night fighting whereas the British had already become adept at the art. Without visual confirmation of the ping on the screen it was difficult to tell friend from foe, so on receiving the news that contact had been made, Cunningham altered course to investigate; at the same time the Italian 1st Division was approaching. In the dark, with visibility below 5,000 yards on a moonless and cloudy night, the searching British cruisers and destroyers were so busy avoiding one another that they ended up avoiding the enemy too.

Admiral Cattaneo aboard the heavy cruiser *Zara* was anticipating a clash with the enemy but he assumed this would take place next day after he had the *Pola* under tow. At 10.10, radar on the *Valiant* located the *Pola* 6 miles to the southwest. When the ships of the British battle fleet were sighted by the *Pola*, it was assumed they were the rescue party and a flare was sent up to advertise its position. Seeing the flare, Cattaneo made for the stricken ship as the *Warspite*, *Valiant*, *Formidable* and *Barham* were approaching from the opposite direction. Unwittingly, Cattaneo was about to cut across their bows. Cunningham had high hopes that they had caught up with the *Vittorio Veneto* before it could reach the safety of its own ground-based air cover and his squadron turned line abreast to the southwest as the Italian cruisers were arriving from the northeast. As everyone aboard the *Warspite* was scouring the horizon to port looking for the battleship, Commodore Edelsten, who was there to gain experience, calmly reported that he could see two large cruisers with a smaller one ahead of them crossing the fleet's bows from starboard to port. Using short-range wireless Cunningham quickly changed course 40 degrees to starboard and ordered the battle-fleet into a line-ahead formation so as to bring all their guns to bear. At the same time the *Formidable* pulled out of the battle line, this was to be no place for a carrier.

At 10.28, to the surprise of Captain Corsi a searchlight from the *Greyhound*, the closest British ship, fixed on the *Zara*. Corsi thought that his comrades on the *Pola* had gone mad, but then at the same instant in one of the most dramatic moments of the war at sea, the enemy battleships opened fire at only 3,800 yards (3,500m). Cunningham described the drama of the moment in his memoirs. There was dead silence on the bridge of the *Warspite* as the gunners lined up their targets until, at point blank range, the Fleet Gunnery Officer gave the final order to open fire:

> Then came the great orange flash and the violent shudder as the six big guns bearing were fired simultaneously. At the very same instant the destroyer *Greyhound* … switched her searchlight on to one of the enemy cruisers, showing her momentarily up as a silvery-blue shape in the darkness. Our searchlights shone out with the first salvo, and

provided full illumination for what was a ghastly sight. Full in the beam I saw our six great projectiles flying through the air. Five out of the six hit a few feet below the level of the cruiser's upper deck and burst with splashes of brilliant flame. The Italians were quite unprepared. Their guns were trained fore and aft. They were helplessly shattered before they could put up any resistance ... The plight of the Italian cruisers was indescribable. One saw whole turrets and masses of other heavy debris whirling through the air and splashing into the sea, and in a short time the ships themselves were nothing but glowing torches and on fire from stem to stem. The whole action lasted no more than a few minutes.

In five minutes the *Fiume* had been crippled by *Warspite* and *Valiant*, and the *Zara* reduced to a blazing wreck by the combined effort of all three battleships. In charge of a searchlight on board *Valiant* was the 19-year-old Midshipman, Prince Philip Mountbatten, the grandson of King George I of Greece and the future Duke of Edinburgh and husband of Queen Elizabeth II. He performed his duties with such courage that he was Mentioned in Despatches and awarded the Greek Cross of Valour. The supporting Italian destroyers also came under attack, and the *Vittorio Alfieri*'s engines were put out of action and its rudder jammed, leaving it slowly turning in a broad circle. The *Gioberti* and the *Oriani*, the second and fourth in line, turned to starboard and managed to escape undamaged, but the *Carducci*, after initially veering to starboard, returned to its old course laying a thick screen of smoke, leaving it the only target in view. The pummelling it received from the British 6- and 4.7-inch guns, that had a devastating effect on the crew, brought it to a stop. The greatest danger for the British now was to hit one of their own ships by mistake in the confusion. At just after 10.30 Cunningham thought he saw one of three Italian destroyers on the port bow fire a torpedo and he ordered the battleships to take evasive action. In fact, they may have been his own destroyers from the 10th Flotilla and a final salvo from the *Warspite* had straddled the *Havock* before he ordered his gunners to stop firing. Cunningham decided to leave his destroyers to deal with the cruisers, but the signal he sent to the battleships to disengage to avoid damage by friendly fire was misinterpreted by Pridham-Wippell and Captain Philip Mack, commander of the 14th Destroyer Flotilla from Force C, to refer to them as well, so they swung away to the north. When Mack sought clarification he was ordered to engage with the enemy first, but it was too late for Pridham-Wippell, who had lost contact and gave up the search for the *Vittorio Veneto*.

The destroyer action, illuminated by star shells and gun flashes, was hard to follow by the participants. There was a high-speed chase as the *Greyhound* and the *Griffin* went after the two still-functioning Italian destroyers. The *Oriani* intended to double back on the other flank and fire off some torpedoes but was hit below the waterline, forcing her to retreat making smoke. The *Gioberti* attempted a similar manoeuvre, but was forced away by the British ships and she retired behind her own smokescreen, the only Italian ship to remain unscathed. Afterwards, the *Gioberti*'s captain explained that they had not deployed her guns because the enemy's searchlights, constantly focused on the Italian ships, concealed their shapes and the flashes of their guns made it impossible for the Italian gunners to get a fix on their target. It may be a coincidence, but this was the very principle of the British secret weapon known as the 'Canal Defence Light' which was being developed by a Greek, Marcel Mitzakis, with the help of Oscar de Thoren, a British naval commander, both veterans of the First World War. The idea was being tested at that very moment at Lowther Castle near Penrith for use by tanks fighting at night (I know this because my father was driving one of the tanks). If deployed by a wall of tanks, the CDL would illuminate the enemy while creating a dazzling screen of light that would make it impossible for them to discern the light source. The CDL was used to effect during the defence of the Ludendorff Bridge at the Battle of Remagen in 1945.

The *Stuart* and the *Havock* homed in on a burning ship like moths to a light. The *Stuart*'s captain, Commander Waller aboard the *Stuart*, thought he saw an enemy cruiser circling so he ordered a torpedo attack and reported that one of the eight had hit the target. It was actually the destroyer *Vittorio Alfieri*, and on board was the son of the Admiral, Ensign Sansonetti, who, as he saw the *Stuart* rush by only 200 yards away, in a desperate attempt helped fire a last round of torpedoes before his ship sank, but the enemy was too close for there to be any hope of hitting the target. As the *Stuart* then turned its attention on the *Fiume*, which capsized and sank at 11.15, with the loss of 812 men, and the *Zara*, another ship suddenly appeared out of the darkness 150 yards away. According to the British accounts this was the *Carducci* but this seems unlikely as it was immobilised by now. The two ships exchanged fire without result, fortunately for them, as in reality it was probably the *Havock*. The *Havock* proceeded on to finish off the *Vittorio Alfieri*, which finally sank with the loss of 211 crew at 11.30, and the *Carducci* went down fifteen minutes later with the loss of 169. Just after midnight the *Havock* reported seeing the silhouette of a stationary undamaged battleship. This was assumed to be the *Vittorio Veneto* and Captain Mack's main objective. The report brought the seven destroyers of the 14th and 2nd Destroyer Flotilla, which had sailed nearly 60 miles westward, rushing back. By the time Mack received a correction that it was not the *Veneto* but a cruiser, it was too late for him to resume the search for the Italian flagship.

The ship the *Havock* had seen was the hapless *Pola*. The crew had been helpless spectators to the carnage going on around them and the captain, believing that the fight was over, ordered the stopcocks to be opened. At first the crew began to abandon ship but finding the water uninviting many returned on board, where they raided the wine store. When Mack's destroyer *Jervis* arrived at the battle zone he found the sea filled 'with boats, rafts and swimming men' and the lit-up target of a cruiser 2 miles away on the horizon. The *Jervis* fired three torpedoes at the glowing wreck, there was an explosion and at 2.40am the *Zara* vanished beneath the waves with the loss of 783 men. The *Pola* continued to remain unscathed as the circling destroyers, *Havock*, *Griffin*, and *Greyhound* had expended all their torpedoes. It was then a question of whether to board the ship or sink it. When Mack took the *Jervis* alongside the *Pola* he found a state of panic stricken confusion. He saved those crewmembers that had not already jumped overboard, saving 257 men; 328 were lost. Then the *Jervis* drew back and with the aid of the *Nubian* torpedoed the *Pola*. It blew up and sank at 4.03, the final action of the battle. The *Vittorio Veneto* was already 40 miles away, making for Taranto. As dawn broke reconnaissance aircraft from the *Formidable*, Greece and Crete tried in vain to locate the battleship, but it had got away.

The Allied ships rendezvoused and to Cunningham's 'inexpressible relief all twelve destroyers were present'; he was afraid that *Warspite* had sunk one of them. When they steamed back to the scene of the battle they found 'the calm sea covered with a film of oil, and strewn with boats, rafts and wreckage, with many floating corpses'. Cunningham despatched all the destroyers he could spare to search for survivors. Approximately 900 men were rescued, though some died later. Their rescue efforts were cut short by the arrival of some German Junker 88 heavy dive-bombers and the fleet retired to the east after signalling the exact position of any other survivors to the *Supermarina*, which sent out the hospital ship, *Gradisca*, saving another 160 lives. The Italians had expected air support and they blamed its lack for the destruction of their fleet. Too late the Germans subjected the Allies to a sustained air attack. It was afternoon when the fighters from the *Formidable* were required to counter their efforts. The fleet reached Alexandria the following day without further incident.

The battle had been fought over a wide area in seas to the south of Cape Matapan, the southern tip of the central peninsula of the Peloponnese. The Italians lost five ships and around 2,400 sailors, killed, missing or captured and, after the disaster at Taranto, the blow to the *Regia Marina* was as much on morale as material. In contrast, the British losses were slight, one torpedo bomber with its three aircrew. Admiral Cunningham was appreciative of the contribution of the Fleet Air Arm, and the intervention of reconnaissance planes and bombers, taking off at sea or from land bases, proved crucial. He agreed with Iachino's assessment that the Italian admiral was let down by his air reconnaissance, but there was also a lack of communication. Iachino had taken no notice of what turned out to be accurate reports of the position of Cunningham's main fleet, persuading himself that the Germans had spotted his own ships not the enemy. This led him to completely misjudge the situation on the evening of the 28th when the *Pola* was damaged in the air attack and the decision was made to help the crippled ship. In his testament of the battle, Iachino laid bare how unprepared the Italian navy was in the technique of night fighting. As Cunningham explained:

> They had not visualized a night action between heavy ships and did not keep their heavy guns manned, which accounts for the turrets of the Zara and Fiume being trained fore and aft when the engagement began. They had good ships, good guns and torpedoes, flashless ammunition and much else; but even their newest ships lacked the radar which had served us so well, while in the art of night fighting in heavy ships they were no further advanced than we had been at Jutland twenty-five years before.

While Cunningham received praise for continuing to engage with the enemy at night in the pursuit of the *Vittorio Veneto*, Admiral Iachino received a chilly reception from the *Regia Marina*'s Chief of Staff, Admiral Riccardi. Mussolini, on the other hand, was more understanding. After listening to Iachino's complaints. he promised to build aircraft carriers to provide the navy with its own reconnaissance.

In Churchill's opinion, 'This timely and welcome victory off Cape Matapan disposed of all challenge to British naval mastery of the Eastern Mediterranean at this critical time.' This was not entirely true: although the Italian navy had suffered severe losses, these were countered by the sinking of the cruisers *York*, blown up by explosive motorboats in Suda Bay, Crete, on 26 March, and *Bonaventure*, torpedoed by the submarine *Ambra* on 31 March, and by July the *Regia Marina* had three battleships

HMS *Warspite* under attack in the Mediterranean c.1941. *(Photo: Arthur Conry, public domain)*

back in action. Meanwhile, the convoys carrying Hurricanes to Malta and Axis troops to north Africa continued. The effect of Matapan was more to constrain the Italian fleet. Realising their technical deficiencies and over-reliance on German support, they decided to avoid offensive action, especially at night, and to not venture far from land-based air support. The next time the Italian fleet would sail out in force was when it surrendered to Admiral Cunningham and the Allies at Malta in September 1943. The first of the promised aircraft carriers, the *Aquila*, converted from the Atlantic passenger liner SS *Roma*, remained uncompleted.

The reluctance of the Italians to venture into open waters would prove to be vital. In the early morning of 6 April, divisions of the German 12th Army crossed the Greek and Yugoslav borders. Piraeus, where the convoys were landing the Allied troops, was so intensively bombed that eleven ships were sunk and the port almost completely ruined, making it necessary to divert supplies to other smaller ports, and the location of Axis air bases in Rhodes meant heavy losses could be inflicted on the convoys with little retaliation. If the Italian surface ships had actively seized the moment to intervene, Cunningham's task in Greece may have become untenable. The German invasion proved as successful as all their previous incursions, and on 15 April Yugoslavia capitulated. As the Allied forces retreated before the German onslaught it would only be a matter of time before Greece followed suit. The fall of Greece came on 24 April and once again the Royal Navy would be called on to evacuate an army. As the Germans had gained air supremacy, the evacuation, organised at sea by Pridham-Wippell, had to take place at night. Cunningham made nearly all of his light ships available, including two cruisers and nineteen destroyers with eleven transport ships. Some 50,662 men, 80 per cent of the force, were safely brought out at the cost of two destroyers and a transport ship. A Greek cruiser, six destroyers and four submarines escaped to Alexandria to continue the fight under the wing of the Royal Navy. Some of the troops were evacuated only as far as Crete.

Commonwealth forces were also on the retreat in north Africa, all their gains wiped out by the reinvigorated Axis forces under Rommel. Attempts to disrupt their supply convoys with submarine and air attacks from Malta were supplemented by the deployment of the 14th Destroyer Flotilla. Captain Mack achieved a notable success on 16 April when he attacked a convoy of three troopships and two munitions ships escorted by the Italian 8th Destroyer Squadron off Sfax in Tunisia. Attacking in the dark early hours of the morning he sank two of the enemy's three destroyers and all five of the German and Italian convoy vessels. The other destroyer was badly damaged and retreated, finally grounding on the Kerkennah Banks to keep from foundering. The *Mohawk* was the only British destroyer to be seriously damaged in the engagement. Despite this success the Axis convoys were still getting through, so it was decided that the 1st Battle Squadron, with destroyers in support and to sweep for mines, would bombard Tripoli harbour from the sea. Just after five in the morning the *Warspite* opened up, followed by the other battleships *Barham* and *Valiant*, and the Italian shore batteries quickly returned fire. Two freighters were sunk and some others damaged, and there was some damage to the port harbour but not enough to disrupt the continued unloading of supplies.

By the end of April, Axis forces had reached the Egyptian border. At the same time, they were poised to attack Crete, where Pridham-Wippell was organising the evacuation of troops to Alexandria. It had been hoped that Crete might be held and the Royal Navy may have been confident that it could protect the island from a sea-borne invasion, but the Germans exploited the Allies' lack of air cover by parachuting in on 20 May, the first large scale invasion of its kind. The stiff resistance put up by the Allied troops and the islanders themselves was not enough to hold back the attackers and by 1 June Crete was taken. Around 17,000 troops were rescued but at a cost. The arrival of the *Fliergerkorps X* dive-bombers had made the running of convoys extremely hazardous and with the aid of some Italian bombers they accounted for three cruisers and six destroyers and many more ships damaged, including three battleships, one of which was the *Warspite*, six cruisers and the *Formidable*. Around 2,011 naval personnel died in the Battle of Crete. In this situation of crisis it was decided to take the risk of running the gauntlet of air and naval attacks by sending a fast convoy, Operation Tiger, carrying tanks and Hurricanes, directly through the Mediterranean rather than round Africa to Wavell's beleaguered army in Egypt. Guarded by the combined efforts of Force H and the Mediterranean Fleet, it managed successfully to dodge enemy torpedoes and bombs and reach Alexandria, with the loss of only one merchant ship that hit a mine off Malta. A return convoy was sent to reinforce Malta.

Further strain was put on the navy by the urgent situation in the Atlantic. The largest warship in any European navy, the German battleship *Bismarck*, and the cruiser *Prinz Eugen* were on the loose, threatening the merchant shipping that Britain relied on for its survival. This meant little could be spared for the Mediterranean Fleet, and in May ships from Force H, including the *Ark Royal* and the pride of the British Navy, the battleship *Hood*, were called away to deal with the threat. In one devastating blow, shells from the *Bismarck* hit the *Hood*'s magazine, causing an explosion that sank it at once with only three survivors from a crew of 1,415. To avenge the loss every available ship was called on to hunt and sink the *Bismark*. After being damaged by the *Prince of Wales* she was hit by a torpedo from one of *Ark Royal*'s Swordfish as she made for the French port of Brest. The torpedo damaged her rudder, leaving her sailing in circles. The *Bismark* fought on, but by now she was an easy target for the gathering Allied ships. Eventually the crew were forced to scuttle her and she sank on 27 May with the loss of 2,200 men; only 110 were saved. The *Ark Royal* did not have long to bask in its success; it was sent straight back on convoy duty with Force H, keeping the lifeline to Malta open.

The convoys continued through the summer of 1941 bringing desperately needed supplies to Malta, particularly the fighters and bombers that would make the island, in Churchill's view, an aircraft carrier in its own right. Some respite came when Hitler changed his strategy and withdrew the Luftwaffe to assist in Operation Barbarossa (22 June), the invasion of Soviet Russia. The Italians continued to attack by air and submarine but practice had made Force H adept in anti-aircraft and anti-submarine tactics. The success of the convoys meant that the Royal Navy and RAF

Fairey Swordfish of 820 Squadron fly over the new HMS *Ark Royal*. The squadron was involved in the attack on the French fleet at Mers-el-Kébir, attacks on Cagliari, the Battle of Spartivento and convoy duty to Malta and famously in the sinking of the *Bismark*. (*Photo: Donald. M. McPherson, public domain*)

were able to go on the offensive from Malta. In the late summer their own air and submarine attacks sank 108 Axis ships bound for Africa, hitting Rommel hard, particularly the loss of fuel for tanks. A further problem for his supply ships was that Tobruk was still in Allied hands. Besieged by Axis troops, the defenders were in turn kept supplied by the 10th Destroyer Flotilla, making almost nightly runs from Alexandria. By November, the attacks on the Axis convoys from Malta were augmented by the cruisers and destroyers of the relocated Force B and Force K; the latter scored a number of successes depriving Rommel of troops, munitions and vehicles. These successes were countered when the *Ark Royal*'s luck finally ran out on a return run to Malta and she was sunk by a German submarine, *U-81*. A few days later the *Barham* was sent to the bottom by *U-331*; the *Kriegs-marine*, the German navy, had entered the Mediterranean. The Germans were critical of Italian efforts and Rommel had requested the intervention of the U-Boats. After the defeat at Matapan, the capital ships of the *Regia Marina* had been mainly confined to port – a planned major sortie in June by their reinvigorated battleships, *Littorio*, *Vittorio Veneto*, *Giulio Cesare*, *Doria* and *Duilio*, had been aborted due to lack of fuel – but this did not stop the larger ships from performing escort duty. In December, Axis efforts were further boosted by the return of the Luftwaffe. In the mean-time, the Royal Navy's resources were becoming depleted and, with Malta surrounded by enemy airbases, only 20 per cent of the convoys were getting through.

Once again the British navy was stretched. In the Pacific the Japanese were using their technological advance to great effect. Their aircraft carriers were larger and more modern, and they had mastered the art of naval air strikes. On Sunday 7 December the Imperial Japanese Naval Air Service launched its attack on the US naval base of Pearl Harbour, bringing America into the war. A few days later the battleships *Repulse* and *Prince of Wales* were sunk by Mitsubishi bombers, and in February the *Exeter* was lost in the Battle of the Java Sea, and worst of all Singapore fell to the Japanese. In a desperate measure Somerville was transferred to the Indian Ocean, with five aged battleships and three aircraft carriers. In Churchill's view, it was 'the most dangerous moment of the war'. In a few months the situation in the Mediterranean had been turned on its head. In November Admiral Raeder had declared that the enemy was operat-ing with complete freedom along the German transport routes, but by January, Cunningham was opining 'our situation in the Eastern Mediter-ranean is depressing in the extreme'. In December, Iachino aboard the *Littorio*, accompanied by the *Doria* and *Cesare*, two heavy cruisers and five destroyer squadrons had managed successfully to repulse a British cruiser and destroyer attack on a convoy off Sirte. Italian morale was on the up. In the meantime, the bombardment of Malta had become constant and the relieving convoys were required to dodge the increasingly-intensive aerial and submarine attacks to get through, suffering heavy losses on the way.

The situation on Malta was becoming critical. The island was under siege, and with food stocks rapidly running out, Cunningham received orders from the Admiralty to get a convoy through to Malta regardless of the risk. On 20 March, the supply ship *Breconshire*, the Norwegian merchantman *Talabot* and the British merchant ships *Pampas* and *Clan Campbell*, carrying between them 26,000 tons of supplies, left Alexandria guarded by three cruisers and three destroyer flotillas under the command of Rear-Admiral Vian aboard the cruiser *Cleopatra*. In anticipation of an attack, 'Hunt' class anti-aircraft and anti-submarine destroyers were sent ahead to sweep for U-boats between Alexandria and Tobruk. During the operation, the *Heythrop* was sunk by a torpedo from the very submarines they were searching for. The other destroyers refuelled at Tobruk before joining the convoy on the morning of 21 March. In the meantime, to forestall air attacks, commando raids were carried out on the enemy's north African airfields. The most dangerous stretches were where the convoy came within the range of bombers from Crete and Libya and the Italian fleet. Due to the lack of refuelling facilities on Malta, by nightfall on the 22nd the larger warships were to leave the convoy with the 'Hunt' class destroyers to make its own way to reach the island before dawn the following morning.

The *Supermarina* realised there was a major operation underway when it received a report of the convoy's position from the Italian submarine *Platino* on the afternoon of 21 March and in response Admiral Iachino set out from Taranto just after midnight that night with the *Littorio* and four destroyers, and Rear-Admiral Parona left Messina with three cruisers and four destroyers an hour later. The Italians thought their movements were unknown to the British, but Iachino's departure was reported by the submarine *P36* and Vian was informed that a powerful enemy fleet was heading his way. At 8.00am the light cruiser *Penelope* and the destroyer *Legion* from Malta's Force K joined the convoy. Vian's orders were to evade the enemy for as long as possible, and once the convoy was safely on its way he was free to attack the enemy. In the afternoon the two fleets made contact amid stormy seas. Parona's ships were ahead of Iachino and he was ordered to hold off. This suited Vian well and he formed his warships into a formation to screen the convoy, making dense clouds of smoke that were blown in the direction of the oncoming Italians. Parona turned north-ward under orders in the hope the British would follow into the arms of Iachino, a more perfected repeat of the tactic he had tried at Gavdos. The Italians opened fire and a long-range shooting match ensued. At the same time the convoy endured an attack by Junkers 88s. A fierce anti-aircraft barrage was put up by the 'H' class destroyers and by 4.00pm Vian was able to report to Cunningham that he had repulsed the enemy. His opti-mism was premature. Iachino's group had joined with Parona's and the Admiral decided, with the light and the weather fast deteriorating, to position himself between the British ships and Malta.

At 4.45 the Italians opened fire. A salvo from the cruiser *Bande Nere* damaged *Cleopatra*'s bridge, killing fifteen men and disabling the radar and radio. A series of exchanges followed, but their accuracy was hampered by the ships changing course as they were tossed about in the gale, and the heavy smokescreen of the British ships led to uncertainty as to their effec-tiveness. The British destroyers attempted a number of torpedo attacks to ward off their attackers, during which the *Kingston* was temporarily brought to a halt when a shell from the heavy cruiser *Gorizia* hit its boiler room. In an attack on the flagship *Littorio*, the *Lively* received a hit to the hull that caused some flooding. In return one of her 4.7-inch shells struck the *Littorio* on the aft deck. By 7.00pm it was all over. The Italians ceased firing and headed for home, having damaged six enemy warships, but importantly the convoy was untouched. In what became known as the Second Battle of Sirte, Vian had fended off two attacks by a powerful Italian fleet, which contained the battleship *Littorio*, the heavy cruisers *Gorizia* and *Trento*, the light cruiser *Giovanni Delle Bande Nere*, and ten destroyers. The escorts had also fought off twenty-eight air attacks by Ju.88s and Heinkel He.111s and Italian S.79 torpedo aircraft, expending nearly all their ammunition in the process. For the Italians it was the rough seas that would prove more dangerous. Two destroyers took on so much water they foundered and sank and the *Bande Nere* and the *Geniere* were severely damaged. On her journey north to make repairs the *Bande Nere* was sunk by the submarine *Urge* on 1 April.

As Vian turned his warships back to Alexandria, the convoy ploughed on to Malta into the teeth of the storm. It was now a matter of each ship making its own way, accompanied by one or two of the Escort Group, the antiaircraft light cruiser *Carlisle*, the 'H' class destroyers, and the two destroyers of Force K. In need of repairs, *Havock* and *Kingston* also chose to head for the Malta repair yards. During the battle the merchant ships had been forced to change course several times, slowing their progress, so the chance of making Malta before dawn was out of the question. This meant they had to make the last miles under constant air attack. The *Talabot* and the *Pampas* reached the Grand Harbour at Valetta at mid-morning. Not so fortunate was the *Clan Campbell*, the slowest member of the convoy, it was sunk 20 miles short of safety, and the *Legion* was damaged and required towing into harbour. Just 8 miles from home the *Breconshire* was disabled and when efforts to tow her into harbour failed she was forced to anchor at Marsaxlokk, a small fishing village at the southeast corner of the island. For four days attempts were made to save the *Breconshire*, during which the destroyer *Southwold* was lost when it hit a mine; until on 27 March the German bombers prevailed in sinking her.

This was not the end of the story. The bombs continued to rain down and on 26 March the *Legion* was sunk in the naval dockyard and the *Talabot* and *Pampas* hit. The *Talabot* was carrying a highly-explosive cargo of ammunition, and had to be scuttled to prevent an explosion, and as much cargo salvaged from the *Pampas* as possible before it sank. In the end it was a disappointing result for all the endeavour expended. Only 5,000 of the 26,000 tons of cargo originally loaded actually reached Malta, along with a limited amount of fuel oil that was saved from the *Breconshire*. Such heavy losses could not be sustained and it was realised that more supplies would only reach the island once its aerial defences were improved. Iachino may have outgunned the British but his failure to touch the convoy only convinced the head of the Luftwaffe, *Generalfieldmarschall* Kesselring, that it would be down to his bombers to neutralise Malta.

The Germans increased their air attacks and in April the island suffered its heaviest bombardment of the war. Taking a number of losses, the Royal Navy's surface ships were forced to withdraw, leaving the Axis convoys greater freedom to ply between Italy and the African coast and the island even more isolated. Slowly Malta was being starved out. To build up the airforce, Spitfires had begun to arrive during March, and they proved a great improvement on the dated Hurricanes. Their journey was a combination of aircraft carrier and flight, an operation enhanced by the loan of the US Navy's carrier *Wasp*. The journey was the easy part: of those delivered on 20 April, only seven survived out of forty-six after a massive attack on the airfield; it was the low point for the island.

During April, Cunningham was replaced by Admiral Henry Harwood, who had made his reputation as the commander of the destroyer squadron that sank the German battleship *Graf Spee* at the Battle of the River Plate in 1939. Cunningham would go on to supervise the Anglo-American landings in North Africa in 1943 (Operation Torch). In June, Harwood

Operation Pedestal: view from the aft of HMS *Victorious* showing Hawker Sea Hurricanes and a Fairey Albacore on the flight deck and HMS *Indomitable* and HMS *Eagle* in the background. (*Photo: L.C. Priest RN, public domain*)

decided on another double convoy from Gibraltar and Alexandria to relieve the island. The Alexandria convoy was forced to retreat by the Italian fleet with the loss of one cruiser and five destroyers, but two merchantmen from the Gibraltar convoy made the Grand Harbour after enduring four days of attacks. 25,000 tons of supplies were delivered, enough with strict rationing to fend off starvation for two months. The cost was a heavy one: four merchantmen, one cruiser and four destroyers. The survival of the island was becoming dependent on the continued supply of Spitfires and the resilience of the RAF pilots. In the aerial battle that followed, Kesselring's belief that the Luftwaffe was winning proved to be misinformed; the Spitfires were making a difference. Critically a plan to capture Malta by combined paratroop and amphibious attack, favoured by the Italians, was postponed by the German high command, who believed the land war in Africa to be the greater priority, and the diversion of aircraft for this purpose gave Malta a small respite during May. On 20 June,

Tobruk fell to Rommel and with the Axis troops advancing as far as El Alamein the situation looked dire for the Allies.

While Rommel was building up his forces in the desert for the final push, another ambitious convoy was being planned, Operation Pedestal, known in Malta as the Santa Marija Convoy. In a reprise of the June operation there would be two convoys, but the one from the east would be a bluff. The dummy convoy would turn back, leaving the larger western convoy the task of breaking through. At such a point in the war, with the Navy's resources stretched to their maximum (the naval escort had to be reinforced by ships from the Atlantic Fleet) and Malta with only days of supplies left, including much needed aviation fuel, the fate of the Allies in the Mediterranean was riding on its success in getting through. Fourteen merchant ships were to be escorted by three aircraft carriers (*Victorious*, *Indomitable*, and *Eagle*), two battleships (*Nelson* and *Rodney*), seven cruisers and twenty-four destroyers. In addition, there were two fleet oilers protected by four corvettes, eight destroyers escorting the carrier *Furious* and eight submarines. The Italians intended to intercept this convoy south of the island of Pantalleria, in the confined seas between Sicily and Tunisia where they had been successful against the previous convoy; but this time the British would be better prepared.

The first contingent of the convoy left Gibraltar on 9 August. Two days later British intelligence knew that the enemy was aware of their position and that submarines had been alerted and cruisers and destroyers were at the ready or at sea. The purpose of the convoy was less certain, and Kesselring ordered units in north Africa to prepare for landings around Tobruk. Before any attack by the Italian fleet, the convoy had to endure four aerial assaults, including one comprised of around a hundred planes. The raids left the *Indomitable* and the *Victorious* damaged and the destroyer *Foresight* and a merchantman out of action. There were submarines too – the *Eagle* was sunk by *U-73* and Italian torpedoes hit the light cruisers *Nigeria*, *Kenya*, *Cairo*, which sank, and the American tanker SS *Ohio* – and Italian torpedo boats fatally damaged the cruiser *Manchester* and sank four merchant ships. This would have been a good moment for the *Regia Marina* to strike, but a lack of coordination and trust between the Axis partners and confidence on the part of the Italians meant a decisive opportunity was missed. The Italian fleet continued to be hampered by lack of fuel, keeping its battleships in port, so the intercepting force consisted of two cruiser divisions (7th and 3rd) and seventeen destroyers under Rear-Admiral Parona. When information was received that a battleship and cruiser were joining the British fleet Parona was called back on the orders of Mussolini. In fact, the aerial reconnaissance report was mistaken and the ships were a light cruiser and two destroyers.

The decoy convoy and an attack on Rhodes (Operation MG 3 and MG 4) in the Eastern Mediterranean had failed to divert the Axis forces from attacking Pedestal, but some of the returning Italian cruisers were ordered to join the 8th Cruiser Division to make an attack on MG 3. They were in fact being lured into a trap. On the morning of 13 August torpedoes from the submarine *Unbroken*, lurking in the straits north of Sicily, hit the *Bolzano* and the *Muzio Attendolo*, putting them out of action for the duration. In the meantime, the aerial barrage on the convoy continued. Finally, at 4.30 that afternoon, five merchant ships, including the oft-damaged *Ohio*, limped into Valetta to a jubilant reception. The 33,000 tons of supplies and 15,000 tons of oil would be enough to keep Malta going for another two weeks or more, a critical breathing space. The convoy had arrived at considerable cost: thirty-four aircraft lost; one aircraft carrier, two light cruisers, one destroyer and nine merchant ships sunk; one aircraft carrier, two light cruisers and three merchant ships damaged. The Luftwaffe and the *Regia Aeronautica* suffered the brunt of the Axis losses (between forty-eight and sixty planes) while for the navies two cruisers were damaged and two submarines sunk. It may have appeared to be a victory for the Axis, but it was a Pyrrhic one. They had inflicted considerable losses on the British but these were losses the British were prepared to take; for, despite all their efforts, the Axis had not pushed home their attack and cut Malta's supply line. Both the German and Italian high command realised that the British had won the strategic battle. As Rear-Admiral Franco Maugeri, head of Italy's naval intelligence, wrote in his diary for 17 August, 'Malta has resumed functioning despite all the losses we inflicted.'

Although navies were still important, the contest was becoming one of air supremacy. Without its aircraft carriers the British would have been impotent and Malta's strategic worth as an airbase grew as the war progressed. As the attack on Taranto and the sinking of the *Bismark* had shown, the days of the battleship were numbered, and the Battle of Cape Matapan would be the last time the Royal Navy engaged fleet to fleet. During Operation Pedestal the opposing fleets never made serious contact, and it was thanks to enough ships being able to weather the aerial storm that Malta could continue to be used as a base for warships, aircraft and submarines to harass the Axis' desert campaign. On 30 August Rommel's assault on Egypt was brought to a halt by Lieutenant General Bernard Montgomery's 8th Army at the Battle of El Alamein. Rommel put

Bomb damage in Kingsway, Valetta, April 1942. (*Photo: Lt J.E. Russell RN, public domain*)

his defeat down to lack of supplies, particularly fuel, and it is claimed Malta-based submarines sank 390,660 tonnes of Axis shipping. By October Rommel was in retreat, and the subsequent loss of Luftwaffe airbases in north Africa eased the path of the last opposed convoy to Malta. In November, in a combined US and British operation (Torch), 160 British warships landed over 100,000 troops in Morocco and Algeria. The tide had turned, but it would still take nearly a year before Admiral Cunningham was able to accept the surrender of the Italian Fleet on 10 September 1943 off the coast of Malta; an event largely made possible because an island slightly smaller than the Isle of Wight had survived the dark days, when it achieved the unwanted distinction of having taken the heaviest sustained bombing recorded, enduring an attack that lasted 154 days and nights with a total of 6,700 bombs dropped during 3,343 air raids. In April and March of 1942 alone 14,500 enemy bombers dropped twice the tonnage of bombs on Malta than on London during the worst twelve months of the Blitz. It was on 15 April 1942 that King George VI awarded the whole island the George Cross for 'heroism … that will long be famous in history'.

Bibliography

General

Anderson, Roger Charles, *Naval Wars in the Levant, 1559–1853*, Princeton University Press, Princeton, 1952.

Arenson, Sarah, *The Encircled Sea: The Mediterranean Maritime Civilisation*, Constable, London, 1990.

Boardman, John, Jasper Griffin and Oswyn Murray (eds), *The Oxford History of the Classical World*, OUP, Oxford, 1986.

Bradford, Ernle, *Mediterranean: Portrait of a Sea*, Penguin, Harmonsworth, 2000.

Flaceliere, Robert, *Daily Life in Greece at the Time of Pericles*, Phoenix Press, London, 2002.

Gabriel, Richard A., 'The Roman Navy: Masters of the Mediterranean', *Military History*, December 2007.

Lavery, Brian, *Empire of the Seas: The Remarkable Story of How the Navy Forged the Modern World*, Bloomsbury, London, 2015.

Mahan, Alfred Thayer, *The Influence of Sea Power on History: 1660–1805*, Bison Books, London, 1980.

Moscati, Sabatino, *The World of the Phoenicians*, Sphere Books, London, 1973.

Parry, J.H., *The Age of Reconnaissance: Discovery, Exploration and Settlement 1450–1650*, Phoenix Press, London, 2000.

Steinby, Christa, *Rome Versus Carthage: The War at Sea*, Pen and Sword, Barnsley, 2014.

Three Decks: Warships in the Age of Sail, https://threedecks.org/index.php?display_type=home.

Wilson, Ben, *Empire of the Deep: The Rise and Fall of the British Navy*, Weidenfeld and Nicolson, London, 2014.

Salamis, 480BC

Aeschylus, *The Persians*, trans. Robert Potter, J. Crouse, Norwich, 1777.

Aristotle, *Nicomachean Ethics*, trans. H. Rackham, Harvard University Press, Cambridge, MA, 1934.

Bowra, C.M., *Periclean Athens*, Weidenfeld and Nicholson, London, 1971.

Connelly, Joan Breton, *The Parthenon Enigma: A Journey into Legend*, Head of Zeus, London, 2017.

Euripides, 'Erechtheus', *Selected Fragmentary Plays*, eds. C. Collard, M. Cropp and J. Gibert, vol. 1, Aris & Phillips Classical Texts, Warminster, 1995.

Hamel, Debra, *Athenian Generals: Military Authority in the Classical Period*, Brill, Boston, 1998.

Herodotus, *Histories*, trans. Aubrey de Sélincourt, Penguin, Harmondsworth, 1964.

Holland, Tom, *Persian Fire: The First World Empire and the Battle for the West*, Little, Brown, London, 2005.

Jordan, Borimir, 'The Crews of Athenian Triremes', *L'Antiquité Classique*, no. 69, 2000, pp. 81–101.

Plutarch, 'The Life of Themistocles', *Parallel Lives*, trans. Bernadotte Perrin, Harvard University Press, Cambridge, MA, 1914.

Plutarch, 'De Herodoti malignitate' ('The Malice of Herodotus', 36), *Moralia*, trans. William W. Goodwin, Little, Brown, and Company, Cambridge, MA, 1874.

Pseudo-Xenophon (The Old Oligarch), *Constitution of the Athenians*, trans. E.C. Marchant, Harvard University Press, Cambridge, MA, 1984..

Strauss, Barry, *Salamis: The Greatest Naval Battle of the Ancient World, 480BC*, Hutchinson, London, 2004.

Thucydides, *The Peloponnesian War*, trans. Rex Warner, Penguin Classics, Harmondsworth, 1954.

Xenophon, 'Agesilaus', *Minor Works*, trans. John Selby Watson, G. Bell, London, 1878.

Actium, 31BC

Augustus, *Res Gestae Divi Augusti* (the achievements of the deified Augustus) 14AD, trans. Thomas Bushnell BSG, 1998.

Cassius Dio, 'How Caesar conquered Antony at Actium (chapters 15–35)', *Roman History*, Book 50, trans. Earnest Cary, Harvard University Press, Cambridge, MA, 1917.

Gabriel, Richard, 'The Roman Navy: Masters of the Mediterranean', *Military History*, December 2007.

Goldsworthy, Adrian, *Antony and Cleopatra*, Phoenix, London, 2011.

Horace, *Odes*, Book 1, trans. C. Smart, revised by Theodore Alois Buckley, Harper & Brothers, New York, 1863.

Lindsay, Jack, *Cleopatra*, Constable & Co. London, 1971.

Livy, *Periochae*, Book 133, trans. Jona Lendering, https://www.livius.org/sources/content/livy/livy-periochae-131-135/.

Plutarch, 'The Life of Antony', *The Parallel Lives*, Vol. IX, trans. Bernadotte Perrin, Harvard University Press, Cambridge, MA, 1914.

Suetonius, 'Augustus: afterwards deified', *The Twelve Caesars*, trans Robert Graves, Penguin Books, Harmondsworth, 1965.

Vellius Paterculus, *Compendium of Roman History*, Book II, trans. F.W. Shipley, Loeb Classical Library, Harvard University Press, 1924, Chapters 59–93.

Virgil, *Aeneid*, trans. Sir Charles Bowen, John Murray, London, 1889.

Lepanto, 1571

Anderson, R.C., *Naval Wars in the Levant: 1559–1843*, University of Princeton, Princeton & Liverpool, 1952.

Braudel, Ferdnand, *The Mediterranean and the Mediterranean World in the Age of Philip II*, BCA, London, 1992.

Crowley, Roger, *Empires of the Sea: The Final Battle for the Mediterranean 1521–1580*, Faber and Faber, London, 2013.

Imber, Colin, *The Ottoman Empire: 1300–1650*, Palgrave, Basingstoke, 2002.

Inalcik, Halil, *The Ottoman Empire: The Classical Age 1300–1600*, Phoenix, London, 1994.

Konstam, Angus, *Lepanto, 1571: The Greatest Naval Battle of the Renaissance*, Osprey, Oxford, 2003.

McPeak, William J., 'The Battle of Lepanto: "The Best Day's Work in Centuries"', *Warfare History Network*, 2 November 2018, https://warfarehistorynetwork.com/daily/military-history/the-battle-of-lepanto-the-best-days-work-in-centuries/.

Setton, Kenneth Meyer, *The Papacy and the Levant, 1204–1571*, Vol. 162, American Philosophical Society, Philadelphia, PA, 1984.

Sterling, D., 'Turning the tide: Venetian contributions to the Battle of Lepanto', *The Virginia Tech Undergraduate Historical Review*, 2014, 3.DOI: http://doi.org/10.21061/vtuhr.3io.21.

Aboukir Bay, 1798

Anderson, R.C., *Naval Wars in the Levant: 1859–1843*, University of Princeton, Princeton & Liverpool, 1952.

Berry, Sir Edward, *An Authentic Narrative of the Proceedings of his Majesty's Squadron, under the Command of Rear-Admiral Sir Horatio Nelson, from its Sailing from Gibraltar to the Conclusion of the Glorious Battle of the Nile; Drawn up from the Minutes of an Officer of Rank in the Squadron*, 3rd edition, London, 1798.

Herold, J. Christopher, *The Age of Napoleon*, Weidenfeld and Nicolson, London, 1963.

Hudson, Roger (ed), *Nelson and Emma*, Folio Society, London, 1994.

James, William, *The Naval History of Britain from the Declaration of War by France in 1793 to the Accession of George IV*, vol. II, Richard Bentley, London, 1837.

Nelson, Horatio, *The Dispatches and Letters of Vice Admiral Lord Viscount Nelson*, Vol. III, CUP, 2011.

Orde, Denis, *Nelson's Mediterranean Command: concerning Pride, Preferment and Prize Money*, Pentland Press, Edinburgh, 1997.

Steel, David, *Steel's Naval Remembrancer: From the Commencement of the War in 1793 to the End of the Year 1800*, CUP, 2010.

Strathern, Paul, *Napoleon in Egypt*, Random House, London, 2008.

Sugden, John, *Nelson: The Sword of Albion*, The Bodley Head, London, 2014.

Navarino, 1827

Anderson, R.C., *Naval Wars in the Levant: 1859–1843*, University of Princeton, Princeton & Liverpool, 1952.

Brewer, David, *The Flame of Freedom: The Greek War of Independence, 1821–1833*, John Murray, London, 2001.

Codrington, Admiral Edward, 'Dispatches to the Admiralty Office, 10 November 1827', *Bulletins and Other State Intelligence & etc: compiled and arranged from the official documents published in the London Gazette, 1827*, London.

James, William, *Naval History of Great Britain, Vol. VI*, Richard Bentley, London, 1837.

McPherson, Charles, *Life on Board a British Man of War: including a full account of the Battle of Navarino, by a British Seaman*, Blackie, Fullerton & Co, Glasgow, 1829.

Winfield, Rif, *French Warships in the Age of Sail, 1786–1861: Design, Construction, Careers and Fates*, Casemate, Barnsley, 2015.

Woodhouse, C.M., *The Battle of Navarino*, Hodder and Stoughton, London, 1965.

Cape Matapan and the Battle for Malta, 1940–42

Caravaggio, Lieutenant Colonel Angelo N., 'The Attack on Taranto: Tactical Success, Operational Failure', *Naval War College Review*: Vol. 59: No. 3, Article 8, 2006.

Churchill, Winston S., *The Second World War, Vol. V: The Grand Alliance, Germany drives East, January 2 – June 22, 1941*, Cassell & Co., London, 1950.

Cunningham, A.B., *A Sailor's Odyssey*, Hutchinson, London 1951.

Holland, James, *Fortress Malta: An Island Under Siege, 1940–1943*, Phoenix, London, 2004.

Lucas, Laddie, *Malta, the Thorn in Rommel's Side: Six Months that Changed the War*, Stanley Paul, London, 1991.

O'Hara, Vincent, *Struggle for the Middle Sea: The Great Navies at War in the Mediterranean, 1940–1945*, Conway, London, 2009.

Wilmot, Chester, *The Struggle for Europe*, Collins, London, 1952.

Index